WRITING HISTORY AT THE OTTOMAN COURT

WRITING HISTORY AT THE OTTOMAN COURT

Editing the Past, Fashioning the Future

Edited by H. Erdem Çıpa and Emine Fetvacı

Indiana University Press

Bloomington and Indianapolis

This book is a publication of

Indiana University Press
Office of Scholarly Publishing
Herman B Wells Library 350
1320 East 10th Street
Bloomington, Indiana 47405 USA

iupress.indiana.edu

Telephone orders 800-842-6796
Fax orders 812-855-7931

♾ The paper used in this publication meets the minimum requirements of the American National Standard for Information Sciences—Permanence of Paper for Printed Library Materials, ANSI Z39.48-1992.

Manufactured in the United States of America

Library of Congress Cataloging-in-Publication Data

Writing history at the Ottoman court : editing the past, fashioning the future / edited by H. Erdem Çıpa and Emine Fetvacı.
pages cm.
Includes bibliographical references and index.
ISBN 978-0-253-00857-2 (cloth : alk. paper) — ISBN 978-0-253-00864-0 (pbk. : alk. paper) — ISBN 978-0-253-00874-9 (e-book)
1. Turkey—Historiography. I. Çıpa, H. Erdem, [date] II. Fetvacı, Emine.
DR438.8.W75 2013
956'.015072—dc23 2012049578

1 2 3 4 5 18 17 16 15 14 13

Contents

Preface

Ottoman scholars of the early modern era produced an unprecedented number of works with historical subject matter. Beginning in the fifteenth century, authors of various backgrounds composed chronicles; biographical dictionaries; hagiographies; local, dynastic, or universal histories; campaign accounts; compilations of letters; and other literary texts with historical content. The Ottoman historical record consisted of verse and prose accounts; Persian, Ottoman Turkish, and some Arabic texts; and a plethora of archival sources and supporting documents. The writers of these historical texts came from several milieus; indeed, very few were career historians: many were scribes, bureaucrats, soldiers, poets, religious scholars, grand viziers, tax collectors, and men of other professions. The roster included supporters of the state, dissenters, and eulogizers, as well as complainers and critics.

Members of the Ottoman dynasty and administration, too, were attuned to the value of historical writing and experimented with appointing official historians. One such experiment began in the sixteenth century and led to the creation of numerous dynastic accounts that were illustrated in luxurious manuscripts.[1] At the end of the seventeenth century another kind of office was created, that of the court chronicler. The holder of this post was given access to archival records and kept a record of important events in Ottoman history.[2] Thus, Ottoman rulers and those around them—in a manner similar to that of other European monarchs, such as the Habsburgs in Spain—sought to create a historical record that favored their interests and concerns.[3] Yet, historical writing was far from being constrained to court-sponsored projects.

Indeed, the historical imagination had such a hold on the Ottomans that authors and readers alike often viewed the present in terms of literary or historical models. Thus we read about Ottoman rulers who are the Alexanders or Solomons of their age and grand viziers called "Asaf," linking them to Solomon's vizier. The first occupants of the office of court historian were charged with writing *Shāhnāma*-like accounts of the Ottoman dynasty, in the same meter and rhyme scheme of the eleventh-century poem by Firdawsī, and in Persian; in its first incarnation the position was called the *şehnāmeci*, or *Shāhnāma*-writer. That the image of the Ottoman sultan was modeled in some instances after *Shāhnāma* figures is as evident in the textual content of the manuscripts as in the visual representations that sometimes accompany them.[4] The history of the Ottoman state and Ottoman historiography developed, not surprisingly, in tandem.[5]

Given the Ottomans' predilection for historical writing and record keeping, modern historians of the Ottoman Empire have had a dazzling array of materials through which to examine the history and historiography of the empire. A certain interest in Ottoman historiography was already evident in the work of such early scholars as Fuat Köprülü (d. 1966) and Paul Wittek (d. 1978), who compared chronicles to establish textual authenticity and reliability.[6] In influential essays on Ottoman historiography, Halil İnalcık, Victor Ménage, and John R. Walsh began to explore the literary dimensions of Ottoman historical writing and took account of audiences and contexts of use.[7] These scholars, however, were not interested in Ottoman historians and their writing as historical phenomena in their own right but rather as sources for the reconstruction of a reliable account of events from Ottoman history.[8] Only in recent years, with the work of Cornell Fleischer and Cemal Kafadar leading the way, have historians been moving away from mining Ottoman historical works for "facts" and focusing on contexts of writing and on literary and stylistic dimensions. The work of historians like Gabriel Piterberg, Giancarlo Casale, and Baki Tezcan, some of whom are contributors to the present volume, has been charting exciting new territory in this regard. In a different fashion, Dimitris Kastritsis combines numerous texts with the study of context and reminds us that there is room for historiographical investigation through the close study of a select few texts, while Tijana Krstić, to great effect, makes ample use of texts not traditionally considered in the historical genre.[9] All of these scholars are also careful to consider contexts of production and use and to examine a body of material in a comparative, or supplementary, way. They interpret the sources at hand in an informed fashion, with attention to authorial intentions and anchored in the historical context.

Recent scholarship on Ottoman historiography has also been moving away from an understanding of fifteenth- and sixteenth-century histories as embodying a single, monolithic ideal of the Ottoman state or dynasty. Texts that have heretofore been assigned an "Ottoman" understanding of world events, or "Ottoman" cultural or political motives and interests, are being reassigned to the motivations of individuals, social groups, or political factions reacting to very specific combinations of events. Building on this new understanding of early modern Ottoman history writing, the essays that constitute the current volume present innovative and nuanced readings of a wide range of historical narratives, revealing the implicit—and at times multiple, or even contradictory—messages conveyed by the texts and illustrations of historical manuscripts. These essays demonstrate that even the histories that appear to operate primarily as imperial propaganda reveal different agendas and represent varied attitudes toward the Ottoman dynasty and the members of its ruling elite. Informed by such disparate fields of inquiry as history, art history, and philology, collectively they offer fresh interdisciplinary insights into the heterogeneous nature of history writing within the context of an early modern Islamic empire.

The essays in the present volume focus on a core group of Ottoman histories and historians from the fifteenth and sixteenth centuries. The only exception is the contribution by Hakan Karateke, which analyzes the nineteenth-century responses to these earlier histories. Through innovative approaches to these well-known sources, the scholars contributing to the present volume advance our understanding of a seminal period in Ottoman history. They turn to the sources to answer such questions as how the Ottomans understood themselves in relation to non-Ottoman others as well as within their own court; how they visualized the ideal ruler; how they defined their culture and place in the world; and what the significance of Islam was in their self-definition. Together, the essays examine the role of historiography in fashioning Ottoman identity and institutionalizing the dynastic state structure. As such, they also shed light on the crucial question of why there was a historiographical explosion in the fifteenth- and sixteenth-century Ottoman Empire.

We have chosen to explore three themes within Ottoman historiography: the question of audience, the significance and implications of genre in historical writing, and the definition of what or who is "Ottoman" through the writing of history. By questioning for whom these histories were written, to what expectations they cater, and in which contexts they were read, the essays consider the oft-neglected consumers of these histories. By grappling with the question of what constitutes history in the Ottoman context, and examining the visual and verbal means in which notions of history are signaled in illustrated works, they also move toward a more nuanced definition of Ottoman historiography. The authors remind us of the multiplicity of genres of historical writing and their blending. They provide evidence of dynastic histories that are written into universal histories, biographical dictionaries incorporated into regional histories, war accounts within universal histories, and so on.

The strongest thread running through the essays is the desire, on the part of Ottoman authors, to define who and what is "Ottoman"—perhaps not surprising, as fifteenth- and sixteenth-century Ottomans were clearly preoccupied with determining the nature and contours of their polity and their place in the world. As the geographic boundaries of the state changed dramatically in the fifteenth and sixteenth centuries, Ottoman identity had to accommodate these changes. A frenzy of legal writing—written with the goal of integrating the peoples and the lands conquered under Sultan Süleyman (r. 1520–1566) and his father Selim I (r. 1512–1520)—helped to give order to the newly expanded empire.[10] More often than not, historiography was used to give shape to the newly expanded empire. Many of the studies in the present volume trace the ways in which this happened.

Dimitris Kastritsis's contribution is a historiographic inquiry into one of the earliest surviving works of Ottoman history. He investigates the style, structure, and content of the text to demonstrate that it is a work of propaganda intended to interpret the Ottoman Civil War in such a way as to justify Mehmed I's (r. 1413–1421) right to rule, serving as a rationalization of the succession process, which of course lies at the core of dynastic identity. The text explores Ottoman identity on multiple registers, highlighting the Ottoman values of justice and social balance.

Focusing on a similar moment in history, Baki Tezcan's study is a careful examination of some of the earliest Ottoman historical narratives and the ways in which they reflect a different relationship between the Ottomans and Mongols than that found in later chronicles. Tezcan's essay is a potent reminder that Ottoman identity is not a fixed notion but one that changed over time, as well as from group to group. Tezcan's recreation of the ways in which the early Ottomans imagined themselves in relation to the Mongols suggests that Turco-Mongol identity was the earliest one espoused by the Ottomans, as they defined themselves as the descendants of Turco-Mongol nomads who settled in Anatolia.

Kaya Şahin's contribution is an analysis of Celālzāde Muṣṭafā's (d. 1567) opus magnum, *Ṭabaḳātü'l-Memālik ve Derecātü'l-Mesālik*. Exploring the links between history writing and identity formation at the Ottoman court of the sixteenth century, Şahin demonstrates that the representations of history in Celālzāde's work helped entrench an Ottoman Sunni identity and a state- and dynasty-centric political ideology. Celālzāde wrote his text addressing the elite Ottoman ruling class, employing a self-consciously "Ottoman" language—a rhyming prose that weaves together Arabic, Persian, and Turkish. Focusing on the literary qualities of the text, Şahin demonstrates that Celālzāde, and, by extension, history writing, were influenced by and addressed the political, cultural, and ideological concerns of their immediate context.

Tijana Krstić's study focuses on narratives of conversion and demonstrates not only that Muslim Ottoman authors were concerned with the phenomenon of conversion to Islam and discussed it in their works but also that these texts served as loci where a different aspect of Ottoman identity was negotiated—the place of the convert to Islam. Because a significant portion of the Ottoman elite consisted of such converts, who had gone through the *devşirme* system, discussions of the roles of converts in Ottoman society also concerned the identity of the Ottoman ruling class. Krstić's study also highlights the dynamic nature of Ottoman identity by focusing on the constantly changing debate (in the Ottoman context) about what made a good Muslim and a good subject of the House of Osman.

Giancarlo Casale's essay on a 1559 printed world map accompanied by Ottoman commentary analyzes Ottoman visions of the world in the sixteenth century and examines the place Ottomans carved for themselves in these visions. The object of Casale's inquiry is a work of historical geography that presents a picture of the Ottoman state defined by its relationship to the legacies of Rome and Alexander the Great. He postulates that the argument put forth by the document and its visual form would have resonated with a specific segment of the Ottoman audience. What is at stake here, again, are definitions of the Ottoman Empire and Ottoman identity, forcefully defined as European—a worldview in competition with others circulating in the Ottoman court and among the scholarly classes. The map and commentary, in Casale's analysis, thus become active participants in sixteenth-century Ottoman discourses on identity.

Sinem Eryılmaz's study focuses on the first volume of the illustrated *Shāhnāma-yi Āl-i ʿOṣmān* by ʿĀrif. This, too, is a text that engages with the issue of dynastic legitimacy, Sultan Süleyman's right to rule, and by extension the definition of the Ottoman sultanate. The text justifies Süleyman's reign as preordained and highlights his roles as spiritual and earthly leader, a prophet-like sultan, in word and image. Eryılmaz engages with the issue of genre by comparing ʿĀrif's text to examples of the *Qiṣaṣ al-Anbiyāʾ* (Stories of Prophets) group of texts, demonstrating the overlap of dynastic, universal, and religious histories and examining the ways in which they are all embedded in the *Shāhnāma-yi Āl-i ʿOsmān* project.

Hakan Karateke's contribution, the final one in the volume, considers the nineteenth-century reception of these multiple visions of Ottoman identity and presents yet another idealized view of the empire. Reacting to contemporary political and intellectual circumstances, the histories written by nineteenth-century authors consider the Ottomans part of a newly redefined world, and world history. Exploring these works reminds us that our twenty-first-century notions of the Ottoman past are equally informed by our own surroundings. In a way, the authors whose texts Karateke examines took a much earlier look at Ottoman historiography than we do and were equally aware of its potency in conversations about identity.

The essays in this volume were originally presented as conference papers at a one-day symposium at Indiana University on October 30, 2009, and generated in-depth discussion focusing on the three themes of audience, genre, and "Ottomanness." Their final versions, included in this volume, incorporate the productive exchanges among symposium participants. Together, they remind us of the fluid nature of Ottoman identity and the significant role played by historians in shaping that identity as they addressed different audiences. We hope that with this volume we, too, have been able to make a contribution to our understanding of the Ottoman past and the deliberate ways in which it was recorded by Ottoman historians seeking to shape their future.

Notes

1. See Christine Woodhead, "An Experiment in Official Historiography: The Post of Şehnameci in the Ottoman Empire, c. 1555–1605," *Wiener Zeitschrift für die Kunde des Morgenlandes* 75 (1983): 157–182; Emine Fetvacı, "The Office of the Ottoman Court Historian," in *Studies on Istanbul and Beyond. The Freely Papers*, ed. Robert G. Ousterhout, 1:6–21 (Philadelphia: University of Pennsylvania Museum of Archaeology and Anthropology, 2007); Fatma Sinem Eryılmaz, "The Shehnamecis of Sultan Süleymān: ʿĀrif and Eflatun and Their Dynastic Project" (PhD diss., University of Chicago, 2010); and Emine Fetvacı, *Picturing History at the Ottoman Court* (Bloomington: Indiana University Press, 2013).

2. Cornell Fleischer, *Bureaucrat and Intellectual in the Ottoman Empire: The Historian Mustafa Âli (1541–1600)* (Princeton, N.J.: Princeton University Press, 1986), 237–238; and Lewis V. Thomas, *A Study of Naima* (New York: New York University Press, 1972), 36–42, 66–73.

3. For official history in the Spanish Habsburg context, see Richard L. Kagan, *Clio and the Crown: The Politics of History in Medieval and Early Modern Spain* (Baltimore: Johns Hopkins University Press, 2009).

4. Serpil Bağcı, "Visualizing Power: Portrayals of the Sultans in Illustrated Histories of the Ottoman Dynasty," *Islamic Art* 6 (2009): 113–127. For a study that follows the changing trajectory of Ottoman imperial depictions, see Fetvacı, *Picturing History at the Ottoman Court*.

5. Cemal Kafadar, *Between Two Worlds: The Construction of the Ottoman State* (Berkeley: University of California Press, 1995); and Gabriel Piterberg, *An Ottoman Tragedy: History and Historiography at Play* (Berkeley: University of California Press, 2003), 30–49.

6. Paul Wittek, *The Rise of the Ottoman Empire* (London: Royal Asiatic Society, 1938); and Mehmet Fuat Köprülü, *Osmanlı Devleti'nin Kuruluşu* (Ankara: Türk Tarih Kurumu, 1959).

7. Halil İnalcık, "The Rise of Ottoman Historiography," in *Historians of the Middle East*, ed. Bernard Lewis and Peter M. Holt (New York: Oxford University Press, 1962), 152–167; V. L. Ménage, "The Beginnings of Ottoman Historiography," in *Historians of the Middle East*, 168–179; and John R. Walsh, "The Historiography of Ottoman-Safavid Relations in the Sixteenth and Seventeenth Centuries," in *Historians of the Middle East*, 197–212.

8. This distinction is one made by Piterberg, *An Ottoman Tragedy*, 51–52, although he does not apply it to İnalcık, Ménage, and Walsh in this way.

9. Fleischer, *Bureaucrat and Intellectual;* Kafadar, *Between Two Worlds;* Piterberg, *An Ottoman Tragedy;* Giancarlo Casale, *The Ottoman Age of Exploration* (Oxford: Oxford University Press, 2010); Baki Tezcan, *The Second Ottoman Empire: Political and Social Transformation in the Early Modern World* (New York: Cambridge University Press, 2010); Dimitris Kastritsis, *The Sons of Bayezid: Empire Building and Representation in the Ottoman Civil War of 1402–1413* (Leiden, Boston: Brill, 2007); and Tijana Krstić, *Contested Conversions to Islam: Narratives of Religious Change in the Early Modern Ottoman Empire* (Stanford: Stanford University Press, 2011).

10. Snježana Buzov, "The Lawgiver and His Lawmakers: The Role of Legal Discourse in the Change of Ottoman Imperial Culture" (PhD diss., University of Chicago, 2005), 190–191.

Note on Transliteration

For the sake of consistency, all Arabic, Persian, and Ottoman Turkish titles of historical works, the names of their authors, and all technical terms have been transliterated. Ottoman, Arabic, and Persian words have been transliterated according to the *International Journal of Middle East Studies* system, with the exception that, in Ottoman words, ḫ has been used for خ and h for ه. The titles of historical works cited throughout the volume are transliterated in accordance with the language of composition.

For the sake of convenience and legibility, personal names of well-known historical figures (e.g., Osman, Mehmed, Timur) and words that appear in standard English dictionaries (e.g., sultan, pasha) have been anglicized. Place names are given in their modern and commonly accepted anglicized forms (e.g., Bosnia, not Bosna), or, where appropriate, in their modern or Ottoman Turkish forms.

Names of individuals are followed by the years of their death (d.), regnal years (r.), or, for authors, the years during which their literary activities flourished (fl.) if their dates of death are unknown. Unless otherwise specified, dates follow the Gregorian calendar.

Acknowledgments

THIS PROJECT BEGAN as a panel on Ottoman historiography at the 2006 annual conference of the Middle East Studies Association. Three years later we were able to convene a larger group of scholars on the same topic at Indiana University. The essays in the present volume are revised versions of the papers presented in Bloomington in October 2009. We are grateful to the participants in these scholarly gatherings for their rigorous scholarship and sincere collegiality as both sessions were filled with intense, constructive discussions from which all participants benefited immensely. We are also indebted to the audiences at these events for their thoughtful questions and valuable suggestions. The papers in this volume were improved with the help of this collective feedback and discussion, and we are most thankful to the authors for their patient revisions. In its final form this volume is a testament to collaboration and support among colleagues and friends.

Thanks are also due to the Stanford Humanities Fellowship, the Peter T. Paul Career Development Professorship at Boston University, the New Frontiers New Perspectives Grant at Indiana University, Bloomington, and the departments of History and Near Eastern Studies as well as the College of Literature, Science, and the Arts at the University of Michigan, Ann Arbor, for their financial assistance.

We would like to thank Gottfried Hagen and the anonymous reviewer for Indiana University Press for their helpful criticisms. Janet Rauscher and Sarah Brown copyedited the manuscript meticulously, Robert Sloan at Indiana University Press supported the project from its inception, and June Silay oversaw its production with great care—we could not have asked for better editors.

We are grateful to Christiane Gruber and Daniel Star for their encouragement and support along the way.

WRITING HISTORY AT THE OTTOMAN COURT

1 The Historical Epic *Aḥvāl-i Sulṭān Meḥemmed* (The Tales of Sultan Mehmed) in the Context of Early Ottoman Historiography

Dimitris Kastritsis

Discussions of the birth of Ottoman historiography often state that the Ottomans only began writing their history in earnest at the end of the fifteenth century. Indeed, a significant number of manuscripts from that time are extant, many bearing the simple title *Tevārīḫ-i Āl-i ʿOṣmān* (Chronicles of the House of Osman). Generally speaking, the works recount the early fourteenth-century birth of the Ottoman state and its gradual growth in importance, to the time when its status as an empire was confirmed by the conquest of Constantinople in 1453 under Mehmed II (r. 1444–1446, 1451–1481). They were written with hindsight at a time when the Ottoman Empire was fully established—but in order to tell their stories, they needed to draw upon earlier sources, which must have been available at the time in manuscript form but now only survive thanks to their incorporation into later works.[1]

This essay considers one of the most important of these, which survives intact in two later manuscripts: the *Codex Menzel* (*Mz*) of the chronicle of Neşrī (Mevlānā Meḥemmed, d. ca. 1520) and the *Oxford Anonymous Chronicle* (*OA*). The text in question is an anonymous account of the Ottoman Civil War of 1402–1413, completed shortly after the end of the war. It originally probably bore a title akin to *Aḥvāl-i Sulṭān Meḥemmed bin Bāyezīd Ḫān* (The Tales of Sultan Mehmed, Son of Bayezid Khan; hereafter *Aḥvāl*), and describes the struggle for supremacy of the Ottoman prince Mehmed, who emerged from the Civil War as the sole Ottoman ruler, Sultan Mehmed I (r. 1413–1421).[2] The purpose of this essay is to provide a concise overall description of *Aḥvāl* and evaluate its significance for the development of early Ottoman historiography.

The Civil War of 1402–1413, which modern historical literature often calls the Interregnum, took place after the crushing defeat of the Ottomans by the central Asian empire-builder Timur (Tamerlane, d. 1405) at the Battle of Ankara (July 28, 1402). In that battle, Mehmed's father Bayezid I (r. 1389–1402) was taken prisoner and forced to witness the dismemberment of his empire by Timur over the course of several months, eventually dying in captivity as Timur's armies started their journey back east. Before leaving, Timur recognized several of Bayezid's sons as his vassals, granting them the right to rule over what was left of their father's domain. Of these sons, Mehmed was eventually able to gain the upper hand through the elimination of his brothers. *Aḥvāl* tells that story from the perspective of the winner. It is one of the earliest Ottoman histories that has survived, in a form very close to the original, and is singular in that it describes events early in Ottoman history almost immediately after they had taken place.[3] The style is that of a *menāḳıbnāme* (book of exploits), which was one of the principal genres of Old Anatolian Turkish literature prevalent at the time.[4] In *Aḥvāl*, whose content suggests that it could have been produced only in Mehmed's court, the genre in question is deployed for political purposes. In fact, as I will suggest below, the work probably was meant to be read aloud to an audience, most probably in a courtly or military setting.

Before analyzing the source in terms of its style, structure, and content, more background is needed about the nature of early Ottoman historiography; this will provide the necessary context for the subsequent discussion of the chronicle itself. It was Bayezid II (r. 1481–1512) and his court who seem to have been largely responsible for the production of the comprehensive chronicles of the late fifteenth century, which generally end in 1484, the date when Bayezid made the only important conquests of his reign, the port cities of Kilia and Akkerman on the northern Black Sea coast.[5] These chronicles include the well-known histories of ʿĀşıḳpaşazāde (d. after 1484) and Neşrī, which are interrelated, as Neşrī uses ʿĀşıḳpaşazāde as one of his principal sources.[6] In fact, it is difficult to find a single Ottoman historical work from the fifteenth century that is not to some extent a compilation, a description that applies even to anonymous chronicles, such as those published by Friedrich Giese.[7] The use of such compilations as historical sources presents a formidable problem—it is difficult to judge the accuracy of a narrative passage when its original date of composition and the identity of its author are unknown. Scholars working in the field of Ottoman history have dealt with this problem in different ways. On the one hand, there are those who believe that it is possible and worthwhile to identify distinct kernels by the careful application of philological and historical analysis; on the other are those who doubt the feasibility or value of such an endeavor.[8]

Needless to say, to dismiss entirely the usefulness of trying to unravel the early Ottoman chronicle tradition is to question the very possibility of studying early Ottoman history at all, at least from an internal point of view. For there are few other sources on the subject available to the modern historian, and those are often equally problematic. Just as the chronicle of ʿĀşıḳpaşazāde is in part an eyewitness account and in part derived from at least one other source—allegedly a *menāḳıbnāme* on the House of Osman that the author read when he was a boy—the same is true of other narrative sources on early Ottoman history, such as the chronicles of the Byzantine authors Doukas (d. after 1462) and Chalkokondyles (d. ca. 1490), which were also completed in the second half of the fifteenth century.[9] As for documentary sources, these are scarce for the period before the reign of Mehmed II, especially from within the Ottoman state itself. If we are to understand the foundation of the Ottoman state and its development prior to the conquest of Constantinople, we need to make judicious use of all of the available sources, including chronicles and other historical narratives, whose value increases to the extent that we can identify and analyze their constituent parts.

Many of these texts can be traced to the years following the collapse of Bayezid I's empire after his defeat by Timur. The two most famous are the *menāḳıbnāme* mentioned above, allegedly seen by ʿĀşıḳpaşazāde in 1413 while he was staying as a guest in the house of its author Yaḫşı Faḳīh (fl. ca. 1413), and a poem by the court poet Aḥmedī (d. 1413), which praises the rulers of the Ottoman dynasty to Emir Süleyman (d. 1411).[10] This poem, which is not as much an account of history as a panegyric meditation on historical events, survives as part of Aḥmedī's *İskendernāme,* a lengthy didactic and encyclopedic work inspired by the legend of Alexander.[11] While the two texts are very different, not least because the exact contents of Yaḫşı Faḳīh's lost work are still unknown, it is nevertheless possible to say that they share a common preoccupation with explaining the origins of the House of Osman and the qualities that made it distinct from its neighbors in Anatolia and other political entities in Islamic history. Thus, both works emphasize the Ottomans' role in expanding the domain of Islam (*dārü'l-İslām*) through the practice of holy raiding against Christians.[12] Moreover, both compare the House of Osman to other dynasties, Aḥmedī contrasting their justice with the injustice of the Mongols, and the parts of ʿĀşıḳpaşazāde attributed to Yaḫşı Faḳīh dwelling on the origins of distinctive Ottoman institutions.[13]

Compared to these two works, *Aḥvāl* treats a more limited subject: the tumultuous rise to power of Mehmed I following Timur's victory at Ankara. This period witnessed events that were of decisive significance for the nascent empire, whose very existence was at stake. During his thirteen-year reign, Bayezid I had led a relentless series of campaigns that aimed to turn the state he had inherited into a full-fledged, centralized empire. Already under his father, Murad I (r. 1362–1389), the Ottoman state had become an empire of sorts. From the 1370s, if not earlier, Murad, the first ruler in the dynasty to call himself sultan, counted among his vassals the Byzantine emperor, whose territory could hardly be termed an empire in any meaningful sense at that point. That designation is more suitable for Murad I's state, which was, however, an empire of vassals. His son Bayezid aspired to something greater: a large, unified empire from the Danube to the Euphrates, with Constantinople as its capital. To achieve that goal, he besieged the Byzantine capital for eight years, threatened his Balkan Christian vassals with elimination, and dispossessed the rival Muslim principalities (*beylik*) of Anatolia that stood in his way, annexing them through a series of campaigns largely carried out by the armies of his Christian vassals. When a crusade was launched against him, he crushed it at Nicopolis on the Danube (1396), killing and taking captive many elite knights from Hungary and western Europe. Had he continued unchallenged by Timur, he might well have achieved his goal of becoming the first Muslim ruler of Constantinople. The full realization of that dream, however, would have to wait a half century, for Bayezid's great-grandson Mehmed II, "the Conqueror." After the defeat at Ankara, Bayezid's sons were forced to fight for their survival against each other and the re-established *beyliks* of Anatolia.

Scholars of Ottoman historiography have made the argument that it was the trauma of 1402 that led to the birth of Ottoman historical consciousness.[14] That may well be true but is difficult, if not impossible, to demonstrate. The *menāḳıbnāme* of Yaḫşı Faḳīh was probably complete by 1413, while the historical section of Aḥmedī's poem was definitely written before 1411.[15] It is conceivable and even likely that both works were composed in the decade after 1402, when the rival Ottoman princes would have felt a strong need to legitimize themselves in the face of an outside threat: the Timurid empire, whose rulers were now their overlords and who contested their claims to regional supremacy and expansion at the expense of other Muslim states. While it is also possible that drafts of these works were already in existence before the Battle of Ankara, it is difficult to establish this with certainty.[16] However, this is not the case for *Aḥvāl,* a historical narrative dealing extensively with events that were still recent when it was written. Before analyzing this narrative in detail, both in terms of its content and mode of presentation, it is worth mentioning that it is not the only literary work composed in the court of Mehmed I whose theme relates directly to the Civil War. Just as the prose *menāḳıbnāme* attributed to Yaḫşı Faḳīh has a verse counterpart in Aḥmedī's poem, in the sense that both recount the rise of the House of Osman ruler by ruler, it is possible to say that *Aḥvāl* has a counterpart in a historical poem by the court poet ʿAbdü'lvāsiʿ Çelebi (fl. ca. 1414), which also deals with the Civil War of 1402–1413 and attempts to explain its outcome. However, unlike *Aḥvāl,* about whose date of composition we can only make an educated guess, it is known with certainty that ʿAbdü'lvāsiʿ's *Ḫalīlnāme,* of which the poem forms a part, was completed in 1414.[17]

I will return to this point in due course, when examining the content and main argument of *Aḥvāl,* which is related to that of ʿAbdü'lvāsiʿ's poem. Before doing so, however, it is necessary to consider the work's overall style and structure. I will begin, then, with a brief description of the text as it survives today before turning to a more complete analysis and evaluation of its content.

Aḥvāl: Language, Structure, Style

Aḥvāl survives only as incorporated into two later chronicles. One of these is the chronicle of Neşrī, more specifically an early draft of Neşrī's compilation known as the *Codex Menzel* (*Mz*), while the other is the manuscript known as the *Oxford Anonymous Chronicle* (*OA*).[18]

In both works, it is possible to identify clearly a text of the *menāḳıbnāme* genre, which reads almost identically when the two manuscripts are placed side by side. The work in question describes in epic style the struggles of Mehmed I to establish himself as the sole Ottoman ruler after the defeat and capture of his father at Ankara.

Both versions begin with a chapter heading that is a variant on the phrase *Aḥvāl-i Sulṭān Meḥemmed bin Bāyezīd Ḫān* (The Tales of Sultan Mehmed, Son of Bayezid Khan), suggesting that the lost original also bore such a title.[19] Another indication that we are dealing with what must originally have been a self-contained work is the fact that in both manuscripts the text in question is a story with a beginning and an end. The beginning is the battlefield at Ankara (July 28, 1402), and the end is the death of Mehmed's brother Musa on another battlefield, that of Çamurlu (near Sofia, July 5, 1413).[20] As we will see, Musa's death is presented as the direct result of his murder of his older brother Süleyman, which provides an element that appears to have been very important to the work's anonymous author(s): narrative closure.

Aḥvāl's style in both *Mz* and *OA* should also be mentioned. The chapter headings follow an archaic Turkish construction (with the exception of the first, which, as I have pointed out, was probably the title of the entire work) and refer to the protagonist simply as "Sulṭān Meḥmed," whereas the chapter headings before and after the relevant section of *Mz* are in Arabic and the rest of *OA* uses more elaborate titles for the Ottoman rulers (e.g., *Pādişāh-ı İslām,* the Padishah of Islam, and *Sulṭānü'l-İslām,* the Sultan of Islam). These elements suggest that we are dealing with a work that was circulating in the late fifteenth century but is now lost—except as incorporated into later works. This was copied almost verbatim by Neşrī into an early draft of his chronicle (*Mz*) and was subsequently edited to bring it closer to the style of the rest of the work. As for *OA*, it is possible to say that *Aḥvāl* represents its core; although it covers little more than a decade of Ottoman history, it accounts for approximately one-third of the entire manuscript. The most likely explanation for this discrepancy in a chronicle that recounts nearly two centuries of Ottoman history is that the anonymous compiler(s) of *OA* simply expanded *Aḥvāl* chronologically with the help of various other sources. During this process, it seems that an attempt was made to mimic the style of *Aḥvāl,* notably in the chapter headings, but this principle was only partly respected, as in the context of the late-fifteenth-century Ottoman Empire it would have seemed inappropriate to refer to illustrious and long-dead ancestors of the current ruler by the simple title "Sulṭān." As we will see, in the context of the political challenge unleashed by Timur and especially the Civil War, such a title represented a significant claim on the part of Mehmed I and his court. Other evidence also suggests that *Aḥvāl* was used in this way,[21] but by the time *OA* was compiled "Sulṭān" on its own seemed less lofty and impressive, and its use without any qualification could lead to confusion in a chronicle covering the reigns of no fewer than eight Ottoman rulers. For that reason, in the chapters of *OA* preceding and following *Aḥvāl,* we find, in addition to the titles already mentioned (e.g., *Pādişāh-ı İslām*), many instances in which rulers are referred to by name (e.g., *Sulṭān Murād, Sulṭān Meḥemmed Ḫān,* etc.) and even some rather elaborate combinations (e.g., *Sulṭānü'l-İslām ve'l-Müslimīn Sulṭān Meḥemmed Ḫān,* The Sultan of Islam and the Muslims Sultan Mehmed Khan, used for Mehmed II).[22] When *Aḥvāl* was first composed, such constructions would have been unnecessary, not only because in the historical context of the early fifteenth century "Sulṭān" was a sufficiently lofty title but also because Mehmed I, the sultan to whom the work refers, was still alive.

Using as a guide the folios of *Codex Menzel,* the contents of *Aḥvāl* can be divided into the following five sections:

1. *Mz*, 98–114 (sixteen folios): Mehmed's struggles in the Amasya-Tokat region
2. *Mz*, 114–123 (nine folios): Mehmed's battles in Anatolia with his brother Isa
3. *Mz*, 123–129 (six folios): the conflict in Anatolia between Mehmed and Süleyman
4. *Mz*, 129–133 (four folios): Musa's crossing to Rumelia and defeat of Süleyman
5. *Mz*, 133–141 (eight folios): Musa's reign and Mehmed's struggles against him[23]

The above calculation reveals a glaring inconsistency between the approximate number of folios in, and the time span covered by, each section. Of a total of forty-three folios in *Mz* containing *Aḥvāl,* a full sixteen (or 37%) deal with events that took place while Timur was still in Anatolia, a period of only eight months. Moreover, a further nine (or 21%) describe Mehmed's battles with Isa, which were almost certainly over by September 1403. If these are added together, we see that while our chronicle spans the entire eleven-year Civil War, nearly 60 percent of it deals with the first year alone. Conversely, the period from Isa's defeat in 1403 to Musa's rise in 1409, during which Mehmed had withdrawn to his home base of Amasya following the onslaught of his brother Süleyman, is covered in a mere six folios (or 14% of the chronicle). This is surprising, given that the period in question comprises more than half of the Civil War. Detailed description only resumes again with the rise and fall of Musa (1409–1413), covered in a total of twelve folios (or 28% of the chronicle). In fact, a little more than one-third of that section is dedicated to Mehmed's final campaign against Musa.

It is interesting to note that in the final sections, in which the account becomes more detailed again, the action shifts at least in part to Rumelia, which until that time had been almost entirely absent from the chronicle. However, when perusing the account of Musa's actions there, the reader might believe that the chronicle's author and audience are in Amasya, for the descriptions have a legendary character. On the other hand, Mehmed's final campaign against Musa is described in great detail, almost resembling a campaign diary. Clearly written by someone who participated in the campaign, it is a little "rough around the edges"; the *Ḫalīlnāme*'s verse account of the same campaign, presented to the sultan in 1414, is much more polished. This roughness at the end of *Aḥvāl* suggests a busy period and that the epic needed to be completed in a hurry, in order to provide a complete narrative of Mehmed's rise to power in light of Musa's defeat. Such an account would have been useful at least until 1416, when Düzme Mustafa ("the Impostor," d. 1423) was challenging Mehmed's rule and when the social revolt associated with Sheikh Bedreddīn (d. 1416) made clear that Musa still had many supporters in Rumelia.[24]

What are we to make of *Aḥvāl*'s uneven treatment of its subject matter? To begin, the chronicle's focus on the first year after Ankara suggests two possible interpretations: that it was begun in the immediate aftermath of the battle, in an effort to rally support for Mehmed as he struggled to re-establish himself in Amasya, or that it was started following Süleyman's victories in Anatolia and Mehmed's withdrawal back to his base, in order to build morale by describing former successes. In either case, the intended audience would have been the same: people in the vicinity of Mehmed's court in Amasya, where the work was presumably read aloud, perhaps to assembled troops, the people repeatedly mentioned in the chronicle as "the brave men of Rūm" and "the commanders of Rūm."[25] That *Aḥvāl* was meant to be read aloud is suggested by the fact that many chapters begin with a summary of the previous chapter and end with Mehmed feasting with his men after another great victory. This aspect of *Aḥvāl*'s style becomes repetitive when the entire work is read from beginning to end, but it would have served a useful function if the epic was read in installments, as was most likely the case. While we may never know the exact performative context and audience for *menāḳıbnāme* works like *Aḥvāl,* there is evidence that in this period storytellers (*meddāḥ, qiṣṣakhwān*) were a common presence in courtly and other public settings, such as army barracks, where they could provide varying styles of entertainment depending on their training and audience.[26] Although the language of *Aḥvāl* suggests an author with a high level of education, its style is very lively and there can be little doubt that it was intended to be read aloud. Its stories are recounted in an entertaining and humorous manner, with vivid dialogue. Take, for example, the following passage:

> He shouted with a loud voice: "You are still a young boy, and your mouth smells of your mother's milk. How can you deem it fitting to call yourself Sultan and demand a kingdom?" . . . He replied: "Old fool! Do you think that all this huffing and puffing makes you a man? It looks like you have whitened your beard at the mill, and have never actually done battle with anyone."[27]

Stories told in a lively narrative style like the above could serve not only to bolster morale among Mehmed's own army and people but also to spread his reputation and intimidate his enemies. Visitors to Mehmed's court would presumably hear them being performed and spread them to neighboring areas, where they would act as propaganda. This pattern might explain why there is so little coverage in *Aḥvāl* of the period between 1404 and 1409, when its protagonist was not faring well, a fact that must have been obvious to contemporaneous audiences.

Having described *Aḥvāl* briefly in terms of its language, style, and overall structure, I will now turn to its content. I will begin with the chronicle's primary political argument, which is also found in ʿAbdü'lvāsiʿ Çelebi's poem, before turning to other aspects of its presentation of events.

Aḥvāl and ʿAbdü'lvāsiʿ's Poem: Two Texts, One Argument

While a detailed analysis of ʿAbdü'lvāsiʿ Çelebi's poem on the Battle of Çamurlu is beyond the scope of this essay, which focuses on *Aḥvāl,* the two texts should be studied side by side, as they share not only an overall theme but also their primary political argument. These similarities suggest that both are products of the same court propaganda effort to interpret the Ottoman Civil War in such a way as to justify Mehmed I's victory over his brothers—while at the same time removing from him any blame for their elimination.[28] This campaign was most likely orchestrated by Mehmed's vizier Bayezid Pasha (d. 1421), who had been Mehmed's tutor and was the de facto ruler of his administration, at least in the immediate aftermath of 1402, when the prince was still an adolescent. While it is only possible to speculate on the circumstances of composition of *Aḥvāl,* which is written in the third person and contains no explicit clues, ʿAbdü'lvāsiʿ makes clear that his entire *Ḫalīlnāme,* including the poem on the Battle of Çamurlu, came into being through the encouragement of Bayezid Pasha. This man, who was probably a palace slave (*ḳul*), is described in *Aḥvāl* in relatively modest but heroic terms as "a special lord (*beg*) of the Sultan, who was his favorite and his vizier."[29]

It is worth discussing ʿAbdü'lvāsiʿ's poem here briefly, as it provides some much-needed context for the anonymous *Aḥvāl.* Like Aḥmedī's historical poem, which was discussed in the beginning of this essay, ʿAbdü'lvāsiʿ's is included in a larger work, his *Ḫalīlnāme,* whose main theme is the life of the prophet Abraham. The historical poem appended to this work describes the Battle of Çamurlu, in which Mehmed I eliminated his brother Musa and reunited the Ottoman realm under his own rule.[30] Although the poem chronicles a single campaign and its outcome—unlike *Aḥvāl,* which covers the entire eleven-year-long Civil War—ʿAbdü'lvāsiʿ Çelebi's work also contains broad allusions to what came before Çamurlu. These references are used for rhetorical purposes, to support ʿAbdü'lvāsiʿ's claim that Mehmed is akin to the Islamic *Mahdī*[31] because he eliminated the discord created by his brothers and thereby healed the world:

> God made him an unmixed good
> He made him king of this world, in order to heal it
> Justice had disappeared, but now has returned
> The world is well-managed, and now wears a smile
> Could this man who healed the world be the *Mahdī*?
> Men have found joy, and all sadness is gone
> If this is not the *Mahdī,* then who is the *Mahdī*?
> He has made a cradle for the child of justice
> The cosmos is joyful, the world is well-administered
> This is a sign of the *Mahdī,* whose disposition is famous
> Wherever he goes, with divine assistance he conquers provinces
> Whenever he makes it his goal, *begs* submit to him
> A great khan, of great lineage and great *devlet.*
> That is the proof that he is the*Mahdī*!
> His name is Muhammad, his custom the sharia
> If the *Mahdī* appears, then so does divine truth![32]

It must be made clear that, unlike ʿAbdü'lvāsiʿ's poem, *Aḥvāl* does not compare Mehmed directly to the *Mahdī.* It does, however, emphasize his justice and willingness to share power with his brothers and others, provided they recognize his position as supreme leader. To present Mehmed in that light, both texts share a common narrative of the events of the Civil War that is most clearly evident in *Aḥvāl*. Broadly speaking, this account is as follows. Of the three brothers competing with Mehmed for the throne after Ankara, Isa (d. 1403?) is presented as treacherous and unwilling to share power with Mehmed in Anatolia; Süleyman (d. 1411) as greedy and unwilling to confine himself to Rumelia (the Ottoman Balkans, where he had established himself after the defeat at Ankara); and Musa (d. 1413) as guilty of the death of Süleyman as well as of betraying his oath to rule Rumelia in Mehmed's name, as it was Mehmed who sent him there in the first place, in order to challenge Süleyman's tyrannical rule. Mehmed, on the other hand, is never blamed for the death of his brothers—in *Aḥvāl*'s version of events, Isa simply disappears after losing several battles and Musa is overcome by Mehmed's overzealous officers on the battlefield of Çamurlu, before Mehmed has had time to arrive on the scene.[33]

Such a presentation of events suggests that in the aftermath of the Civil War there was a need to justify the fact that Mehmed I had emerged as sole ruler over what was left of Bayezid I's Ottoman Empire, although this authority had resulted in part from the elimination of his brothers. Of course, Mehmed was not the first Ottoman ruler to come to power by killing his relatives. After the death of Murad I at the Battle of Kosovo, the accession of Bayezid I had been ensured by the elimination of his brother Yakub (d. 1389), and there were probably earlier cases as well.[34] Well before 1402, the Ottoman ruling elite had apparently realized that, in the absence of a clear system of succession, the only way to ensure the smooth transition of power so important for a tax-based agrarian empire was by ensuring that only one candidate succeeded to the throne. Others had to be eliminated, either at court or on the battlefield, in a practice to which modern historians generally refer as fratricide.[35] However, the fact that fratricide was being practiced does not suggest that it was considered acceptable. By the time *Aḥvāl* was written there was a long history of dynastic power sharing in the Middle East, and audiences could point to many examples from the Seljuk and Mongol empires, among other states. After 1402, Timur and his successor Shahrukh (r. 1405–1447) ostensibly supported such ideas of power-sharing, demanding that the Ottoman princes jointly rule the provinces left to them, alongside other Timurid vassals.[36]

To further complicate matters, although the Ottomans did not have a clear succession system, apparently seniority of age was an argument that was being made and needed to be addressed. When the Civil War began, Süleyman and Isa were Mehmed's seniors and he was only a boy. Perhaps for that reason, they found themselves in a more advantageous position. Süleyman was based in the unconquered province of Rumelia and had the support of most of his father's administration, while Isa controlled the Anatolian city of Bursa, which at that time was still considered the principal Ottoman capital.[37] If Mehmed was to succeed and his success was to be explained, each of these arguments had to be systematically rebutted. And indeed, both *Aḥvāl* and ʿAbdü'lvāsi''s poem attempt to do so. On several occasions in *Aḥvāl* there is discussion of a power-sharing arrangement, in which Mehmed would play the role of supreme ruler and his brothers would govern provinces in his name; the same idea is clearly present in 'Abdü'lvāsi''s poem.[38] Moreover, the narrative of *Aḥvāl* also succeeds in absolving Mehmed of all guilt for his brothers' deaths. Finally, the age argument is systematically rebutted by invoking the supernatural concept of *devlet*—one that is difficult to translate but might be rendered as "royal charisma," "talent," or "fortune," a divine mandate to rule that is innate and does not depend on age. Despite its charismatic quality, however, *devlet* is subject to fluctuation and must be proven repeatedly on the battlefield.

Having described *Aḥvāl* in general terms and compared it to 'Abdü'lvāsi''s poem and other historical literature that has survived from the early fifteenth century, I will now examine the chronicle more closely, starting at the beginning.

Aḥvāl: Content Analysis

As we have seen, Mehmed's struggles in the Amasya-Tokat region compose more than a third of the chronicle yet describe events that took place over a period of only eight months. The extensive coverage given to such a short time span can be explained in a number of ways. It has been suggested that Mehmed and his court had a need for a narrative for propaganda purposes, as in the months after Ankara the Ottoman prince was struggling to re-establish his rule in the Amasya area against a number of local adversaries. In fact, those months were highly exceptional by any account. Following his victory at Ankara, Timur occupied Anatolia with his large armies, moving from town to town and devastating the countryside. According to the Byzantine chronicler Doukas, "when the spring came and that harsh and tumultuous winter passed, there was a strong famine and pestilence in all the provinces on which the Scythians set foot, and civil wars."[39] *Aḥvāl* gives us a singular insight into this situation, not least because it focuses on Amasya and Tokat, a region about which little is otherwise known.

First, it is of some interest to note that the chronicle refers most frequently to Tokat, despite the fact that Mehmed's court was in Amasya. Both towns were located in the province of Rūm, the part of Anatolia where the nomadic ideals championed by Timur were arguably the strongest. In pre-Mongol times it had been the core territory of the Danishmendids, who had a more nomadic orientation than the centralizing Seljuks. In Mongol times the nearby town of Sivas had become the seat of the local Ilkhanid governor. Fifty years later, the Mongol governorship was transformed into the *beylik* of Eretna, founded by an Ilkhanid officer. By the end of the fourteenth century what was left of the *beylik* was being ruled by the vizier Kadi Burhaneddin (d. 1398) of Sivas. It was from this man that Bayezid I eventually wrested control of the province. He appointed his young son Mehmed governor in Amasya in 1392 and a year later received the support of some of the most important local tribes.[40] Regarding these tribes, it is clear that in 1402 there was still a strong nomadic presence in the area, with Türkmens inhabiting both the Amasya-Tokat region and the province of Canik to its north. It is also important to note the proximity of the *beylik* of Kastamonu (*İsfendiyār*), located immediately to the north of the corridor connecting Mehmed's base of Rūm with the Ottoman homelands in Bithynia. These factors of politics, geography, and demography provide explanation as to why Mehmed's administration had such difficulty re-establishing itself there while Timur was still present in Anatolia.

Let us take a brief look, then, at the ways in which this situation is represented in the relevant chapters of *Aḥvāl*. Even more than other parts of the chronicle, the early section reads like a *menāḳıbnāme* whose hero is "the Sultan," namely, the young prince Mehmed. Especially in this section, the epic-legendary style can obscure the true nature of events, which is all the more difficult to discern because these are of a local character. After fleeing the battlefield at Ankara, Mehmed reaches Tokat, "killing an incalculable number of the Tatars that came before him."[41] In a distraught state as he contemplates the captivity of his father and the plight of the Ottoman realm and subjects (*re'āyā*), he wishes to attack the Timurid armies in order to save his father but is dissuaded by his advisers, who suggest that he should instead follow the enemy from afar. With this aim in mind, he sets out heading west, where he is confronted by a hostile force led by Kara Yahya, the nephew of Isfendiyar of Kastamonu, on whose territory he is encroaching. A military confrontation ensues in which Kara Yahya is defeated and flees. Mehmed's army pursues the forces, killing those they can reach and plundering their belongings. The description of this first victory (*fetḥ*) of Mehmed is heroic and sets the tone for many more to come. Here we also find a first glimpse of some supernatural elements underlying the chronicle's presentation of events. Mehmed's *devlet* is mentioned for the first time, as is divine predestination (*taḳdīr-i rabbānī*), which "brings things forth from the world of the unseen."[42] Throughout the chronicle, its actors are forced to react to such forces: after Kara Yahya's attack, Mehmed and his *beg*s deliberate on the deeper significance of what happened, saying "now that the world has shown us this face, what is to be done?" They then decide to "climb up into the steep mountains and watch the state of the world."[43] While we might be tempted to dismiss such phrases as mere topoi, in fact they play a significant role in a narrative that aims to present Mehmed's rise to power as an event that was destined to happen.

A significant aspect of the way such deeper forces seem to work is through the absence or loss of *devlet*. As we have seen, this concept is used on several occasions in *Aḥvāl* to explain why Mehmed, "who is only a young boy," has the right to confront various enemies, including his two older brothers. In the early chapters of *Aḥvāl*, first Kara Yahya and then Kara Devletşah face Mehmed in battle and both are presented as doubting his authority because of his age. Mehmed, however, soundly defeats them, thereby proving that he has the right to rule. When Kara Yahya confronts Mehmed again a few chapters later, the Ottoman prince is presented as smiling and telling his men: "Has this man whose *devlet* was defeated come up against us again? Is he totally devoid of shame and honor? We must take care of him."[44] The same concept is deployed later to explain Mehmed's proposal to his brother Isa, namely, that Mehmed should keep Bursa and the surrounding territory in Bithynia, while Isa should take Aydın, Saruhan, Germiyan, Karasi, and Karaman, territories that at this time were no longer under Ottoman rule. It should come as no surprise to the chronicle's audience that Isa objects, as he is the older brother and Bursa is already in his control. The chronicle makes clear, though, that primogeniture is irrelevant: the right to rule is intrinsic and God given, to be proven in battle. After Isa rejects Mehmed's proposal, Mehmed says: "It is inevitable that we must fight with this man. At least now the fault will not have been ours" and leads his army into battle. As the battle intensifies, everyone wonders "to which side will *devlet* turn?"[45] Of course, Mehmed wins, thereby establishing that he is the supreme ruler, a fact that is proven beyond doubt by three additional victories over Isa. When Mehmed's other older brother, Emir Süleyman, hears that the former has defeated Isa and been enthroned in Bursa, he objects that Mehmed "is but a boy, since when is he suitable for the throne?" However, his advisers reply that the matter is for God to decide, "for even if that person is young in age, he is made great by his *devlet*. Whoever has confronted him in the past was eventually defeated."[46]

That the epic *menāḳıbnāme* style of *Aḥvāl* is strongest in its early chapters has already been stated. These chapters describe a number of confrontations with tribes,[47] the siege of an unidentified fortified town, and Bayezid Pasha's operation to "smoke out the bandit" (*ḥarāmī*) Mezid from a mosque in Sivas.[48] Indeed, there is a striking resemblance here to other early Ottoman chronicles, specifically Giese's anonymous *Tevārīḫ* and the parts of ʿĀşıḳpaşazāde attributed to Yaḫşı Faḳīh. As with those texts, it is tempting to dismiss such stories as little more than legends created to serve political aims. However, there is more to all of this than seems evident: it is thanks to *Aḥvāl* alone that we learn of the appointment by Timur of a certain Kara Devletşah to rule over Amasya. We are told explicitly that he circulated his diploma of appointment (*nişān, yarlıġ*), saying "Timur has granted this province to me." Based on Timur's policies in other parts of Anatolia, it seems likely that this man was from a family with claims dating to pre-Ottoman times, and we are told that he had with him an army of Kurds. As for Mezid, he was apparently the son-in-law of Kadi Burhaneddin, the pre-Ottoman ruler of Sivas.[49] With the exception of Kara Devletşah, who is killed in battle, all of Mehmed's adversaries escape alive and become part of his government. The Ottoman prince thus emerges from these skirmishes as the ruler of a tribal confederacy in the region of Rūm, ready to enter into a marriage alliance with the neighboring principality of Dulkadir.

However, Mehmed first must respond to another marriage proposal, which would make him the son-in-law of Timur himself. This scenario comes as part of a story consisting of three chapters.[50] The section occupies an intermediate position in the narrative, between the local struggles that we have already seen and the rest of the chronicle, in which the focus is Mehmed's dealings with his brothers and the *beyliks* of Anatolia. It describes the Ottoman prince's response to an invitation from Timur to visit his court while the central Asian conqueror is still wintering in Anatolia. There is much exaggeration here—we are expected to believe that in the months after Ankara, Mehmed had become so powerful that even Timur feared him:

> While Timur was wintering in the province of Aydın, a Tatar came to him and said: "There is no young warrior in the world today as brave and valorous as Sultan Mehmed. Unlike his father, he is a difficult enemy! He has taken the heads of many men from your army. He has settled on the road passing through that province, and doesn't give a chance to those who fall into his hands, but destroys them all. Unless you take care of him, you too are in danger. There is a chance that he won't let you pass through there."[51]

How can we interpret such stories? Aside from the question of their veracity, we must consider the narrative function they fulfill in a historical account such as this, which was clearly meant to be performed in public. The mention, here and elsewhere in the chronicle, of "Tatars" (namely, Mongols) is significant: to an Ottoman (or otherwise *Rūmī*) audience, Timur and his armies represented a revival of the Mongol presence in Anatolia, especially in an area like Amasya, which had been near the center of local Ilkhanid rule. As in other early Ottoman chronicles, a clear rivalry is present between *Rūmī*s and Tatars, who are presented as wicked and unworthy of trust.[52] This can be seen again later in *Aḥvāl*, when Mehmed is betrayed by a Tatar named Toyran (*Doyıran*? lit. "he who fills up"), who had pledged to support him against his brother Süleyman but instead raided the countryside around Ankara "like a bandit" (*ḥarāmī*).[53]

In fact, banditry is one of the principal accusations in *Aḥvāl* against Mehmed's enemies, few of whom are actually Tatars. We have already seen the term used for Mezid in Sivas, and it is also applied to Kara Devletşah, the Türkmen Gözleroğlu, and, on one occasion, even Mehmed's brother Musa Çelebi, who "escaped to the mountains, becoming a bandit."[54] The implication is that anyone who lives as a nomad or engages in otherwise disorderly behavior is opposed to the stable, sedentary administration represented by Mehmed, his court, and his army. People who wander the mountains and countryside raiding settled populations are mischievous and antisocial elements to be subdued or eliminated. Our source employs considerable skill in stigmatizing its hero's enemies in this way, exploiting what must have been residual anti-Mongol and antinomadic feeling in an audience more or less loyal to what had become by then a sedentary Ottoman state. However, as we will discover in the chronicle's presentation of Emir Süleyman and Çandarlı Ali Pasha (d. 1406), there can also be a negative side to sedentary rule.

Let us return to the story of Mehmed's aborted visit to Timur and try to understand its context and significance. After his victory at Ankara, Timur considered himself overlord of the entire realm formerly ruled by Bayezid I and gave diplomas of appointment to local rulers to administer parts of it in his name. These included Ottoman princes—there is evidence that both Isa and Musa were given diplomas to rule over Bursa and its surrounding region of Bithynia. However, the differences between Bithynia, where the original Ottoman emirate had been formed, and Mehmed's province of Rūm, which was a recent acquisition, were significant. Under the circumstances, it was reasonable for Mehmed to fear that Timur's invitation was a trap, one that would lead not to the granting of a diploma of appointment to the governorship of Amasya and Tokat but instead to his imprisonment. The chronicle tells us as much when it relates that Mehmed's advisers discouraged him from answering the invitation, which was part of Timur's plan to "get hold of [Mehmed] without using violence." Of course, in typically heroic fashion, the protagonist of the chronicle rejects their advice because "his mind became set on the idea that of course he must answer Timur's invitation."[55] When he is attacked along the way, though, he is finally persuaded that a visit to Timur is too risky. By means of an ambassador, Mehmed presents his apologies to Timur, who responds with news of Bayezıd's death and departs for the east immediately thereafter.[56]

Perhaps the real purpose of the story of Mehmed's aborted visit to Timur is to explain why—unlike his brothers and the other rulers of Anatolia reinstated as Timur's vassals when the central Asian conqueror departed for the east—Mehmed was left without a diploma of appointment. In the immediate post-Timurid situation this represented a serious problem of legitimacy. For that reason, our chronicle presents Timur as responding to what was allegedly the will of the late Ottoman sultan Bayezid, namely, that Bayezid's corpse and his young son Musa, who had been taken captive at Ankara, be surrendered to Mehmed. To the chronicle's audience, this act would confer on Mehmed the legitimacy of an heir apparent selected by Bayezid and recognized as such even by Timur. It is important to note here the crucial role of the Germiyanid ruler Yakub II (r. 1387–1390, 1402–1411, 1413?–1429), who was certainly an ally of Mehmed's at this time and who appears to have been responsible for obtaining the corpse of Bayezid along with the captive prince Musa. Mehmed was able to use these relatives (both dead and alive) to great advantage when seizing Bursa from his older brother Isa, for it seems that Musa had been granted a diploma for the city by Timur in order to bury his father there. With the young Musa in his court, Mehmed could claim to be entering Bursa in order to bury his father, acting as regent for an underage brother, who held a diploma of appointment from Timur.[57] Much is made of all of this by our chronicle, which of course points to Mehmed's need to legitimize himself in the immediate aftermath of Timur's departure from the area. Perhaps the strongest expression of that need is the fact that the only coin on which an Ottoman prince's name appears alongside that of Timur was minted by Mehmed around this time.[58]

Turning to a different theme, I have already suggested that *Aḥvāl*'s presentation of Tatars and its general *menāḳıbnāme* style are not the only elements that it shares with ʿĀşıḳpaşazāde and other early Ottoman historical literature. Another is the vilification of the Çandarlı family, a vizierial dynasty that played a central role in the development of the early Ottoman state.[59] Specifically, *Aḥvāl* takes aim at Emir Süleyman's grand vizier Çandarlı Ali Pasha, who had also held that post under Bayezid I and was arguably the most important member of Bayezid I's administration. Following the Battle of Ankara, Ali Pasha had rescued Süleyman from the battlefield and taken him to Rumelia, where he played an instrumental role in ensuring the continuity of the Ottoman administration following the disaster of 1402. As we have seen, the transition was much less smooth in the case of Mehmed in the province of Rūm, where Mehmed's tutor and vizier Bayezid Pasha played a similarly central role. We have seen that Bayezid Pasha was definitely behind the *Ḫalīlnāme* of 'Abdü'lvāsi' Çelebi and probably also *Aḥvāl*—if so, then it is possible to consider *Aḥvāl* 's vilification of Çandarlı Ali at least in part as an expression of the rivalry between grand viziers. This would have been more than just personal: because Bayezid was probably a *ḳul*, and the Çandarlı family belonged to the scholarly class (*'ulemā'*), the two would have represented different tendencies within the early Ottoman state at a time when Bayezid I's centralization project and its demise had revealed severe divisions within Ottoman society. These are clearly visible, if not always easy to understand, in the early Ottoman chronicle tradition; for example, in the anonymous *Tevārīḫ* edited by Giese, the vilification of the Çandarlı has been traced to frontiersmen and other social elements opposed to centralization. The Çandarlı family and other "schoolmen" coming from the Anatolian hinterland are blamed for importing from farther east such classic Middle Eastern institutions as taxation based on land surveys, Islamic judges, and slave armies—the famous Janissary corps was created by Ali Pasha's father, Çandarlı Halil Hayreddin Pasha (d. 1387).[60]

In this light, it is interesting to note that while in the first third of *Aḥvāl* the villains are largely unruly tribal elements accused of oppressing the peasant population (*re'āyā*), with Emir Süleyman's arrival on the scene the focus shifts to that Ottoman prince's corrupt courtly habits and wily grand vizier. Ali Pasha makes two appearances in the chronicle, both involving deception by means of letters, a fitting crime for someone perceived by his enemies as a corrupt scholar. In the first appearance he intercepts an order from Mehmed to the officer guarding the fortress of Ankara and changes its content, resulting in the surrender of the fortress to Süleyman. In the second, during a long operation of Mehmed against Süleyman, Ali Pasha sends a letter to Mehmed warning him of treason in his ranks, thereby causing him to abandon the operation. To make matters worse, Süleyman is presented as receiving news of Mehmed's impending attack from an official sent to carry out a land survey, whom he receives in the bath while drinking wine.[61] Elements such as these serve to create a negative image of Süleyman's administration—which is of course headed by Çandarlı Ali Pasha—as burdened by greed, deception, and other ills of an overcivilized courtly life. On the other hand, Mehmed and his grand vizier Bayezid Pasha represent a government based on justice and acceptance of divine order. Through military vigor and constant vigilance, they are able to maintain a balance between nomads, peasants, and town-dwellers. Thus it can be said that, apart from the concept of royal charisma (*devlet*) decreed by divine predestination and proven in battle, the chronicle's worldview is also infused with ancient Near Eastern ideas of justice and social balance. When reading of the struggles of Prince Mehmed against his brothers and numerous other adversaries, what comes to mind is the so-called circle of justice, a metaphor for a social order in which each class works to maintain the balance that is a sine qua non of royal power and prosperity.[62]

The same idea is evident in the final part of *Aḥvāl,* which treats the rise and demise of Mehmed's brother Musa. We have already seen that Musa's crimes include killing Süleyman and betraying his oath to rule in Mehmed's name, but the Ottoman prince is also presented as guilty of alienating important magnates. According to *Aḥvāl,* Musa "marched and conquered all of Rumelia for himself, and started to eliminate renowned *begs* from among the *begs* of Rumelia." These included Ali Pasha's brother Çandarlı Ibrahim Pasha (d. 1429), who fled to Constantinople and sent a message to Mehmed "informing him of Musa Çelebi's abominable actions and of the hatred that the *begs* harbored for him." This story comes immediately after the chapter describing Emir Süleyman's downfall, precipitated by his dishonorable treatment of several officers, including one whose beard is shaven. Thus both brothers become guilty of disturbing the natural order of society, according to which a ruler must respect his lords. Mehmed, however, is guilty of no such crime. According to *Aḥvāl,* upon receiving news of Musa's actions from Çandarlı Ibrahim, "he sent a letter with a robe of honor and invited him with various displays of respect to join him."[63] Mehmed's generosity can also be seen in the large banquet he hosts for the entire army before setting out on his final campaign against Musa in 1413. On that occasion he is presented as so overwhelmed by zeal to defeat his treacherous brother that he gives away everything in his sight to the prince of Dulkadir, his brother-in-law and ally, while also bestowing robes of honor and other gifts to the rest of his officers and men. As he does so, he states that all he needs in life is a horse, sword, and mace:

> In the course of friendly conversation, the Sultan warmed up, and gifted to Dulkadiroğlu the clothes that he was wearing, the horse he rode on, and every sort of banqueting utensil in the room: goblets, decanters, and various other gold and silver utensils. And he donated robes of honor to his *begs* and men, bestowing endless bounty on each and every one of them. Then the Sultan became passionate, and said: "Let everyone know that I am campaigning in Rumelia. I have a horse, a sword, and a mace, and they are enough for me! Whatever else is won is to be shared with my companions!"[64]

Aḥvāl's presentation of its hero as someone who is not without material wealth, but who is only interested in the honor and well-being of his fighters and subjects, was probably intended to resonate with elements of a society that felt threatened by the centralization policies of Bayezid I. However, more research on that period of Ottoman history is needed before it will be possible to make any pronouncements on the exact causes and nature of the social tensions so clearly echoed in this and other early works of Ottoman historical literature. What is clear is that the collapse of 1402 was a watershed and that Bayezid's centralizing, imperialist tendencies were widely viewed as responsible for his downfall. In light of Timur's victory, and of the depredations caused by his armies in the months that followed, writers like ʿAbdü'lvāsiʿ, Aḥmedī, Yaḫşı Faḳīh, and the anonymous author(s) of *Aḥvāl* emphasized in descriptions of their patrons and the entire Ottoman family certain values: justice, humility, self-sufficiency, bravery against all odds, and pious acceptance of the divine will. Because, like other works, *Aḥvāl* was incorporated verbatim into later histories, it is possible to say that the social and political concerns that it reflects continued to play an important role in shaping the image and historiography of the Ottoman Empire, even into the modern era.

Notes

1. Halil İnalcık, "The Rise of Ottoman Historiography," in *Historians of the Middle East*, ed. Bernard Lewis and Peter M. Holt (London: Oxford University Press, 1962), 152–167; V. L. Ménage, "The Beginnings of Ottoman Historiography," in *Historians of the Middle East*, 168–179; Ménage, *Neshrī's History of the Ottomans: The Sources and Development of the Text* (London: Oxford University Press, 1964); and Cemal Kafadar, *Between Two Worlds: The Construction of the Ottoman State* (Berkeley: University of California Press, 1995), 90–105.

2. The work in question was first identified by İnalcık and Ménage. See İnalcık, "The Rise of Ottoman Historiography," 157, 161; Ménage, "The Beginnings of Ottoman Historiography," 176; and Ménage, *Neshrī's History*, 13–14. For a critical edition and English translation, see *Aḥvāl-i Sulṭān Meḥemmed bin Bāyezīd Ḫān*, ed. and trans. Dimitris Kastritsis as *The Tales of Sultan Meḥmed, Son of Bayezid Khan*, (Cambridge, Mass.: Harvard University, Department of Near Eastern Languages and Civilizations, 2007). *Mz* was lost during the Second World War; thankfully, there is a published facsimile: [Mevlānā Meḥemmed] Neşrī, *Ǧihânnümâ: Die altosmanische Chronik des Mevlânâ Meḥemmed Neschrî*, Vol. 1, ed. Franz Taeschner (Leipzig: Harrassowitz, 1951). The page numbers in these notes refer to Taeschner's facsimile edition. There is also a published facsimile of *OA*: [Oxford] Anonymous, Oxford University, Bodleian Library, Marsh 313, published as *Rûhî Târîhi*, with transcription, by Yaşar Yücel and Halil E. Cengiz (Ankara: Türk Tarih Kurumu Basımevi, 1992). Unfortunately, it is mistakenly attributed to the historian Rūḥī (d. 16th c.), the folios are not numbered, and one double set of pages that exists in the original is missing from the facsimile. The numbers below refer to the original folios.

3. On the Ottoman Civil War, see Dimitris Kastritsis, *The Sons of Bayezid: Empire Building and Representation in the Ottoman Civil War of 1402–1413* (Leiden: Brill, 2007); *Encyclopedia of Islam*, 2nd ed. (hereafter cited as *EI²*), s.v. "Meḥemmed I" (Halil İnalcık); and Elizabeth Zachariadou, "Süleyman Çelebi in Rumili and the Ottoman Chronicles," *Der Islam* 60, no. 2 (1983): 268–290. Despite its obvious bias, it is the contemporary nature of *Aḥvāl* that makes it so useful for the reconstruction of events. While the more important battles, skirmishes, and territorial gains or losses would have still been fresh in the minds of its audience a generation later, when the Ottoman state had recovered from Ankara and its aftermath, most such events would have seemed obscure.

4. On this broader genre in the Islamic world, see *EI²*, s.v. "Manāḳib" (Charles Pellat). For the immediate context of Old Anatolian Turkish literature, see "Introduction," in *The Battalname, an Ottoman Turkish Frontier Epic Wondertale*, ed. and trans. Yorgos Dedes (Cambridge, Mass.: Harvard University, Department of Near Eastern Languages and Civilizations, 1996), 1–84.

5. Ménage, "The Beginnings of Ottoman Historiography," 171; and Kafadar, *Between Two Worlds*, 97.

6. ʿĀşıḳpaşazāde, *Die altosmanische Chronik des ʿĀşıḳpaşazāde*, ed. Friedrich Giese (Leipzig: Harrassowitz, 1929); Ménage, *Neshrī's History*; Neşrī, *Kitâb-ı Cihan-nümâ. Neşrî Tarihi*, 2 vols., ed. Faik Reşit Unat and Mehmed A. Köymen (Ankara: Türk Tarih Kurumu, 1949–1957); and Neşrī, *Ğihânnümâ: Die altosmanische Chronik des Mevlânâ Meḥemmed Neschrî*, 2 vols., ed. Franz Taeschner (Leipzig: Harrassowitz, 1951–1959).

7. Anonymous, *Die altosmanischen anonymen Chroniken: Teârîh-i Âl-i ʿOsmân*, ed. Friedrich Giese (Breslau: self-published, 1922).

8. Kafadar, *Between Two Worlds*, 90–105; and Colin Imber, *The Ottoman Empire 1300–1481* (Istanbul: Isis Press, 1990), 1–5.

9. Ménage, "The Menākib of Yakhshi Faqīh," *Bulletin of the School of Oriental and African Studies* 26 (1963): 50–54; Doukas, *Istoria Turco-Bizantină (1341–1462)*, ed. Vasile Grecu (Bucarest: Editura Academiei Republicii Populare Romîne, 1958); Doukas, *Decline and Fall of Byzantium to the Ottoman Turks*, trans. Harry J. Magoulias (Detroit: Wayne State University Press, 1975); and Laonikos Chalkokondyles, *Laonici Chalcocandylae historiarum demonstrationes*, 2 vols., ed. Jeno Darkó (Budapest: Academia Litterarum Hungarica, 1922–1927).

10. Ménage, "The Menākib of Yakhshi Faqīh"; and Aḥmedī, *Tevārīḫ-i Mülūk-i Āl-i ʿOṣmān ve Ġazv-i İşān Bā-Küffār: Tāceʾd-Dīn İbrāhīm bin Ḫıżır Aḥmedī*, critical ed. Kemal Silay (Cambridge, Mass.: Harvard University, Department of Near Eastern Languages and Civilizations, 2004).

11. Aḥmedī, *İskender-nāme: İnceleme, Tıpkıbasım*, ed. İsmail Ünver (Ankara: Türk Tarih Kurumu, 1983); and Ménage, "The Beginnings of Ottoman Historiography," 169–170.

12. This is a controversial point, as in the ʿĀşıḳpaşazāde-Yaḫşı Faḳīh compilation such passages can be attributed to the compiler rather than his source.

13. These include white headgear instead of red and the practice of standing at attention when military music is heard. Aḥmedī, *Tevārīḫ*, ed. Silay, chap. 1, verses 3–12; Aḥmedī, *İskender-nāme*, ed. Ünver, 65b; Paris Bibliotheque Nationale Turc 309, 289a; ʿĀşıḳpaşazāde, *Die altosmanische Chronik*, ed. Giese, 13–14 (chap. 8), 37 (chap. 31); and Kafadar, *Between Two Worlds*, 146, 152.

14. Kafadar, *Between Two Worlds*, 94–96.

15. The Ottoman prince Emir Süleyman, to whom the *İskendernāme* is dedicated, died on February 17, 1411. See Kastritsis, *Sons of Bayezid*, 153–158. The oldest surviving manuscript is from 1416 (Paris, Bibliotheque Nationale, MS Turc 309). See Aḥmedī, *Tevārīḫ*, ed. Silay, viii, xviii–xix; and Aḥmedī, *İskender-nāme*, ed. Ünver, 24–27. Ünver's edition reproduces the oldest and most complete manuscript in Turkey (İstanbul Üniversitesi Kütüphanesi, MS TY 921). This is also the manuscript on which Silay based his edition.

16. İnalcık, "The Rise of Ottoman Historiography," 152, cites the demonization of Çandarlı Ali Pasha in the passages of ʿĀşıḳpaşazāde attributed to Yaḫşı Faḳīh as proof that the latter was writing under Mehmed I. Ali Pasha had sided with Mehmed's rival Emir Süleyman—see the last part of this essay for further discussion of this theme.

17. ʿAbdüʾlvāsiʿ Çelebi, *Ḫalīlnāme*, ed. Ayhan Güldaş (Ankara: T. C. Kültür Bakanlığı, 1996), 9. According to Güldaş, the work was probably written over the course of one or two years in Amasya, which had been Mehmed's base during the Civil War. On ʿAbdüʾlvāsiʿ Çelebi and his work, see also Günay Alpay, "Abdülvâsi Çelebi'nin Eseri ve Nüshaları," *Türk Dili Araştırmaları Yıllığı: Belleten* 33 (1969): 201–226.

18. For details on these manuscripts see note 2.

19. *Mz*, 98: "Aḥvāl-i Sulṭān Meḥemmed bin Bāyezīd Ḫān bin Murād Ḫān bin Orḫān bin ʿOṣmān"; *OA*, 46b: "Fī beyān aḥvāli's-Sulṭān Meḥemmed Ḫān bin Bāyezīd Ḫān."

20. *OA*, 46b–103a; *Mz*, 98–141. For the events in question, see Marie Mathilde Alexandrescu-Dersca Bulgaru, *La campagne de Timur en Anatolie (1402)* (Bucharest: Monitorul Oficial si Imprimeriile

Statului, 1942); Klaus-Peter Matschke, *Die Schlacht bei Ankara und das Schicksal von Byzanz: Studien zur spätbyzantinischen Geschichte zwischen 1402 und 1422* (Weimar: Bohlau, 1981); and Kastritsis, *Sons of Bayezid*, 41–50, 188–194.

21. Examples include coins minted by Mehmed and the anonymous *Chronicle of the Tocco* (completed after 1422), which calls Musa "the emir" and Mehmed "his brother, the sultan." See the coin chart in *EI*², s.v. "Meḥemmed I" (Halil İnalcık), 974; Cüneyt Ölçer, *Yıldırım Bayezid'in Oğullarına Ait Akçe ve Mangırlar* (Istanbul: Yenilik Basımevi, 1968); Anonymous, *Cronaca dei Tocco di Cefalonia di anonimo*, ed. Giuseppe Schirò (Rome: Accademia nazionale dei Lincei, 1975), 360–363; and Kastritsis, *Sons of Bayezid*, 198–199.

22. *OA*, 152b.

23. The corresponding pages in *OA* are 46b–66b (I); 66b–79a (II); 79a–87a (III); 87a–92a (IV); and 92a–103a (V).

24. Other arguments for this dating of the chronicle can be found in Kastritsis, *Sons of Bayezid*, 28–33. Recent literature on the revolt of Sheikh Bedreddīn with up-to-date references includes Kastritsis, "The Revolt of Şeyh Bedreddin in the Context of the Ottoman Civil War of 1402–13," in *Halcyon Days in Crete 7: Political Initiatives "From the Bottom Up" in the Ottoman Empire* (Rethymno: University of Crete Press, 2012), 233–250; H. Erdem Çıpa, "Contextualizing Şeyḫ Bedreddīn: Notes on Ḫalīl b. İsmā'īl's Menāḳıb-ı Şeyḫ Bedreddīn b. İsrā'īl," in *Şinasi Tekin'in Anısına: Uygurlardan Osmanlıya* (Istanbul: Simurg, 2005), 285–295.

25. *Rūm dilāverleri* (*OA*, 46b; *Mz*, 98); *Rūm serverleri* (*OA*, 47b; *Mz*, 99 and passim).

26. "Introduction," *Battalname*, ed. Dedes, 61–64.

27. *OA*, 50b; *Mz*, 101: "Sen henüz bir ṭıfıl oğlan olub anañ südi ağzuñda ḳoḳar. Ne liyāḳat-ü-isti'dād ile aduñı sulṭān ḳoyub memleket ṭaleb idersin? . . . eyitdi ki 'İy pīr ḫerīf! (*OA*: ḥaref) Bir nice hay ve huy idüb (*Mz*: bunca hay ḥuy idüb) gendüñi bir ādem mi ṣanursın? Beñzer ki saḳaluñ degirmende ağardub kimsenüñ żarbın ve ḥarbın görmemişsin."

28. Kastritsis, *Sons of Bayezid*, 195–220.

29. *OA*, 61b; *Mz*, 110: "meger gendünüñ bir ḫāṣṣ [*OA*: ḥażır] begi vardı, aña Bāyezīd Paşa dirlerdi. Sulṭān'uñ maḳbūli idi ve hem vezīri idi." This is part of the story of Mezid Beg, allegedly a bandit but actually a local claimant to power in Sivas, who is smoked out of a mosque by Bayezid Pasha (*OA*, 61b–62b; *Mz*, 110–111). When Bayezid takes him before Sultan Mehmed, the latter forgives him and confirms him as his vassal, at which point Mezid "made many wishes for the well-being of Bayezid Pasha and went about his business" (*Bāyezīd Paşaya çoḳ du'ālar idüb işine meşġūl oldı*). On Bayezid Pasha's *ḳul* and Albanian origins, see Doukas, *Istoria Turco-Bizantină*, ed. Grecu, chap. 22:10, 164–167. The chronicler provides a rich description of Bayezid's important connection to Mehmed and his family, which should be taken seriously, if viewed critically. However, Aydın Taneri suggests instead that the vizier was born in Amasya, without even mentioning Doukas (see *Diyanet Vakfı İslam Ansiklopedisi* (hereafter cited as *DİA*), s.v. "Bayezid Paşa (ö. 824/1421)." On the Mezid incident, see Kastritsis, *Sons of Bayezid*, 75–76.

30. 'Abdü'lvāsi' Çelebi, *Ḫalīlnāme*, ed. Güldaş, 254–278 (verses 1,731–1,924). An English translation is in Kastritsis, *Sons of Bayezid*, 221–232.

31. Literally, "the rightly guided one," a messianic, eschatological figure expected to appear and rule before the end of the world. See *EI*², s.v. "Al Mahdī" (Wilferd Madelung). In the early Ottoman context the views of Ibn 'Arabī (d. 1240), other Sufis, and even the Shi'a should be taken into account.

32. 'Abdü'lvāsi' Çelebi, *Ḫalīlnāme*, ed. Güldaş, verses 1,738–1,745: "Anı bir ḫayr-ı maḥż itmişdür Allāh / Bu 'ālem oñmağ içün 'āleme şāh // 'Adālet gitmiş idi geldi şimdi / 'İmāret oldı 'ālem güldi şimdi // Meger Mehdī budur kim oñdı 'ālem / Ferahlar buldı ādem gitdi hep ġam // Eger Mehdī degülse ḳanı Mehdī / Ol itdi ma'dilet ṭıflına mehdi // Cihān ḫoşlıḳda 'ālem oldı ma'mūr / 'Alāmet Mehdīden budur ḫō [*sic*?] meşhūr // Ne yire varsa illerdür müyesser / Ḳaçan ḳaṣd itse beglerdür müsaḫḫar // Ulu aṣl ulu devletlü ulu ḫān / Anuñ mehdīligine uşbu bürhān // Muḥammed-ismdür

resm-i şerī'at / Ḳoparsa Mehdī uş ḳopdı ḥaḳīḳāt." A full translation is in Kastritsis, *Sons of Bayezid,* 221–232.

33. The relevant passages are the following: ʿAbdü'lvāsiʿ Çelebi, *Ḫalīlnāme,* ed. Güldaş, verses 1,750–1,770; *OA,* 68a–69a, 77a–78b, 91a–91b, 102a–103a; *Mz,* 115, 121–122, 132, 140–141. See also Kastritsis, *Sons of Bayezid,* 206–220.

34. Kafadar, *Between Two Worlds,* 105–108, 136–137; Cemal Kafadar, "Osman Beg and His Uncle: Murder in the Family?" in *Studies in Ottoman History in Honour of Professor V. L. Ménage,* ed. Colin Heywood and Colin Imber (Istanbul: Isis Press, 1994), 157–163; and Mehmet Akman, *Osmanlı Devletinde Kardeş Katli* (Istanbul: Eren, 1997), 43–58.

35. The term is not entirely accurate, as rivals could also include uncles and other first-degree male relatives.

36. This attitude can be seen in Shahrukh's letter to Mehmed I, in which Shahrukh reprimands Mehmed for killing his own brothers, stating that such behavior goes against the custom of the Ilkhanid Mongols (*Töre-i İlḫānī*). See Ferīdūn Aḥmed, *Münşe'ātü's-Selāṭīn. Mecmū'a-i münşe'āt-ı Ferīdūn Bey* (Istanbul: Dārü'ṭ-ṭıbā'ati'l-ʿāmire, 1264–1265 [1848–1849]), 150–151; English translation and analysis in Kastritsis, *Sons of Bayezid,* 203–205.

37. See *EI*^{2}, s.v. "Meḥemmed I" (Halil İnalcık), 975; and Kastritsis, *Sons of Bayezid,* 46, 79–100. It was apparently the Timurid devastation of Anatolia in 1402–1403 that made Edirne appear a safer and more attractive capital once the Civil War was over; after all, it had functioned as such under Süleyman and Musa.

38. In *Aḥvāl* the best example is Mehmed's alleged power-sharing proposal to Isa before the Battle of Ulubad (spring 1403): *OA,* 68b–70a; *Mz,* 115–116. Others are Süleyman's unwillingness to confine himself to Rumelia and Musa's alleged betrayal of his oath to rule in Mehmed's name: *OA,* 71b; *Mz,* 117; *OA,* 87a; *Mz,* 129; ʿAbdü'lvāsiʿ Çelebi, *Ḫalīlnāme,* ed. Güldaş, verses 1,748–1,753, 1,762–1,770.

39. Doukas, *Istoria Turco-Bizantină,* ed. Grecu, chap. 18:3, 113. My translation.

40. İsmail Hakkı Uzunçarşılı, *Osmanlı Tarihi* (Ankara: Türk Tarih Kurumu, 1947), 1:260–268, 275–278; Yaşar Yücel, *Kadı Burhaneddin Ahmed ve Devleti (1344–1398)* (Ankara: Ankara Üniversitesi Basımevi, 1970); Elizabeth Zachariadou, "Manuel II Palaeologos on the Strife between Bayezid and Kadi Burhan al-Din Ahmad," *Bulletin of the School of Oriental and African Studies* 18 (1980): 471–481; and John E. Woods, *The Aqquyunlu: Clan, Confederation, Empire* (Salt Lake City: University of Utah Press, 1999). For additional references, see Kastritsis, *Sons of Bayezid,* 64–66.

41. *OA,* 46b; *Mz,* 98: "öñine gelen Tatardan bī-ḥadd u bī-ḳıyās ḳırub."

42. *OA,* 48b–49a; *Mz,* 100: "görelüm ki taḳdīr-i rabbānī ʿālem-i ġaybdan ne iẓhār ider. El-ḥamdü li-llāh ki Allāh ʿināyetinde ve sulṭānumuz devletinde vaḳtumuz ḫoş ve niʿmetümüz bī-nihāyedür."

43. *OA,* 48b; *Mz,* 100: "Çün ʿālem bu vech ile ṣūret gösterdi, ne itmek gerek? Maṣlaḥat oldur ki bu aradan ḳalḳub aşaġa ṭarafa gidevüz, ṣarp ṭaġlara çıḳub ʿālemüñ ḥāline naẓar idevüz."

44. *Mz,* 112: "Bu devleti ṣınmış gişi yine üstümüz mi geldi? Bunuñ ḫōd ʿār u ġayreti yoġımış. Bunuñ ḥaḳḳından gelmek gerek."

45. *OA,* 68b–69a; *Mz,* 115: "Sulṭān . . . eyitdi ki "Bunuñla lā-cerem ceng itmek gerekdür. Hele yaramazlıḳ bizden olmadı" diyüp . . . iki ʿasker cūş u ḫurūşa gelüb . . . meydān erenleri ilerü yöriyüb "Devlet ḳanḳı ṭarafa müteveccih ola?" dirken . . ."

46. *OA,* 71b; *Mz,* 117: "Henüz bir ṭıfıl oğlandur, taḫta ḳaçan lāyıḳdur? İmdi ḫāṭırum şöyle ister ki Anaṭolı ṭarafına geçüb taḫtı elinden alam . . . begler eyitdiler ki 'İy şāh! Eyü dirsiz, ammā iş Allāh'uñdur. Zīrā egerçi ol gişi yaşda giçidür, devletde ulu gibidür. Her gişi ki anuñla muḳābil oldı āḫirü'l-emr münhezim olup ṣındı."

47. For example, İnaloğlu, Köpekoğlu, Gözleroğlu.

48. *OA,* 51a–62b; *Mz,* 102–111; Kastritsis, *Sons of Bayezid,* 63–77; and *EI*^{2}, s.v. "Meḥemmed I" (Halil İnalcık), 974.

49. See note 29.
50. *OA*, 62b–67a; *Mz*, 111–114.
51. *OA*, 62b–63a; *Mz*, 111: "Temür Aydın İlinde ḳışlar iken bir Tatar gelüp Temüre eyitdi ki 'Bugün (Mz: tekevvün-i) 'ālem içinde Sulṭān Meḥemmed gibi pehlivān ve bahādur yigit yoḳdur. Atasına beñzemez, şarp yağıdur. Leşkerüñden çoḳ gişinüñ başın almışdur, bu yolda ṭurub ele girenin mecāl virmeyüb helāk ider. Eger anuñ ḳaydın görmezseñ saña daḫı ḫaylī iḥtiyāṭ vardur. İḥtimāl var ki seni ol ṭarafa geçürmeye' didi."
52. There are some good examples in the section of 'Āşıḳpaşazāde's chronicle attributed to Yaḫşī Faḳīh. For some of these, see 'Āşıḳpaşazāde, *Die altosmanische Chronik*, ed. Giese, 13 (chap. 7), 25–26 (chap. 21). As we have seen above, it is likely that Yaḫşī Faḳīh was writing after 1402, which might explain why he focuses on Tatars, as they were associated with the central Asian and pro-Mongol Timur. See also the story in the same chronicle in which the captive Bayezid I begs Timur to take the Tatars with him when he leaves Anatolia: 'Āşıḳpaşazāde, *Die altosmanische Chronik*, ed. Giese, 72 (end of chap. 27).
53. *OA*, 79b–80b; *Mz*, 123–124.
54. *OA*, 89a; *Mz*, 130: "Mūsā Çelebi bu ḳażiyyeye muṭṭali' olıcaḳ şınub ḳaçub ṭağlara düşüb ḥarāmi oldı."
55. *OA*, 63a–64b; *Mz*, 111–112: "Çün Temür bunı işitdi be-ġāyet münfa'il oldı, ammā 'aḳlı reyi birle tedbīr idüb bu melāleti iẓhār itmeyüb 'Aḥsen-i vech ile Sulṭānı şāyed ele getürem' didi . . . Sulṭān'uñ mecmū'-ı vezīrleri ve begleri şöyle maṣlaḥat gördiler ki Sulṭān bir ḳadem Temürden yaña mütevec-cih olmayub . . . Sulṭān çün beglerinden ve vezīrlerinden bu ḫaberi işidicek fikri bunuñ üzerine muṣammem oldı ki, el-bette Temürüñ da'vetin icābet ide (*Mz*+ Ḥaḳḳ te'ālā ezel-i āzālde' başına ne yazub yazılan ne nesne idügin göre)."
56. Kastritsis, ed., *The Tales of Sultan Mehmed*, 13–15.
57. For the document proving the alliance between Mehmed and Yakub II of Germiyan, see Şinasi Tekin, "Fatih Sultan Mehmed Devrine Âit bir İnşâ Mecmuası," *Journal of Turkish Studies* 20 (1996): 296; and Kastritsis, "Çelebi Meḥemmed's Letter of Oath (*Sevgendnāme*) to Ya'ḳūb II of Germiyan: Notes and a Translation Based on Şinasi Tekin's Edition," in *Şinasi Tekin'in Anısına:Uygurlardan Osmanlıya* (Istanbul: Simurg, 2005), 442–444. See also Kastritsis, *Sons of Bāyezīd*, 81–89. Apparently Mehmed's mother was also Yakub's sister: see *EI*[2], s.v. "Germiyān-oghulları" (Irène Mélikoff).
58. For the coin, see Ölçer, *Yıldırım Bayezid'in Oğullarına Ait Akçe ve Mangırlar*; İbrahim Artuk and Cevriye Artuk, *İstanbul Arkeoloji Müzeleri: Teşhirdeki İslami Sikkeler Kataloğu* (Istanbul: T.C. Millî Eğitim Bakanlığı, Eski Eserler ve Müzeler Genel Müdürlüğü, 1970–1973); and *EI*[2], s.v. "Meḥemmed I" (Halil İnalcık), 974 (chart). See also Kastritsis, *Sons of Bayezid*, 49.
59. On the Çandarlı family, see İsmail Hakkı Uzunçarşılı, *Çandarlı Vezir Ailesi* (Ankara: Türk Tarih Kurumu, 1974); Franz Taeschner and Paul Wittek, "Die Vezirfamilie der Ğandarlyzāde (14./15. Jhdt.) und ihre Denkmäler," *Der Islam* 18 (1929): 60–115; and *EI*[2], s.v. "Djandarlı" (V. L. Ménage).
60. *EI*[2], s.v. "Yeñi Čeri" (Rhoads Murphey); Anonymous, *Die altosmanischen anonymen Chroniken*, ed. Giese, 31; and Bernard Lewis, *Islam from the Prophet Muhammad to the Capture of Constantinople*, 1:139–140.
61. *OA*, 80b–85b; *Mz*, 124–128.
62. On this concept, see Ibn Khaldūn, *The Muqaddimah: An Introduction to History*, trans. Franz Rosenthal (Princeton, N.J.: Princeton University Press, 1967), 40–41. For a discussion and citation of Ottoman authors, see Ariel Salzmann, *Tocqueville in the Ottoman Empire: Rival Paths to the Modern State* (Leiden: Brill, 2004), 76–77. See also Halil İnalcık, *The Ottoman Empire: The Classical Age* (New York: Praeger, 1973), 65–69.
63. *OA*, 92a–92b; *Mz*, 133: "Mūsā Çelebi . . . yöriyüb tamām Rūmilin żabṭ-u-ḥıfẓ idüb Rūmili beglerinden be-nām be-nām begleri helāk itmege başladı . . . İbrāhīm Paşa . . . Sulṭāna ḫaber

gönderüb, Mūsā Çelebinüñ afʿāl-ı şenīʿesin iʿlām idüb begler andan (*Mz:* beglerinden) nefret itdügin bildürdi. Sulṭān çün bu ḫaberi istimāʿ itdi, mektūb u ḫilʿat gönderüb envāʿ-i taʿẓīm birle anı daʿvet itdi." For the story of Süleyman's ill treatment of his *begs*, see *OA*, 89b–91a; *Mz*, 131–132.

64. *OA*, 98a; *Mz*, 137: "Andan Sulṭān (*Mz*+ germ olup) vezīrlerine ve beglerine eyitdi ki: "Her kim var ise (*Mz:* dilerse) bilsün ki Rūmiline sefer iderem. Bir atum ve bir ḳılıcum ve bir çomaġum vardur, baña kifāyet ider. Bāḳī ne ele gelürse (*Mz:* girürse) mecmūʿı yārān ile der-miyāndur."

2 The Memory of the Mongols in Early Ottoman Historiography

Baki Tezcan

THIS ESSAY EXPLORES the ways in which fourteenth-century historiography reflects the Ottomans' relationship with their ultimate overlords, the Mongols. When Osman, the founder of the Ottoman dynasty, started his military operations in Byzantine Bithynia (in northwestern Anatolia, to the east of the Marmara Sea) around 1300, most of Anatolia was under the direct rule of the Ilkhans, a dynasty that was established in Azerbaijan by Genghis Khan's grandson Hulagu (d. 1265), the Mongol ruler who conquered Baghdad in 1258 and brought the Abbasid Caliphate to an end. Most Ottoman historical sources, however, either do not refer to the Mongols or mention them only as troublemakers in Anatolia. Rather, they anachronistically cast the Ottomans into a relationship of vassalage with the Anatolian Seljuks, a Turkish dynasty that ruled most of Anatolia from the late eleventh to the thirteenth century, when they became vassals of the Ilkhans before gradually disappearing from the political scene altogether.

I argue that some of the earliest Ottoman historical narratives reflect a different way of imagining the Mongols. According to this alternative historical construction, the Mongols were the cousins of the Ottomans and the Ottomans did not need the blessing of the Seljuks to establish political rule in Anatolia. This particular depiction of the relationships among the Mongols, the Ottomans, and the Seljuks was forgotten in the fifteenth century, the early years of which witnessed the last remnants of Mongol power in Anatolia leaving the land. Fortunately, ʿĀşıḳpaşazāde (d. after 1484),[1] arguably the most important Ottoman historian of the late fifteenth century, had access to a historical source that predated this memory loss.

There is a rather graphic story in ʿĀşıḳpaşazāde's account of the exploits of Osman, the founder of the Ottoman dynasty. Sultan Alaeddin, who is supposed to be a Seljukid ruler, is besieging Karaca Hisar, which is probably the fortress of Inönü in the vicinity of Eskişehir, in the northwestern corner of central Anatolia. Osman is there to help him. After a few days of warfare, messengers arrive to inform Alaeddin that a certain Mongol named Bayinjar attacked Ereğli,[2] killed its inhabitants, and burnt the whole city. Upon hearing the news, the Seljuk sultan leaves the siege to Osman and rushes to Ereğli. Bayinjar encounters Alaeddin along the way, and Seljuk and Mongol forces face each other in a place called Biga Öyüğü (*Bīġā Öyügī*), engaging in a fierce battle for two days and two nights. In the end, the Seljuks overcome Bayinjar's Mongol forces:

> They decimated them so [badly] that they cut their testicles, sewed the testicle skins to each other, covered [them] with felt, [and] constructed awnings [with them] to make a name [for themselves]. Even now they call that plain the Plain of Testicle[s].[3]

This essay begins with an analysis of this striking story. Following Zeki Velidî Togan's suggestion that this story carries the memory of a Turco-Mongol rebellion, which was crucial to the foundation of the Ottoman political enterprise in Bithynia around 1300, I argue that the earliest Ottomans considered themselves close relatives of the Mongols—in contrast to their post-1402 descendants, who were forced to rebuild their polity in the aftermath of their traumatic defeat against Timur (d. 1405), the Turco-Mongol victor of the Battle of Ankara (1402). Coming to the verge of political annihilation in Mongol hands, the Ottomans revised the representation of Mongols in their chronicles. Moreover, once Ilkhans lost their political power over Anatolia, and once most of the descendants of the thirteenth-century Mongol conquerors left for Central Asia in the company of Timur in the first years of the fifteenth century, political genealogies in Anatolia set the Mongols aside and focused on the Turcomans (Turkish nomads) instead, as the remaining political power holders in Anatolia were mostly of Turcoman origin. In such a climate, the Anatolian Seljuks, a dynasty whose founders had originated from one of the Turkic Oghuz tribes in the eleventh century, became much more appropriate role models and retrospective lords than the Mongols. Furthermore, after the Ottomans embraced the political legitimacy provided by the sixteenth-century adoption of Sunni orthodoxy, a close association with the Mongols could prove to be embarrassing, as the Mongols with whom the earliest Ottomans were in contact were the sons or grandsons of those who had sacked Baghdad in 1258 and brought the Abbasid Caliphate to an end. Connecting the Ottomans directly with the Seljuks, the saviors of the Abbasid Caliphate from the Shi'ite Buyids earlier in 1055, provided a much more legitimate genealogy.

Thus, the close relationship between Ottoman rulers and Mongols in the fourteenth century was conveniently forgotten in the fifteenth century, when the Ottomans constructed their past in such a way as to prove themselves noble Turcomans. After they reinvented themselves as the political representatives of Sunni orthodoxy in the sixteenth century, they had more reasons not to remember their Mongol connections. In the early twentieth century, when a lively debate about the origins of the Ottomans commenced, Togan pointed to the possibility of their Mongol origins. His voice was silenced, however, by that of Mehmet Fuat Köprülü, who was keen on securing the Turkish credentials of the Ottomans, as he was building a nationalist school of historiography for the young Turkish Republic.[4]

Leaving the questions of why and how the memory of the Mongols was conveniently omitted from the Ottoman historiography of the fifteenth, sixteenth, and twentieth centuries—and how closely the early Ottomans were indeed associated with the Mongols—to a different occasion, this essay aims to recreate the manner in which the early Ottomans imagined themselves in relation to the Mongols. I will first analyze the story of the "Plain of Testicles" with a view to establishing both the significance it holds in early Ottoman historiography and the clues it provides to the foundation of the Ottoman polity as a Mongol vassalage. Next, I explore ʿĀşıḳpaşazāde's text for further clues about the memory of the Mongols in early Ottoman historiography, arguing that the earliest Ottomans imagined their forefathers arriving in Anatolia in the company of the Mongols. Thus, the earliest self-definition found in Ottoman historiography is a Turco-Mongol one.

The "Plain of Testicles"

The striking story of the "Plain of Testicles" must have been associated with a significant event in early Ottoman memory, as it seems to have been retold many times, leading to its entry, in several versions, into early Ottoman chronicles. In the early fifteenth century, Aḥmedī (d. ca. 1412) mentions that while Ertuğrul (Osman's father) was in the company of Alaeddin engaged in *ghaza,* the Seljuk sultan returned to Konya to attend to the Mongols who broke their peace agreement with him.[5] In Şükrullāh's (d. after 1464) account from the mid-fifteenth century, Ertuğrul assists Alaeddin in the siege of Karaca Hisar. The name of the Mongol leader, the town he attacked, and the place where the Mongol and Seljuk forces face each other are not yet mentioned, but the awning (or tent) made out of testicle skins is.[6] Rūḥī (d. 1522) presents a similar account, but in his version Alaeddin and Ertuğrul besiege Kara Hisar-ı Sahib (modern Afyon in the western part of central Anatolia) as opposed to Karaca Hisar, and he states that the sultan rushed back to Konya.[7] Neşrī (d. ca. 1520) follows Şükrullāh in attributing the event to the lifetime of Ertuğrul but parallels ʿĀşıḳpaşazāde in naming Ereğli as the place that the Mongols attacked and identifying the leader as Bayinjar—he differs only in the spelling of the site of the battle: Boğa Öyüğü (*Būġā Öyügī*).[8] Kemālpaşazāde (d. 1534) places the incident in the lifetime of Ertuğrul, too; he identifies both Ereğli and Biga Öyüğü and mentions the infamous awning/tent as well but names the Mongol leader Baçu.[9] Oruç (d. after 1503) does not name the leader of the Mongols and differs from others in identifying the site that was attacked by Mongols as Ablistan (*Āblistān*), which stands for modern Elbistan (in the southeastern corner of central Anatolia), the pre-Ottoman spelling of which was Abulustayn. Yet he is in agreement with others in the description of the fate of Mongol bodies.[10] In short, most fifteenth- and early sixteenth-century Ottoman chroniclers agree that the Seljuks defeated the Mongols and made awnings from the testicle skins of their enemies.

However, Müneccimbaşı (d. 1702), an Ottoman historian of the late seventeenth century well known for his world history in Arabic, noted that such a battle might not have taken place because the Seljuks could not possibly fight the Mongols in this period, during which the former were like prisoners to the latter.[11] While Müneccimbaşı is most certainly correct, the graphic description of the fate of Mongol bodies and the vivid testimony of the place name, the "Plain of Testicles," are narrative features shared by most of the chroniclers who related this anecdote—suggesting that this is not a fictive battle. While one could invent a historical battle, it is difficult to imagine concocting such lively details that have circulated so widely. While it might reasonably be argued that such a battle must have taken place, perhaps the Mongols actually won or the battle was between different parties. More than sixty years ago, Togan suggested the latter.[12] The more recent work of Rudi Paul Lindner, who underlines the early Ottomans' vassalage to the Mongols, along with the implications of Togan's suggestion, which point toward a closer relationship between the earliest Ottomans and the Mongols, together strengthen the arguments of both Lindner and Togan, as will be shown below.

The story of the "Plain of Testicles" might have been inspired by several military confrontations. Two major battles were fought between the Mongols and the Seljuks: the well-known battle of Kösedağ in northeastern Anatolia in 1243, after which the Seljuks recognized Mongol suzerainty, and the battle around Sultanhanı in central Anatolia in 1256, after which large contingents of Mongols settled in Anatolia. In both of these battles the Mongol forces were led by Baiju, whose name might well have been the source of the name Baçu in Kemālpaşazāde's account. The reference to Elbistan in the account of Oruç might be related to the memory of the Battle of Elbistan (1277), in which the Mamluk sultan Baybars defeated a Mongol force. As for the mention of Ereğli, it probably reflects the memory of the Mongol response to the Turcoman attacks in 1291. Gaykhatu, the Mongol ruler of the Ilkhanate, had come to Anatolia on the invitation of the Seljukid sultan Mesud (d. 1308), who was unable to contain the Turcomans. The Mongol forces spread fear with a series of massacres that started in Ereğli.[13] Thus, the story of the Mongol-Seljuk confrontation found in early Ottoman chronicles seems to have been a composite account built from the memories of different military encounters in which the Mongols constituted one of the opposing parties.

Togan's interpretation of the story, however, was based on a military engagement in which both of the parties included Mongols. Both ʿĀşıḳpaşazāde and Neşrī identify the Mongol leader as Bayinjar, which reminds one of the Mongol governor Bayinjar, who was sent to Anatolia in 1298 by the Ilkhanid ruler Ghazan Khan (r. 1295–1304).[14] Bayinjar was defeated—and killed—by Sulamish, another Mongol commander and the grandson of Baiju, the general of the victorious Mongol armies at Kösedağ in 1243 and at Sultanhanı in 1256, as well as the commander of the first Mongol contingents to settle in Anatolia after 1256. Sulamish was offended by the appointment of Bayinjar and advocated for an independent state in Anatolia under his own leadership. His rebellion in the winter of 1298–1299 was supported by many Turcoman groups. The recently appointed Seljuk sultan Kayqubad III (r. 1298, 1301–1302) left his throne and ran away. Eventually, Sulamish was caught in the vicinity of Ankara, perhaps on his way to the Turcomans of the Kastamonu region in search of more troops. While narrating the end of Sulamish in 1299, Aḳsarāyī, a contemporary administrator of Seljuk finances in Anatolia, notes with relief that the "rebels of the marches" had finally quieted down.

Rashīd al-Dīn (d. 1318), another contemporary historian who was also a close adviser of Ghazan Khan, states that the army of Sulamish included soldiers from the Anatolian marches and that Sulamish was distributing insignia of rule to his supporters.[15] Togan suggests that one should substitute the Mongol Sulamish for the Seljukid Alaeddin in the story narrated by ʿĀşıḳpaşazāde and speculates that it was from Sulamish that Osman should have received the insignia of local rule in Bithynia.[16]

As a textual support to his argument, Togan cites ʿĀşıḳpaşazāde's positive attitude toward a comrade of Osman who is supposed to have come to Bithynia in the company of Ertuğrul but later moved slightly northeast to Mudurnu, leaving Ertuğrul in Söğüd. The name of this comrade is Samsa Çavuş. While Samsa does not seem to be a Turkish name, *çāvuş* is an old Turkish title. What makes Samsa of special interest to this discussion is that his brother's name, Sülemiş, is identical to that of the Mongol commander Sulamish. The story recounted by ʿĀşıḳpaşazāde includes clear indications of an alliance established between Osman and Samsa, with the purpose of engaging in joint raids in the area across the river Sakarya/Sangarius, where Samsa had the advantage of local knowledge. Perhaps because of this advantage, Samsa appears to be the senior partner of the alliance: Osman agrees to accept "whatever Samsa Çavuş says."[17] While there is no evidence that connects Samsa and his brother Sülemiş with Mongols—other than the names of Sulamish and Sülemiş—Togan suggests that the memories of Osman's relations with Sulamish the Mongol commander might have been projected on his relations with Samsa.[18]

Two pieces of circumstantial evidence provide further support to Togan's suggestion. While little else is known about Samsa and Sülemiş, Göynük, which is in the vicinity of the area in which they settled, is mentioned by an early fourteenth-century source as a locality ruled by a Mongol emir named Jaku.[19] Thus, Samsa might well have been Jaku's Mongol predecessor in the area. At least we can be certain that Osman had some Mongol neighbors. Second, ʿĀşıḳpaşazāde records the alliance with Samsa and his brother Sülemiş in the same year as the battle against Bayinjar. The year in which both of these events are recorded, 687/1288–1289, is about ten years too early for the historical date of the battle between Bayinjar and Sulamish; however, the fact that the memory of the battle is associated with an alliance reached with a possibly Mongol senior partner whose brother's name is recorded as Sülemiş makes one give further consideration to Togan's suggestion.

Most recently, Lindner followed Togan with additional evidence gathered from numismatic sources. Lindner asserts that the numismatic evidence does not support Togan's suggestion about Osman's reception of insignia of rule from Sulamish, and he argues that Osman recognized Ghazan Khan as his overlord;[20] the evidence that he presents, however, does not rule out the possibility of both options. It is now well demonstrated that Osman recognized the Mongol Ilkhans as his suzerain. In 1999, Aydın Ayhan and Tuncer Şengün presented a coin on which the name of Abu Said (r. 1316–1335), the last powerful Mongol Khan in Persia, is followed by that of Osman, indicating the latter's vassalage of the former.[21] Osman's acceptance of a vassal status, however, probably dates to the reign of Ghazan Khan and possibly to 1300. There are several coins minted in various parts of Anatolia in the name of Ghazan Khan that bear the date of 699/1299–1300, many of which originate from the Turcoman marches, possibly including the territory of Osman.[22] While this is not surprising, as the Mongols had been the suzerains of the Seljuks for quite some time, it is important to note that in this year there was "a spike of over forty mints compared with the much lower numbers for preceding and following years."[23] According to Lindner, these coins, which symbolize the political authority of Ghazan Khan over the territories that are mentioned on them as mint locations, suggest that the suzerainty of the Mongol Khan in Persia was reasserted in Anatolia in 1300 with a special effort to include the Turcoman marches.

It is quite possible, however, that Osman might have both received insignia of rule from Sulamish during the latter's rebellion in return for a promise of support and recognized Ghazan Khan as his overlord after the crush of Sulamish's forces. The Seljuk sultan Kayqubad III had left his throne during the Civil War and could not secure Ghazan's reapproval of his sultanate until much later.[24] In short, in 699/1299–1300 Ghazan Khan was not simply the suzerain of a Seljuk sultan but the direct ruler of Anatolia. Thus, political logic would dictate that Osman recognize Ghazan Khan as his suzerain at this time. If Osman indeed supported Sulamish during the Civil War as Togan surmises,[25] then he had even more reason to recognize the suzerainty of Ghazan Khan—lest he be regarded as a rebel. As suggested by Lindner,[26] the year 699/1299–1300, which traditionally has been regarded as the official beginning of Ottoman independence from the Seljuks, might well be the beginning of Ottoman vassalage under the Mongols.

Between Togan and Lindner, other scholars—such as İsmail Hakkı Uzunçarşılı, Irène Beldiceanu-Steinherr, and Halil İnalcık—have recognized the early Ottomans' relationship of vassalage with the Mongols.[27] In addition, there is documentary evidence for this vassalage relationship, as suggested by the copy of a Persian document from 1350 that unequivocally identifies Osman's son Orhan (r. 1324–1362) as a lord of the Anatolian marches paying tribute to the Mongols.[28] What is not there, however, is the recognition of this relationship in Ottoman chronicles. While Togan's suggestion—that the infamous battle on the "Plain of Testicles" was between Sulamish and Bayinjar—might never be proven, it is worth following his lead in looking for further clues about the relationship between the Mongols and the Ottomans in the chronicle of ʿĀşıḳpaşazāde, as the text does indeed have a much more Mongol-friendly tone in its first parts than other early Ottoman chronicles.[29] The possibility that the great-great-grandfather of ʿĀşıḳpaşazāde, Muhlis Pasha, was a close associate of Sulamish during his rebellion in 1298–1299 makes him an even more attractive source for an attempt to reconstruct early Ottoman attitudes toward the Mongols.[30]

A Turco-Mongol Genesis for the Ottomans

Having established the significance of the event whose memory was transformed into the "Plain of Testicles" story that is so commonly found in early Ottoman chronicles, I have suggested that the event that inspired this story might be the victory of the Turco-Mongol rebels led by Sulamish against the Mongol governor Bayinjar. Whether or not Osman supported this rebellion and secured certain privileges in Bithynia from Sulamish, gave his allegiance to Ghazan Khan, or did the latter after the former, as of 1300 he was most likely a Mongol vassal operating in Bithynia. Because we also know—based on numismatic evidence—that Osman recognized the Mongol ruler Abu Said as his overlord later in the first half of the fourteenth century, and because documentary evidence suggests that his son Orhan inherited this legacy, one would expect to find traces of an association with the Mongols in the fourteenth-century self-definition of the Ottomans. In this section I demonstrate that association and argue that in their genesis story the early Ottomans defined themselves as the descendants of Turco-Mongol nomads who settled in Anatolia.

Before considering this genesis story, however, I would like to emphasize the singularity of this story found in the chronicle of ʿĀşıḳpaşazāde by demonstrating that most Ottoman chronicles produced in the fifteenth and early sixteenth centuries display a conscious effort to distance the Ottomans from the Mongols and connect them with the Seljuks.[31] It is important to underline the singular nature of the story, which suggests that this particular genesis story in ʿĀşıḳpaşazāde probably circulated during the time of Orhan, Osman's son and the second ruler of the Ottoman dynasty. ʿĀşıḳpaşazāde identifies one of his sources as a chronicle by Yaḫşı Faḳīh, the son of Isḥāḳ Faḳīh, who, in turn, was the imam of Orhan. Whereas some scholars thought that Yaḫşı Faḳīh's chronicle must be the source of those parts of the text of ʿĀşıḳpaşazāde that were shared by other early Ottoman historical works, such as the corpus of texts known as the "anonymous chronicles," Victor Ménage demonstrated that Yaḫşı Faḳīh's chronicle should be sought in those passages of ʿĀşıḳpaşazāde that "have no counterpart in the 'Anonymous chronicles.'" Thus, if ʿĀşıḳpaşazāde's genesis story is indeed unique, it could well be ascribed to Yaḫşı Faḳīh, who must have reflected the sensibilities of Orhan's reign when his father was the imam of Orhan, who was counted among the frontier vassals of the Mongols.[32] That is not to say, however, that all Mongols mentioned by ʿĀşıḳpaşazāde are friendly. Yet when Mongols are mentioned negatively, there is always a reason why they deserve reproach, as in the case of the "Çavdar" Mongols, who attack Ottoman territory only to be defeated by Orhan (yet Osman makes a truce with them), and treacherous Mongols, who join Timur's forces during the Battle of Ankara.[33]

Most early Ottoman chronicles claim that Osman, the founder of the Ottoman dynasty, and/or his father served the last Anatolian Seljuk sultan(s); thus, the

Ottomans legitimately received their ancestral homeland in northwestern Anatolia from the Seljuks in return for their services.[34] Some of these accounts also assert that Osman received his insignia of rule from a Seljuk sultan.[35] Aḥmedī's *İskendernāme* offers a very clear example of the contradiction created by ignoring the Mongol connection while building a fictitious relation to the Seljuks. The section on the Ottoman dynasty is not the only historical part of Aḥmedī's work. It is rather the concluding section of a longer part devoted to the history of the kings who reigned after Alexander the Great; this section includes a life of Muhammad followed by a history of the four caliphs, the Umayyads, and the Abbasids. Following his account of the last Abbasid caliph of Baghdad, Aḥmedī recounts the history of Genghis Khan and his descendants, the Ilkhans who invaded Persia, Iraq, and Anatolia. The last kings mentioned by Aḥmedī before he begins his account of the Ottomans are the Jalayirids, who were the leaders of a Mongol tribe and replaced the Ilkhans in Azerbaijan and Iraq in the mid-fourteenth century. The Seljuks do not figure prominently in Aḥmedī's summary of Islamic history; there is no section devoted to them.[36] This absence reflects the political reality of the late Middle Ages in the eastern parts of the Islamic world, where political legitimacy was tied to a lineage dating to the Mongols, the last conquerors of the contemporaneous eastern Islamic world—Timur, too, had Mongol ancestry.

Yet, when Aḥmedī begins his account of Ottoman origins, he starts with "Sultan Alaeddin," who is not so much a real person as the default Seljuk king who came to represent all Anatolian Seljuks in early Ottoman historiography. According to Aḥmedī, Osman's father Ertuğrul was serving Alaeddin in the frontiers of the Seljuk kingdom.[37] Once Timur left Anatolia, taking with him the last remnants of the Mongol troops who numbered 30,000–40,000 families and had been using the Anatolian pastures since the mid-thirteenth century,[38] the Anatolian principalities, most of which relied on Turcoman military power, embraced the legacy of the Anatolian Seljuks, who were of Turkic origin, and started competing for that legacy.[39] Aḥmedī's section on Ottoman history, then, stands at the midpoint between a past in which the Mongols reigned supreme and a future that looked promising to Turcoman political power.

In the next major piece of Ottoman historical writing, a universal history by Şükrullāh, an Ottoman man of letters and diplomat of the mid-fifteenth century, one observes that during the decades that passed between Aḥmedī and Şükrullāh the Mongols must have lost their prominence in world history to the Seljuks. Şükrullāh does not devote any chapter to the Mongols but instead ends his section on the Seljuks with the invasion of the Mongols, whom he describes as a cruel force, and moves on to the Ottomans. It is also not surprising that Şükrullāh claims an Oghuz genealogy for Ertuğrul, Osman's father, and states that he had come to Anatolia together with the Seljuks—a chronological impossibility, as the branch of the Seljuk family that established the Anatolian Seljuk dynasty moved to Anatolia in the late eleventh century, two centuries before the period in which Ertuğrul is supposed to have lived.[40] More sophisticated versions of this attempt to connect the Ottomans and the Seljuks took this fact into consideration and claimed that it was one of the ancestors of Ertuğrul who made it into Anatolia.[41]

Although early Ottoman historical writing seems to be quite concerned with erasing the memory of the relationship between the earliest Ottomans and their Mongol overlords—creating instead a connection between the Seljuks and the Ottomans—ʿĀşıḳpaşazāde, thanks to his use of Yaḫşı Faḳīh's chronicle, includes in his text the remnants of a past in which the Ottomans imagined themselves closer to the Mongols. While some of the early Ottoman chronicles bring Osman's forefathers to Anatolia in the company of the Seljuks, others place them in Khurasan and claim that they left their ancestral home because of the Mongol invasions and immigrated to Anatolia.[42] Thus, they either came with the Seljuks or were running away from the Mongols. ʿĀşıḳpaşazāde, however, has a different story to tell. He places the immigration of Osman's ancestors to Anatolia in the context of Islamic history. In a very insightful summary of Islamic political history, ʿĀşıḳpaşazāde states that, first, the Arabs dominated the Persians. Then, the Persians used nomadic Turks as soldiers to overpower the Arabs before sending them to Anatolia under the leadership of Süleymanşah, who is supposed to have been the grandfather of Osman but seems to be a fictive character inspired by the historical Süleymān, the founder of the Anatolian Seljuk kingdom and a member of the Seljuk dynastic family.

ʿĀşıḳpaşazāde's inspiration comes from the Great Seljuks in more ways than only the name of Osman's grandfather. The Great Seljuks had embraced Persian culture and were not interested in Anatolia, which was a frontier zone for them. Nevertheless, they used the territory as a final destination for the Turkic nomadic tribes that had helped them gain military ascendancy but became a liability because of their unruly lifestyle. Claiming that Persians used Turkic nomads to obtain political power but then sent them to Anatolia under the leadership of a certain Süleyman would dovetail well with Seljuk history despite the fact that ʿĀşıḳpaşazāde is careful not to mention the Seljuks themselves.[43] It is in this framework that ʿĀşıḳpaşazāde brings the Turks and the Mongols together:

> They moved Süleymanşah Gazi, who was one of the great men among the nomads, forward. They gave him about fifty thousand nomadic Turcoman and Tatar households.[44]

If we remember that although "Tatar" does not suggest "Mongol" today—the term referred to Mongols in medieval Arabic, Persian, and Turkish as well as in Western languages[45]—we can see that in ʿĀşıḳpaşazāde's account nomadic Turks and Mongols move to Anatolia together. After relating the well-known story of Süleymanşah's death on his way back to the east, while crossing the Euphrates in Syria, ʿĀşıḳpaşazāde states that some of the nomads who followed him dispersed around Syria while others returned to Anatolia:

> Some of them returned to Anatolia. Some of these [who returned to Anatolia] are Tatars, others Turcomans. The Tatars and Turcomans found in Anatolia now originate from that group.[46]

Thus, according to ʿĀşıḳpaşazāde, Anatolia was settled by Turks and Mongols together and the arrival of Osman's forefathers had nothing to do with the Mongol invasions, which, according to other accounts, had pushed them west from their ancestral home.

Not only are the Mongol invasions not invoked by ʿĀşıḳpaşazāde as a cause for the arrival of the forefathers of Osman in Anatolia, but, I would argue, the historical account in ʿĀşıḳpaşazāde is constructed in such a way that both the Turcoman and Mongol nomads seem to have arrived *before* the establishment of the Seljuk dynasty in Anatolia. ʿĀşıḳpaşazāde claims that a member of the Seljuk dynasty, Alaeddin, came to Anatolia and became the king of the country *after* the death of Süleymanşah, during the lifetime of Ertuğrul. While historically the Anatolian Seljuks indeed form an offshoot of the main branch of the Seljuk dynasty farther east, and were thus established by a member of the latter, Alaeddin was not the first Anatolian Seljuk ruler. ʿĀşıḳpaşazāde not only makes Alaeddin the first ruler of the Anatolian Seljuks but also the only one. There is no other Seljuk king mentioned by ʿĀşıḳpaşazāde anywhere in his chronicle, and the identity of Alaeddin is left obscure. Three Anatolian Seljuk kings whose reigns spanned most of the thirteenth century, roughly 1220–1300, carried the honorific Alaeddin.[47] Not only do we not know which of these three Alaeddins was the ruler meant by ʿĀşıḳpaşazāde in a particular episode, but also, as noted by later Ottoman historians, there are cases in which none of the three fits into an episode in which the name Alaeddin is mentioned as a participant.[48] Thus, ʿĀşıḳpaşazāde's Alaeddin is a mythical character meant to stand for all of Anatolian Seljuk history truncated into the thirteenth century. By collapsing 250 years of Anatolian Seljuk history into the lifetime of a single sultan, a non-specified Alaeddin who is basically ahistorical, ʿĀşıḳpaşazāde prepared the ground for a claim that the grandfather of Osman, Süleymanşah, had come to Anatolia *before* the Seljuks, which he accomplishes by making Osman assert at the moment of his declaration of independence:

> And if he says "I descend from the Seljuk dynasty," I myself would say "I am the offspring of Gök Alp [one of the sons of Oghuz, the eponymous ancestor of Turcomans]." And if he says "I came to this land before them," my grandfather Süleymanşah himself came before him.[49]

In short, ʿĀşıḳpaşazāde carries in his text the remnants of a past when the Ottomans imagined themselves as the offspring of the first settlers of Anatolia, who included both Mongol and Turkish nomads and preceded the arrival of the Seljuks, a very creative fiction that legitimizes both the Ottomans' claim to political power and their close alliance with the Mongols.

A final reminder of this Mongol-friendly past is the use of a Mongol name as the ancestor of the Turcoman tribes in Cilicia. During the reign of Bayezid II (r. 1481–1512), when the Mamluks and the Ottomans contested this territory, a genealogical narrative that connects the House of Ramazan in Cilicia with that of the Ottomans was put into circulation. The most complete version of this narrative is found in two manuscripts of the chronicle of Oruç. After noting Süleymanşah's death while crossing the Euphrates, the author states that the nomadic Mongol tribes dispersed:

> Among these Tatar lords there was a great king; they used to call him Bacu, who was either from the Boz-ok or the Üç-ok tribes. He had six sons. They used to call them Yüregir, Kosun, Varsak, Kara Isa, Üzer, Gündüz, and Kuş-temür.[50]

After the death of Bacu Han, Yüregir became the leader of the tribes in the area. He was succeeded by Ramazan, the founder of the House of Ramazan. Here we witness a Mongol leader fathering sons, some of whom are named after Oghuz tribes, including such major ones as Varsak and Yüregir; the Ottomans claim common ancestry with them.[51] Perhaps most striking is the name Bacu, which must have reminded the contemporary readers of Baiju, the commander of the Mongol armies that defeated the Seljuks in 1243 and 1256 and the man who led the settlement of the Mongol contingents in Anatolia. The Ottomans could not construct a better Turco-Mongol past than making Baiju, the grandfather of Osman's contemporary Sulamish, arrive in Anatolia in the company of Süleymanşah, the fictive grandfather of Osman.

It is not surprising that in the fourteenth century, while Ottoman rulers were regarded as Mongol vassals and tens of thousands of Mongol families still were moving from summer to winter pastures in Anatolia, a historiographical tradition of common origins shared by Turks and Mongols developed in Ottoman lands. In central Asia, where Mongols and Turks continued to mingle together for a much longer period, such a tradition of common origins began developing around the same time and took deep roots during the fifteenth century, in parallel to the increasing prestige of the Timurid lineage, which was the embodiment of the Turco-Mongol tradition in many ways.[52] Perhaps what is most surprising is that the Ottoman historiographical tradition shed its fourteenth-century legends so quickly and thoroughly that, with the exception of ʿĀşıḳpaşazāde, they were nowhere to be found after Timur left Anatolia, taking with him the descendants of the Mongols who had settled there 150 years before.[53]

In short, the Ottomans seem to have creatively aligned themselves with the Mongols by declaring them their cousins in the fourteenth century, when it was in their political interest to do so. Once Mongol power subsided and the Mongols left Anatolia permanently in the early fifteenth century, the Ottomans forgot about their Mongol lords and underlined their supposed loyalty to the Seljuks. Historiography, or the construction of collective memory, thus seems to be just as creative as literary fiction, especially if one considers genesis stories.

Notes

This chapter is dedicated to Heath Lowry whose passion for early Ottoman history led me to this study. I thank the participants and organizers of the symposium that sparked this volume, the editors, Emine Fetvacı and Erdem Çıpa, and Gottfried Hagen and an anonymous reviewer for their comments, which helped me revise the original presentation. The remaining shortcomings are mine.

1. Halil İnalcık suggests that ʿĀşıḳpaşazāde died around 1502. See İnalcık, "How to Read ʿĀşık Paşa-zade's History," in *Studies in Ottoman History in Honour of Professor V. L. Ménage*, ed. Colin Heywood and Colin Imber (Istanbul: Isis Press, 1994), 142.

2. Either Konya Ereğlisi in Central Anatolia or perhaps modern Karadeniz Ereğlisi on the western Black Sea coast.

3. ʿĀşıḳpaşazāde, *Tevārīḫ-i Āl-i ʿOsmān*, in *Osmanlı Tarihleri*, ed. N. Atsız (Istanbul: Türkiye Yayınevi, 1947), 97: "Şöyle kırdılar kim hayalarını kesdiler. Derisin birbirine dikdiler. Keçeye kapladılar. Sayvanlar etdiler ad içün. Şimdi dahı ol yazuya Daşak Yazusı derler." All transliterations are rendered as they appear in the works from which they are excerpted.

4. Ahmet-Zeki Velidî Togan, "Die Vorfahren der Osmanen in Mittelasien," *Zeitschrift der deutschen morgenländischen Gesellschaft* 95 (1941): 367–373; and M. Fuat Köprülü, "Osmanlı İmparatorluğu'nun Etnik Menşei Mes'eleleri," *Belleten* 7 (1943): 219–303.

5. Aḥmedī, *Tevārīḫ-i Mülūk-i Āl-i ʿOsmān ve Ġazv-i İşān Bā-Küffār: Tāce'd-Dīn İbrāhīm bin Ḫıżır Aḥmedī*, critical ed. Kemal Silay (Cambridge, Mass.: Harvard University, Department of Near Eastern Languages and Civilizations, 2004), 3–4 [27–28].

6. Şükrullāh, *Bahjat al-tawārīkh*, excerpt ed. and trans. Theodor Seif, in "Der Abschnitt über die Osmanen in Šükrüllāh's persischer Universalgeschichte," *Mitteilungen zur osmanischen Geschichte* 2 (1923–1926), 78, 79.

7. Rūḥī, *Rûhî Târîhi*, ed. Halil Erdoğan Cengiz and Yaşar Yücel, *Belgeler* 14/18 (1989–1992): 376–377.

8. Neşrī [Mevlānā Meḥemmed], *Kitâb-ı Cihan-nümâ*, ed. Faik Reşit Unat and Mehmed A. Köymen (Ankara: Türk Tarih Kurumu, 1949), 1:64–67.

9. İbn-i Kemāl, *Tevārīḫ-i Āl-i ʿOsmān* (I. Defter), ed. Şerafettin Turan (Ankara: Türk Tarih Kurumu, 1970), 55–56.

10. Oruç bin ʿĀdil, *Oruç Beğ Tarihi*, ed. Necdet Öztürk (Istanbul: Çamlıca, 2007), 9–10. This section reads differently in other Oruç manuscripts and thus may belong to an anonymous author or redactor. See Oruç bin ʿĀdil, *Oruç Beğ Tarihi*, ed. Atsız (Istanbul: Tercüman, 1972), 27; and Oruç bin ʿĀdil, *Die frühosmanischen Jahrbücher des Urudsch nach den Handschriften zu Oxford und Cambridge erstmals herausgegeben und eingeleitet*, ed. Franz Babinger (Hannover: H. Lafaire, 1925), 10.

11. Müneccimbaşı, *Jāmiʿ al-duwal*, in *Camiü'd-düvel: Osmanlı Tarihi, 1299–1481*, ed. and trans. Ahmet Ağırakça (Istanbul: İnsan Yayınları, 1995), 22–23 [translation: 73–74]; and Müneccimbaşı, *Ṣaḥā'if ül-aḫbār* [Ottoman Turkish translation of *Jāmiʿ al-duwal*], trans. Nedīm (Istanbul: Maṭbaʿa-i ʿāmire, 1285/1868), 3:275.

12. Ahmet-Zeki Velidî Togan, *Umumî Türk Tarihine Giriş*, vol. 1, *En Eski Devirlerden 16. Asra Kadar* (Istanbul: Hak Kitabevi, 1946), 319.

13. For a political history of the Mongol period in Seljukid Anatolia, see Claude Cahen, *The Formation of Turkey: The Seljukid Sultanate of Rūm: Eleventh to Fourteenth Century*, trans. and ed. P. M. Holt (Harlow: Longman, 2001); Osman Turan, *Selçuklular Zamanında Türkiye: Siyasî Tarih, Alp Arslan'dan Osman Gazi'ye (1071–1318)* (Istanbul: Turan Neşriyat Yurdu, 1971); and Faruk Sümer, "Anadolu'da Moğollar," *Selçuklu Araştırmaları Dergisi* 1 (1969): 1–147.

14. The identification of "Bayıncar Tatar" with the Mongol governor Bayinjar is also suggested by Sümer. See Sümer, "Anadolu'da Moğollar," 118, n. 37.

15. Fadlallāh Rashīd al-Dīn, *Geschichte Ġāzān-Ḫān's aus dem Ta'rih-i-Mubārak-i-Ġāzānī*, ed. Karl Jahn (London: E. J. W. Gibb Memorial, 1940), 121–122, 124; cf. Halil İnalcık, "Osmān Ghāzī's Siege of Nicaea and the Battle of Bapheus," in *The Ottoman Emirate (1300–1389)*, ed. Elizabeth Zachariadou (Rethymnon: Crete University Press, 1993), 82; and Kerīmüddīn Maḥmūd Aḳsarāyī, *Musāmarat al-akhbār*, in *Müsâmeret ül-ahbâr: Moğollar Zamanında Türkiye Selçukluları Tarihi*, ed. Osman Turan (Ankara: Türk Tarih Kurumu, 1944), 270–271. For Sulamish's activities in Damascus and Cairo, see the contemporary source Baybars al-Dawādār Manṣūrī, *Zubdat al-fikrah fī tārīkh al-hijrah* (Berlin: Das arabische Buch, 1998), 319.

16. Togan's suggestion is noted in İnalcık, "Osmān Ghāzī's Siege of Nicaea," 82.

17. 'Āşıḳpaşazāde, *Tevārīḫ-i Āl-i 'Oṣmān*, 99–100: "Osman Gaziyile ahd ü peymān etdiler kim Samsa Çavuş her ne der ise anı kabul edeler."

18. Togan, *Umumî Türk Tarihine Giriş*, 320.

19. 'Umarī, *Masālik al-abṣār fī mamālik al-amṣar*, excerpt ed. Franz Taeschner, in *Al-'Umarī's Bericht über Anatolien in seinem Werke Masālik al-abṣār fī mamālik al-amṣār* (Leipzig: Otto Harrassowitz, 1929), 22, n. E; 'Umarī, "Notice de l'ouvrage qui a pour titre Masalek alabsar fi memalek alamsar, Voyages des yeux dans les royaumes des différentes contrées (ms. Arabe 583)," trans. E. Quatremère, *Notices et Extraits des manuscrits de la Bibliothèque du Roi* 13 (1838): 340; and Togan, *Umumî Türk Tarihine Giriş*, 317–318, 484, n. 5, 11.

20. Rudi Paul Lindner, *Explorations in Ottoman Prehistory* (Ann Arbor: University of Michigan Press, 2007), 93, n. 29, 101.

21. Aydın Ayhan and Tuncer Şengün, "Anadolu Beyliklerinin ve Osmanlı Beyliği'nin İlhanlılar Adına Kestirdiği Sikkeler," in *XIII. Türk Tarih Kongresi (Ankara: 4–8 Ekim 1999)—Kongreye Sunulan Bildiriler* (Ankara: Türk Tarih Kurumu, 2002), 3, part 2:1168, and Plate 3.

22. Ayhan and Şengün, "Sikkeler," 1164–1166. Lindner argues that one such coin seems to have been minted in Söğüt, at the center of Ottoman ancestral lands; see Rudi Paul Lindner, "How Mongol were the Early Ottomans?" in *The Mongol Empire and Its Legacy*, ed. Reuven Amitai-Preiss and David O. Morgan (Leiden: Brill, 1999), 287. See also Rudi Paul Lindner, "Between Seljuks, Mongols and Ottomans," in *The Great Ottoman-Turkish Civilization*, ed. Kemal Çiçek (Ankara: Yeni Türkiye, 2000), 1:118; and Lindner, *Explorations in Ottoman Prehistory*, 97–98.

23. Lindner, "How Mongol were the Early Ottomans?" 286.

24. Aḳsarāyī, *Musāmarat al-akhbār*, 278.

25. Togan, *Umumî Türk Tarihine Giriş*, 320.

26. Lindner, *Explorations in Ottoman Prehistory*, 101.

27. See, for example, İsmail Hakkı Uzunçarşılı, *Osmanlı Tarihi* (Ankara: Türk Tarih Kurumu, 1947), 1:30–31; Irène Beldiceanu-Steinherr, *Recherches sur les actes des règnes des sultans Osman, Orkhan et Murad I* (Munich: Societatea Academică Română, 1967), 66–70; and İnalcık, "Osmān Ghāzī's Siege of Nicaea," 81–82.

28. Togan called this document a "budget," and in that sense it is a predecessor of the Ottoman type that Ömer Lûtfi Barkan was to label a "budget" as well; see Togan, "Mogollar Devrinde Anadolu'nun İktisadî Vaziyeti," *Türk Hukuk ve İktisat Tarihi Mecmuası* 1 (1931): 31. Unlike modern budgets that list the anticipated treasury income and expenditure for a coming year, such documents summarize the actual income and expenditure of the treasury in a past year. Thus, this Persian document dating from 1350 summarizes the income and expenditure items of the Ilkhanid treasury during the fiscal year of 750 AH (March 22, 1349–March 10, 1350). It was reproduced by Māzandarānī around 1363 in his *Risāla-i Falakiyya*, a fiscal manual that aims to teach aspiring secretaries the arts of bookkeeping. See Māzandarānī, *Die Resālä-ye Falakiyyä des 'Abdollāh Ibn Mohammad Ibn Kiyā al-Māzandarānī: ein persischer Leitfaden des staatlichen Rechnungswesens (um 1363)*, ed. Walther Hinz (Wiesbaden: Franz Steiner Verlag, 1952), 153–172. Orhan's name stands as one of the lordships of the marches (Turkish *uç*, Arabic pl. *ujāt*) that, together with the central Anatolian cities,

produced 3,000,000 dinars for the Ilkhanid fisc; Māzandarānī, *Resālä,* 162. It seems that this amount was raised by a tax collector from Khoy named Khwājeh Najm al-Dīn al-Khūʾī and that 2,800,000 dinars of it were spent locally, leaving a net contribution of 200,000 dinars for the Ilkhanid treasury; Māzandarānī, *Resālä,* 170, 172. This document might represent a template based on an earlier example, as the Ilkhanid authority around 1350 may well have been much weaker than the picture drawn by this summary document, which claims items of income from a large geographical range. However, it might also represent the actual state of affairs, as Togan reminds us that coins were struck in the name of the Mongol ruler Togha(y) Temür in various cities of Anatolia during his reign (1338–1353); Togan, "Mogollar Devrinde Anadolu'nun İktisadî Vaziyeti," 33. Another point that strengthens the document's credibility is the closeness of the income figure cited in it to another contemporary source, *Nuzhat al-qulūb* by Qazwīnī from 1340. According to Qazwīnī, the taxes raised in Anatolia amounted to 3,300,000 dinars, which is definitely within the same range as the figure cited by Māzandarānī. Moreover, accounting for the contributions of Orhan and his fellow lords of the Anatolian marches might explain the arithmetic gap in Qazwīnī that Togan identifies but fails to adequately address. Togan notes that the Anatolian tax resources cited by Qazwīnī amount to less than 2,000,000 dinars and states that the gap between this figure and 3,300,000 dinars, which is supposed to be the total, might be due to the taxes of a few cities whose contributions were not noted, the most important ones being Konya and Sivas. A look at the list prepared by Togan, however, suggests that the taxes raised in a few cities might not explain this significant gap. The gap may, however, arise from the fact that Qazwīnī does not cite individually any tribute collected from the lords of the marches, while he probably includes these tributes in his figure for the total; see Togan, "Mogollar Devrinde Anadolu'nun İktisadî Vaziyeti," 22–25; Qazwīnī, *The Geographical Part of the Nuzhat-al-qulūb composed by Ḥamd-Allah Mustawfī of Qazwīn in 740 (1340),* ed. and trans. Guy Le Strange (Leiden: E. J. Brill and Luzac & Co., 1915–1919), 1:94–100 [2:95–100]; and Philip Remler, "New Light on Economic History from Ilkhanid Accounting Manuals," *Studia Iranica* 14, no. 2 (1985): 157–177.

29. Here I must emphasize that this Mongol-friendly tone does not necessarily continue in the later parts of ʿĀşıḳpaşazāde's chronicle, a point of which my colleague Erdem Çıpa reminded me.

30. Sulamish sent a certain al-Mukhlis al-Rumi to Egypt, seeking Mamluk help in his campaign for power in Anatolia. Togan identifies this man as Muhlis Pasha; Togan, *Umumî Türk Tarihine Giriş,* 320. Muhlis Pasha was indeed involved in politics and also had been to Egypt in his youth, an experience that would have made him a good candidate for an ambassadorial job, as attested to by his grandson Elvān Çelebi's hagiographical work on Muhlis Pasha's father, Baba Ilyas, *Menāḳıbü'l-ḳudsiyye fī menāṣıbü'l-ünsiyye.* Erünsal and Ocak, the editors of this work, suggest that Muhlis Pasha probably died around 1280–1290, while Tulum argues for an earlier date, which, if correct, would make it impossible to identify Muhlis Pasha with al-Mukhlis al-Rumi; see Tulum, "Elvan Çelebi'nin Menâkıbu'l-kudsiyye Adlı Eserinin İkinci Baskısı Münasebetiyle—III," *Türk Dünyası Araştırmaları* 106 (1997): 53–104.

31. The fact that Seljuk heritage became much more prestigious may be seen even in hagiographical sources; see H. Erdem Çıpa, "Contextualizing Şeyḫ Bedreddīn: Notes on Ḫalīl b. İsmāʿīl's Menāḳıb-ı Şeyḫ Bedreddīn b. İsrāʾīl," in *Şinasi Tekin'in Anısına: Uygurlardan Osmanlıya* (Istanbul: Simurg, 2005), 286–287.

32. ʿĀşıḳpaşazāde, *Tevārīḫ-i Āl-i ʿOṣmān,* 91; and V. L. Ménage, "The Menākib of Yakhshi Faqīh," *Bulletin of the School of Oriental and African Studies* 26 (1963): 52.

33. See, for example, ʿĀşıḳpaşazāde, *Tevārīḫ-i Āl-i ʿOṣmān,* 108, 144.

34. See, for example, Aḥmedī, *Tevārīḫ-i Mülūk-i Āl-i ʿOṣmān,* 2–4 [27–28].

35. See, for example, Şükrullāh, *Bahjat al-tawārīkh,* 78–79.

36. Aḥmedī, *İskender-nāme,* 42–45.

37. Aḥmedī, *Tevārīḫ-i Mülūk-i Āl-i ʿOṣmān,* 2–3 [27].

38. John Masson Smith, "Mongol Nomadism and Middle Eastern Geography: qīshlāqs and tümens," in *The Mongol Empire and Its Legacy,* ed. Reuven Amitai-Preiss and David O. Morgan (Leiden: Brill, 1999), 48–49.

39. That is not to say that this legacy had been forgotten. To the contrary, there had been anti-Mongol uprisings that had recourse to Seljuk legitimacy in the second half of the thirteenth century. Yet Mongols had been the dominant power of Anatolia, either in the form of Ilkhans, their governors, or autonomous local rulers, well into the late fourteenth century. One should also note that the relationship between Turcomans and Anatolian Seljuks was not necessarily a happy one before the Mongol domination in Anatolia. The Seljuks had actually not cared for their ethnic identity and instead embraced Persian high culture wholeheartedly; for them, Turkish nomads meant mostly trouble. Further, the Turcomans engaged in uprisings against Seljuk political authority, which they found oppressive.

40. For a detailed table of contents for Şükrullāh's chronicle, see Joseph von Hammer-Purgstall, *Geschichte des Osmanischen Reiches* (Pest: C. A. Hartleben, 1827), 9:177–180; *Türkiye Diyanet Vakfı İslâm Ansiklopedisi,* s.v. "Şükrullah" (Sara Nur Yıldız); and Şükrullāh, *Bahjat al-tawārīkh,* 76–79.

41. I do not mean Süleyman, Ertuğrul's alleged father, but ancestors who are multiple generations removed from Ertuğrul; see, for instance, Enverī, *Düstūrnāme,* in *Fatih Devri Kaynaklarından Düstûrnâme-i Enverî: Osmanlı Tarihi Kısmı (1299–1466),* ed. Necdet Öztürk (Istanbul: Kitabevi, 2003), 13–21.

42. Enverī, *Düstūrnāme,* 13–21; Şükrullāh, *Bahjat al-tawārīkh,* 76–77; Anonymous, *Die altosmanischen anonymen Chroniken: Tevârīh-i Âl-i 'Osmân,* ed. Friedrich Giese (Breslau: self-published, 1922), 1:4–5; and *Rûhî Târîhi,* ed. Cengiz and Yücel, 375.

43. As Gottfried Hagen reminded me in his review of this essay, this critique of the Persians for using Turkic nomads and then dispensing with them by sending them to a territory that was insignificant to the Persians might well be read in the context of the uneasy relationship between the Ottomans and their own nomadic population, which was an important topic at the time when 'Āşıḳpaşazāde was writing his chronicle. Many nomadic tribes in Anatolia were soon to shift their allegiances to Shah Ismail (r. 1502–1524), as they were frustrated with Ottoman attempts to settle and tax them.

44. 'Āşıḳpaşazāde, *Tevārīḫ-i Āl-i 'Oṣmān,* 92: "Süleymanşah Gaziyi ilerü çekdiler kim ol göçer evlerün ulularından idi. Elli bin mıkdarı göçer Türkman ve Tatar evin koşdılar."

45. *İslâm Ansiklopedisi,* s.v. "Tatar—Orta Şark'ta Tatarlar" (Faruk Sümer); in western usage "Tatar" was transformed to "Tartar."

46. 'Āşıḳpaşazāde, *Tevārīḫ-i Āl-i 'Oṣmān,* 93: "Bazısı gene Rûma döndiler. Kimi Tatar ve kimi Türkmandur. Şimdiki halda Rûmda olan Tatar ve Türkman ol tayfadandur."

47. They are Kayqubad I (r. 1220–1237), Kayqubad II (r. 1249–1257, jointly with two other Seljuk kings), and Kayqubad III (r. 1298, 1301–1302); Clifford Edmund Bosworth, *The New Islamic Dynasties: A Chronological and Genealogical Manual* (New York: Columbia University Press, 1996), 213.

48. Müneccimbaşı, *Jāmi' al-duwal,* 23; [73–74]; and Müneccimbaşı, *Ṣaḥā'if ül-aḫbār,* 3:275.

49. 'Āşıḳpaşazāde, *Tevārīḫ-i Āl-i 'Oṣmān,* 103: "Ve ger ol, ben Âl-i Salçukvan der ise, ben hod Gök Alp oğlıyın derin. Ve ger bu vilâyete ben anlardan öndin geldüm der ise, Süleymanşah dedem hod andan evvel geldi."

50. Oruç bin 'Ādil, *Oruç Beğ Tarihi,* ed. Öztürk, 4: "Bu Tatar begleri içinde Boz-oklu, Üç-oklu dahı dirler, bir ulu han vardı, Bacu Han dirlerdi. Anuñ altı oglı vardı. Birinüñ adı Yüregir, birinüñ adı Kosun, birinüñ adı Varsak, birinüñ adı Kara Îsâ, birinüñ adı Üzer, birinüñ adı Gündüz, birinüñ Kuş-temür dirlerdi."

51. Oruç bin 'Ādil, *Oruç Beğ Tarihi,* ed. Öztürk, 4–6.

52. See Mihály Dobrovits, "The Turco-Mongolian Tradition of Common Origin and the Historiography in Fifteenth Century Central Asia," *Acta Orientalia Academiae Scientiarum Hungaricae* 48 (1994): 269–277.

53. Here I must note that one can find references to Mongols who remained in Anatolia even after Timur had left with his troops; see, for example, ʿĀşıḳpaşazāde, *Tevārīḫ-i Āl-i ʿOṣmān*, 152–153; I would like to thank Erdem Çıpa for this reference. Also, the Ottomans continued to ally with the descendants of Genghis Khan elsewhere, notably in Crimea, where the Crimean Tatars enjoyed political autonomy as an Ottoman protectorate until the late eighteenth century.

3 Imperialism, Bureaucratic Consciousness, and the Historian's Craft

A Reading of Celālzāde Muṣṭafā's Ṭabaḳātü'l-Memālik ve Derecātü'l-Mesālik

Kaya Şahin

Celālzāde Muṣṭafā's (d. 1567) *Ṭabaḳātü'l-Memālik ve Derecātü'l-Mesālik* (Echelons of the Dominions and Hierarchies of the Professions), hereafter *Ṭabaḳāt,* continues to surprise readers with its large volume and ambitious scope.[1] It begins with a concise treatment of Selim I's rule (1512–1520) and then focuses on the events of Süleyman's reign (1520–1566) from the enthronement of the sultan to the opening of the Süleymaniye Mosque in 1557. The work is written in a language that is often metaphor-laden, rich and thick, a product of Muṣṭafā's conviction that the first half of the sixteenth century represented an unprecedented era in Ottoman history. Muṣṭafā believed that this era deserved to be recorded in a language worthy of its achievements and that a correct version of its history should be produced and circulated by those few with access to the inner workings of the Ottoman government.[2]

Ṭabaḳāt is both a reflection and a repository of thematic, linguistic, political, and cultural trends that fully blossomed in the sixteenth century and are, in this regard, truly "Süleymanic." It describes an exceptional period during which what subsequently has been called the Ottoman "empire" was built and its institutions, culture, and identity were formed. Produced independently, without any direct patronage, it addresses an elite audience of fellow literati, madrasa graduates, poets, historians, scribes, and religious scholars who not only could recognize the message of the work but also appreciated its linguistic and stylistic aspects.

Ṭabaḳāt has been granted almost canonical status by Ottoman historians of the following generations as well as modern scholars of the Ottoman Empire. Muṣṭafā 'Ālī (d. 1600), Peçevī (d. ca. 1650), Ṣolaḳzāde (d. 1657 or 1658), and Ḳaraçelebizāde (d. 1658) referred to *Ṭabaḳāt* extensively while narrating the reign of Süleyman and clearly regarded Muṣṭafā as a prominent cultural figure to be emulated.[3] *Ṭabaḳāt* is one of the primary sources on Süleyman's reign cited in works as varied as Joseph von Hammer-Purgstall or İsmail Hakkı Uzunçarşılı's general surveys of Ottoman history, İsmail Hami Danişmend's chronological compendium, Fahrettin Kırzıoğlu's work on Ottoman activities in Eastern Anatolia and the Caucasus, and Walter Posch's monograph on the Alqas Mirza (d. 1550) revolt.[4] In each of these studies *Ṭabaḳāt* is treated as the official history of Süleyman's reign and is utilized in a rather positivistic fashion, as a primary source of extraordinary richness for the events of a tumultuous era.

While it is true that Muṣṭafā's desire was to write an authoritative history of the period, his work supersedes the narrow confines of an official history. Reading the work as a multilayered text allows us to reach beyond positivistic and empiricist approaches and to discuss history writing as a dialectical and dialogical activity that both influenced and was influenced by the political, cultural, and ideological concerns of a specific period. In this essay I will focus on *Ṭabaḳāt* as a text in order to better illustrate its more personal aspects as well as the narrative and cultural strategies utilized by an Ottoman historian of the sixteenth century to defend the imperial edifice and project.

Introducing *Ṭabaḳāt*

Celālzāde Muṣṭafā's *Ṭabaḳāt* is striking in its language, which both entices and deters its readers with an elaborate weaving of Turkish, Arabic, and Persian through the intermediary of rhyming prose. Although it is possible to identify three distinct linguistic registers throughout the work—aptly classified by Petra Kappert as elaborate, middlebrow, and simple[5]—Muṣṭafā's vivid descriptions often project themselves to the fore at the expense of other passages. A typical portrayal of Süleyman, for instance, calls him a sultan whose slaves and soldiers are as numerous as the stars and a world conqueror whose glory is comparable to that of ancient Persian kings.[6] This triumphalist language, which brings together poetic metaphors, historical themes, and religious references, is similarly used in developing a discourse of military, religious, and cultural superiority over the Mamluks, the Hungarians, the Safavids, and the Habsburgs.[7] Muṣṭafā's insistence on developing and utilizing a highly literary language turns his historical production into a veritable work of art that conveys a profoundly aesthetic reading of sixteenth-century Ottoman history.

Although *Ṭabaḳāt* is primarily preoccupied with Süleyman's rule and image, it also offers its readers a theatrical succession of figures whose lives, personalities, and actions constitute positive and negative moral lessons. Such "rebels" as Janbirdi al-Ghazali (d. 1521) and Şehsuvaroğlu Ali Beg (d. 1522), whom Muṣṭafā knew only through official reports or the testimonies of others, are described with regard to their poor political judgments, which led to their eventual demise.[8] Those whom he knew and respected, such as the historian, scholar, and chief jurisconsult Kemālpaşazāde Aḥmed (d. 1534) and the historian, soldier, and artist Maṭrāḳçı Naṣūḥ (d. 1564), make brief but powerful appearances.[9] Muṣṭafā's mentor Piri Mehmed Pasha (d. 1532), Süleyman's first grand vizier, together with the sultan, dominates the early chapters of the work.[10] Individuals against whom Muṣṭafā harbors grudges, including Ahmed Pasha "the Traitor" (*Ḫā'in*, d. 1524), the nemesis of Piri Mehmed, play negative roles in various dramatic sequences.

Ahmed is portrayed as a veritable bête noire who acts out of pure self-interest, disrupts imperial council meetings, schemes against other viziers, and finally rebels while he is the governor of Egypt.[11] The work's personal dimension is enhanced by the narration of events to which Muṣṭafā was privy, such as Ibrahim Pasha's (d. 1536) travel to Egypt in 1524–1525, after Aḥmed's rebellion, or Molla Kabız's trial in 1527 for allegedly preaching Christianity's superiority over Islam. *Ṭabaḳāt* is also the repository of Muṣṭafā's views on bureaucratic merit, the role of reason (*'aḳl*) in administration, and personal and political loyalty. It thus becomes a vessel for Muṣṭafā's selective remembering and creative narration of his personal and professional observations and experiences.

Beyond the highly personal opinions and values that crisscross the text, Muṣṭafā's endeavor as a historian is in itself impressive. Despite some chronological gaps between chapters,[12] his methodical use of chronology within chapters, based on various campaign diaries (*rūznāme*) and quite likely his personal notes, provides his readers with a secure sense of time. He reproduces "documents," such as the diploma (*berāt*), dated 1529, that appointed Ibrahim Pasha commander in chief (*ser'asker*) and endowed him with quasi-sultanic prerogatives.[13] Similarly, part of the official correspondence between the Ottomans and the Safavids in the period leading to the accord of Amasya in 1555 is provided in the relevant chapter.[14] Muṣṭafā's eye for detail is not limited to official matters and diplomatic issues but extends from descriptions of cities and fortresses to Ottoman siege technology and weaponry. The detailed metaphors, the personal opinions and observations, and the various forms of evidence and specifics culminate in a powerful, often ceremonious, "effect of the Real"[15] that enthralls and at times overwhelms the reader.

Reading *Ṭabaḳāt*

The present reading of *Ṭabaḳāt* is inspired by a number of studies within and outside the field of Ottoman history. Cemal Kafadar and Cornell Fleischer have demonstrated the rich variety of genres, themes, linguistic registers, and political attitudes encountered in fifteenth- and sixteenth-century Ottoman works of history. Their studies reveal links between history-writing and identity formation on both individual and communal levels.[16] Kafadar and Fleischer have also proven that works that were cast aside by modern scholars as highly partisan official/court histories or unreliable literary exercises often defy these hasty categorizations. Gabriel Piterberg brings together the insights provided by Kafadar and Fleischer with lessons drawn from an open-minded assessment of modern debates on literary theory and historiography.[17] His use of Gabrielle Spiegel's studies of medieval European historiography introduces a particularly fresh perspective to the field of Ottoman studies. While recognizing the essential narrativity/textuality of works of history, Spiegel proposes to read them within the contexts that produce their narrative, structural, and thematic aspects rather than as autonomous artifacts that exist in a phenomenological vacuum.[18] Frank Ankersmit's search for "the *juste milieu* between the extravagances of the literary approach to historical writing and the narrow-mindedness of empiricists" is also particularly relevant for the purposes of the present study.[19]

In addition to the insights of these scholars, four "mental tools" proposed by Elizabeth Clark for a creative reading of the patristic literature provide potential avenues into a better understanding of Muṣṭafā's historiographical imagination:

> (1) an examination of "authorial function" that calls into question attributions of intention and context; (2) symptomatic and Derridean readings that attend to the gaps, absences, and aporias in texts; (3) ideology critique, especially helpful in unpacking the early Christian writers' representations of various "Others," including women; and (4) postcolonial discourse theory that helps to illuminate the ways in which Christianity and Empire intertwined.[20]

The "authorial function" in *Ṭabaḳāt* manifests itself as a bureaucratic view of Ottoman history that promotes scribal ideals and defends the idea of an empire based on merit, law, and Sunni Islam. The historical narrative serves these purposes through separate chapters that undergird and corroborate these larger themes. The most conspicuous absence of the text, which creates a thread of tension that traverses the whole work, results from the author's refusal to recognize Ottoman reversals on the military and ideological fronts. Muṣṭafā's enthusiastic insistence on the unbridled achievements of Ottoman imperialism shows us the fault lines of the imperial project. For example, the author's representation of the European Christians, the Mamluks, and the Safavids through a strong sense of alterity provides clues to the construction of an Ottoman elite identity in opposition to the real and perceived enemies of the imperial enterprise. Within this context, the empire is always intertwined with an overarching religious discourse and is legitimized with references to the sultan's identity as a messianic conqueror and the caliph of Sunni Islam.

Before proceeding with a closer look at the work itself, it is necessary to delve into the historical context to better illustrate the environment that determined and constrained Muṣṭafā's "authorial function" and produced the dynamics that eventually led to his notions of alterity, imperialism, and religion.

Introducing Celālzāde Muṣṭafā

Celālzāde Muṣṭafā's[21] father Celaleddin, whose name his sons would later adopt as a genteel-sounding patronymic, hailed from Tosya in north-central Anatolia and served as a low-ranking judge in the Balkans. Like so many of his peers in the sixteenth century, Muṣṭafā entered the scribal service after a madrasa education. He was hired in 1516 as *dīvān kātibi,* a scribe of the imperial council, on the recommendation of Piri Mehmed Pasha and Seydi Beg (a career scribe and future chancellor, d. 1534). Muṣṭafā distinguished himself very quickly in the midst of the still-embryonic Ottoman chancery and worked closely with Piri Mehmed. He survived the Pasha's fall in 1523 and was given a more prominent role under the new grand vizier Ibrahim. He became

Ibrahim's close collaborator and was appointed chief secretary (*re'īsü'l-küttāb*) in 1525. During the eastern campaign of 1534–1536 the chancellor (*nişāncı*) Seydi Beg passed away and Muṣṭafā took the place of his old mentor.

Until his retirement in 1557 (amidst rumors that he had been forced out by Rüstem Pasha, d. 1561), Muṣṭafā remained a highly visible figure in the Ottoman administration, in which he presided over various activities pertaining to imperial jurisdiction (*ḳānūn*), and the *tımar* system, managed the sultan's correspondence, and drafted his edicts. Süleyman himself felt a deep appreciation for Muṣṭafā. Upon his retirement, on the sultan's personal request, Muṣṭafā was appointed the chief of the *müteferriḳa* corps, the group of notables who had access to the palace without any official position; he was also allowed to keep his stipend in his retirement.

During his retirement, Muṣṭafā's home in Istanbul's Eyüb Sultan quarter became a magnet for poets, literati, friends, and acquaintances. His image as the savant of Ottoman bureaucratic practice and a patron of poetry, already an important tenet of his reputation during his professional career, was consolidated in this period.[22] He finally had time to bring together the independent chapters of *Ṭabaḳāt*, written since the 1520s, edit them, and add new sections. He shared parts of his various works with his visitors[23] and probably circulated copies through his social and cultural network. In 1566, in the army camp in Szigetvar, he witnessed Süleyman's death and was made *nişāncı* a second time. He remained in this position for slightly more than a year, until his death in 1567.

Muṣṭafā enjoyed an extraordinary bureaucratic career: he never held an appointment outside Istanbul, worked closely with the sultan and his grand viziers, and lived the life of a trusted insider. His reputation as an exceptionally gifted scribe was established during his lifetime, and both his bureaucratic prowess and his historical output became sources of emulation for future generations.[24] Muṣṭafā and his fellow scribes made crucial contributions to the extension of Ottoman control over newly conquered territories in the sixteenth century; they were also natural allies to the rulers in helping create and enforce sultanic prerogatives. Muṣṭafā realized that, as the smallest distinct group in Ottoman administrative circles (the other two consisting of the military men and religious scholars), scribes had a relatively vulnerable position. He tried to solve this dilemma by producing an enthusiastic endorsement of Ottoman imperialism that emphasized reason, merit, loyalty, and law (both *ḳānūn* and sharia) as some of the fundamental values of the new polity.

Contextualizing *Ṭabaḳāt*

Celālzāde Muṣṭafā came of age in a time characterized, not only for the Ottomans but also for the inhabitants of the entire Eurasian continent, by sudden and radical changes in economic activity and political organization, as well as religious and cultural identity or—to borrow a concept from Ernst Kantorowicz via Sanjay Subrahmanyam—"political theology."[25] The tensions created by these struggles exerted a great impact on the Ottoman realm and radically changed the nature of the Ottoman enterprise.[26]

The last decade of the fifteenth and the early years of the sixteenth century witnessed the rise of Shah Ismail (r. 1501–1524) to power in the lands of the Akkoyunlu Türkmen confederation. Ismail's ancestors, the founders of the Safaviyya religious order, had utilized their networks and dynastic marriages to create a politico-religious movement in the second half of the fifteenth century. Ismail carried their legacy to new heights, and under his leadership the Safavid movement became a powerful vortex for various groups in the Middle East, including the subjects of the Ottoman sultan. Turkish-speaking nomads, as well as townsmen and even disgruntled *timar* holders, joined the Safavid movement.[27] The ensuing rebellions rocked the Ottoman polity to its core; a corollary of this crisis was the power struggle among the sons of Bayezid II (r. 1481–1512) and the eventual victory of Selim I, who expanded the Ottoman domain considerably by toppling the Mamluks of Egypt and successfully stopped the Safavid expansion.[28] Süleyman continued his father's aggressive imperial policies on two fronts. He emerged as a powerful rival of the Habsburgs both politically and ideologically during a period in which the Habsburg dynasty itself was undergoing a process of transformation and consolidation. He also pursued an anti-Safavid policy in the east that included three major campaigns as well as an insistent claim on the Ottoman leadership of Sunni Islam.[29]

These developments led to the creation of a new Ottoman imperialism. The Ottoman enterprise became, militarily and economically, considerably more powerful in the first half of the sixteenth century. In order to perpetuate this power, however, it needed to control the tremendous expanse of land that was gained in the scope of a few decades. This led to the enlargement of the Ottoman chancery, the recruitment of new scribes, and the introduction of a new level of legal and administrative activity.[30] The new Ottoman imperialism also sought a new level of ideological legitimacy, or, as mentioned above, a new "political theology." This new political theology portrayed the Ottomans' struggles with the Habsburgs and the Safavids in a messianic vein, as a prelude to the eventual establishment of a universal empire under the aegis of the Ottoman dynasty. The Safavids' promotion of a non-Sunni Islam gave a particular vehemence to Ottoman claims to represent the true religion.[31] When decades of struggles failed to produce the desired universal monarchy or usher in the messianic era, around the middle of the sixteenth century, the Ottoman enterprise came to rest on a less dynamic but equally religio-political definition of the Ottoman sultan as the leader of Sunni Islam.[32]

Ottoman subjects from different walks of life were pulled into these debates and felt the need to state their positions, assert their identities, gain audiences, curry favor, or circulate criticism. Historiography became an especially relevant field of activity in this environment. Süleyman's reign, in the words of Robert Mantran, witnessed a "historiographical explosion."[33] The Ottoman palace had been active in the patronage of historical works since the second half of the fifteenth century. It now promoted the composition and circulation of historical and literary works whose unifying characteristic was a concern with Süleyman's glory.[34] This effort eventually culminated, around the middle of the century, in a more direct attempt at producing palace-sanctioned *şehnāmes*.[35] The palace's wish to reach out to the subject population in this period is also seen in the emergence of new public ceremonies such as weddings, circumcisions, the sultan's departures and arrivals from and to Istanbul, and the like.[36]

It is also true that various works were produced without any patrons. Ottoman historiography became an instrument for actors from different backgrounds to participate in debates concerning the nature of the Ottoman polity, the identity of the Ottoman sultan, or the meaning of true religion. The Ottoman-Habsburg and Ottoman-Safavid struggles were central to many historical works; the "Safavid problem" especially preoccupied many authors because it raised questions related to each of the issues mentioned above.[37] More importantly, new audiences came to the fore in this period. Bureaucrats, whose numbers increased, became both producers and consumers of historical material; they were joined in this activity by many others living around the Ottoman palace, religious scholars, and some members of the urban middle classes.[38] Gabrielle Spiegel's description of thirteenth-century French historiography is applicable to the Ottoman case as well: "social groups most affected by changes in status tend to be the most conscious of alternative modes of discursive behavior, that they are, in other words, most sensitive to the power of language to register social transformations."[39]

Ottoman history-writing, which emerged in thc first decades of the fifteenth century and expanded later on, had always been a conduit for a variety of political opinions. Stories reconstructing the origins of the Ottoman enterprise and describing the fortunes of the Ottoman dynasty often differed in tone and content, reflecting their authors' positions and their audiences' needs and expectations.[40] One of the major achievements of fifteenth-century Ottoman historians was the promotion of history-writing as the genre par excellence of historical and political debate. Even after the emergence of political advice (*naṣīḥatnāme*) literature as the privileged locus of political debate in the last decades of the sixteenth century, Ottoman historiography preserved this fundamental characteristic.[41]

Fifteenth-century historians were also instrumental in the creation of genres including dynastic *tārīḫ/tevārīḫ*, event-based *fetḥnāmes*/*ġazāvatnāmes*, universal histories, and narratives about the reign of a single sultan. These works reflected a rich linguistic variety—Turkish, Arabic, Persian, Greek—and were written in different registers of Ottoman Turkish ranging from the colloquial to the sophisticated *inşā'*.[42] Thus, sixteenth-century Ottoman historians had at their disposal a significant number of forms and styles.[43] On the other hand, while the obsession of fifteenth-century historians with the origins of the polity did not completely disappear, primacy was now given to the interpretation of the recent past and the immediate present. Muṣṭafā lived in this rich environment, in which political debate was often conducted through historiography. *Ṭabaḳāt* is a response to the larger political developments of his age and to this particular historiographical environment.[44]

Writing *Ṭabaḳāt*

In the long introduction to *Ṭabaḳāt,* composed some time after the 1540s and finished probably during his retirement, Celālzāde Muṣṭafā presents his readers with three historiographical objectives. The first is to hail Süleyman's singular, unprecedented achievements. No earlier ruler had conquered so many countries and captured so many fortresses, and, although the task of writing on Süleyman was an arduous one, Muṣṭafā decided to rise to the challenge.[45] The second objective is to portray the population and the Ottoman "protected realm" (*memālik-i maḥmiyye*) itself: the learned men (*'ulemā', fużalā*), the subject population (*re'āyā*), the soldiers (*sipāh u 'asker*), the fortresses (*ḳılā'*), the territories (*memālik u eḳālīm*), the riches (*ḫazā'in, cihāz, cevāhir, emvāl, ma'ādin*).[46] The third objective is to disclose the truth hidden behind various events of Süleyman's reign. All of these objectives are directly related to Muṣṭafā's assessment of previous historians' works: he considered such works similar in terms of content and style (i.e., without originality); believed that they had failed to represent the realm; and concluded that earlier authors did not have access to the truth of the matter.[47] Each of these objectives represents a distinct stage in Muṣṭafā's historiographical imagination and *Ṭabaḳāt*'s composition.

In Praise of Süleyman

The first sections of what would become *Ṭabaḳāt* were composed as individual campaign narratives. In tone and content these were similar to *fetḥnāme*s and *rūznāme*s. Muṣṭafā, as *re'īsü'l-küttāb* and then *nişāncı,* wrote some of the official *fetḥnāme*s after campaigns. He composed one each following Süleyman's victory at Mohacs in 1526, the "German campaign" of 1532–1533, the Moldavian (*Ḳaraboğdān*) campaign of 1538, and the eastern campaign of 1548–1549.[48] The corresponding chapters in the *Ṭabaḳāt* rely on these earlier versions but considerably expand them.[49] The official *fetḥnāme*s are notable for their elaborate introductions and conclusions praising the sultan in a highly metaphorical and somehow impersonal fashion as well as their concise but quite comprehensive narratives of each campaign's progression. Muṣṭafā began to conceive of these texts in the early 1530s as the first constituent parts of a regnal history-in-progress, a *şehnāme.* This is demonstrated by an anecdote added to *Ṭabaḳāt* most probably during Muṣṭafā's retirement: when he entered Tabriz with the Ottoman army in 1534, Muṣṭafā sought the famous rhetoricians and historians of the city and presented sections of his *şehnāme* to them, apparently receiving high praise.[50]

In all of these earlier versions the sultan is the chief figure; indeed, he is the only actor in the narrative. Muṣṭafā's claim to authority as a historian rests on his individual participation in the campaigns. Writing *fetḥnāme*s was related to Muṣṭafā's duty as a scribe, but his subsequent inclusion and reorganization of them in a *şehnāme* was his own initiative. It is possible that he was encouraged by the sultan or the viziers; it is also very likely that the ambitious scribe wanted to distinguish himself and to follow the ideal of the scribe/littérateur that was represented in the previous generation by figures such as Tacizade Cafer Çelebi (d. 1515), who served as *nişāncı* under Selim I. Moreover, by using the same flowery language in imperial correspondence, peace treaties, *fermāns*, and history, Muṣṭafā produced and propagated a form of expression that unified bureaucratic practice and history-writing.[51]

In terms of audience, the *fetḥnāmes* had a wide circulation. They were sent to Muslim and non-Muslim rulers as well as various Ottoman officials as statements of political and cultural superiority. Ottoman district judges were often instructed to have these texts recited in public, further proving the emergence and existence of new audiences in this period. *Fetḥnāmes* were also read as cultural and textual models by the literati of the empire. Finally, as Muṣṭafā's meetings in Tabriz demonstrate, the Safavid literati were among the intended audience. Muṣṭafā's campaign narratives, written in the new prose of the scribes, could thus be used as an asset in the political and cultural competition between the Ottomans and the Safavids. One of the noteworthy aspects of Muṣṭafā's historiographical imagination is that he would soon feel the need to expand his vision of empire toward a more structural understanding of the realm. This would not necessarily render the *fetḥnāmes* redundant but would lead Muṣṭafā to consider a larger and more ambitious historical project.

The Empire as System

In the late 1530s, after having composed a few independent but interrelated narratives on the sultan's campaigns, Muṣṭafā developed the idea that he could compose a panorama of the empire. Sehī Beg (d. 1548), who finished his biographical dictionary around the same time, praises Muṣṭafā for his literary skills and remarks that Muṣṭafā is writing a work called *Ṭabaḳātü'l-Memālik*. This information is repeated by Laṭīfī (d. 1582), who wrote in the late 1540s.[52] These are the first references to the title of the work: *Ṭabaḳātü'l-Memālik ve Derecātü'l-Mesālik* (Echelons of the Dominions and Hierarchies of the Professions). Muṣṭafā is no longer writing a mere *şehnāme*. The outline of this larger work survives in the form of a table of contents in the extant versions of the *Ṭabaḳāt*[53] and in a few scattered references.

The table of contents reveals that *memālik* referred, in Muṣṭafā's mind, to the lands under the control of the Ottoman dynasty, while *mesālik* denoted the various professional groups who served the sultan both in his household and in the provinces of the empire. The projected work includes thirty sections. The first twenty-nine sections describe the empire and consist of three hundred and seventy-five subsections; the last section is devoted to Süleyman's reign. The first section contains different professional groups whose salaries are paid from the central treasury and who serve the sultan, from food tasters to gardeners and the palace troops. The second section enumerates the different governorates-general (*beglerbeglik*) and mentions the Holy Cities; the third section lists the fortresses of the empire; the following sections are on the auxiliary troops (four and five), the fleet (six), and Istanbul (seven). Sections eight to twenty-nine are individual studies of the twenty-one *beglerbeglik* and the Holy Cities, and the last section is about Süleyman's reign. Muṣṭafā's goal is to provide his readers with a panorama of the empire and then explain, in the final chapter, the political and military processes that produced this panorama. Among these sections, only Muṣṭafā's account of Süleyman's reign survives.

Probably after becoming *nişāncı*, Muṣṭafā appears to have developed the idea that an empire is the sum total of its various constituent parts (human, material, physical/geographical) and decided to use his considerable bureaucratic knowledge to describe them. The table of contents reflects Muṣṭafā's desire to represent the world within hierarchically/organizationally bound, recognizable, and bureaucratic categories. He formulates the fiction that every individual part of the empire, from the smallest *tımar* to the corps of falconers in the palace, is tied together within a system surrounding the sultan, the ultimate lynchpin of a neo-Platonic system.[54] This stage in Muṣṭafā's historical thinking represents an important departure from his earlier work, in the sense that the author's claim to historical authority is now based not only on his experiences as an eyewitness but on his knowledge. The main actor of history is not only the sultan but also the empire itself.

The desire to realize this feat persisted until the end of Muṣṭafā's life. In a number of manuscripts, reproduced after a copy made by his son Hüseyin, readers are told that, for the sake of brevity, the first twenty-nine sections will be placed into a second volume, which was never written.[55] While mentioning a plague outbreak in Egypt in 1523, the author inserts a comment informing his readers that he will provide more details on this event in the appropriate section on Egypt.[56] Although he wouldn't be able to carry this ambitious project to fruition, Muṣṭafā's inclusion of the table of contents in the last version of *Ṭabaḳāt* reveals that he believed in the historiographical—and cultural—value it carried.

History as Personal Testimony

The third stage in *Ṭabaḳāt*'s composition started during Muṣṭafā's retirement and represents yet another historiographical step: the reign of the sultan is now conceived as a process that does not merely consist of campaigns but includes a series of other events as well.[57] More importantly, in this last stage Muṣṭafā inserts himself, his own values and perspectives, into the story of Süleyman's reign. In the first two stages the authority of the historian is based on his gaze as witness and his knowledge as bureaucrat. In the third the historian's recollections, judgments, and analyses are added to the narrative. As Patrick Geary suggests in the case of medieval Europe around the year 1000, every act of memory has the particular purpose of influencing historical, collective, or group memory; especially in the hands of someone with Muṣṭafā's career and reputation, the claim to remember and the outcome of this remembering become powerful instruments.[58]

An important component of Muṣṭafā's historical work during his retirement is his editing and expanding previous materials that existed as *fetḥnāmes* and *rūznāmes* composed by him and others. For example, in his chapter on the Ottoman capture of the island of Rhodes in 1522, Muṣṭafā weaves together the march of the army to southwestern Anatolia under the command of the sultan and the progress of the Ottoman navy (with which he traveled) toward Rhodes, creating a powerful feeling of simultaneity. He adds more depth to the narrative by inserting the news of a fortress captured from the Hungarians and by describing the near-simultaneous campaign of Ferhad Pasha's (d. 1524) punitive expedition in central Anatolia against Şehsuvaroğlu Ali Beg.[59] While recalling the Ottoman army's crossing of the Danube toward Moldavia, Muṣṭafā reminds his readers that this is the same river the army had crossed on the way to Vienna in 1529, thus establishing narrative continuity between an earlier chapter and the current one.[60]

The third stage is further characterized by the insertion of highly personal passages into the existing *fetḥnāme* structure, which transforms the impersonal campaign narratives into a backdrop for Muṣṭafā's opinions on various issues and individuals. In his chapters on the Belgrade (1521) and Rhodes (1522) campaigns, for instance, the driving dynamic of the narrative becomes the enmity between Piri Mehmed Pasha and Ahmed Pasha, an issue that could not be covered, for structural as well as political reasons, in a *fetḥnāme*.[61] Another example is the campaign against the Safavids in 1548–1549, organized in order to place the renegade Safavid prince Alqas Mirza on the Safavid throne.[62] Muṣṭafā presents a detailed historical background of the whole affair, describes the arrival of Alqas in the sultan's palace, criticizes the Ottoman viziers for having been misled by Alqas's empty promises, and relays anecdotes about God's punishment of those who leave the fold of Sunni Islam. These passages exist side by side with elaborate descriptions of Süleyman mounting his horse and leaving the capital or the visit of the Ottoman princes to the army camp. Muṣṭafā's dissatisfaction with Alqas and the outcome of the campaign is openly stated throughout the narrative.

Authorial activity is not limited to these editorial additions, however. The composition of chapters focusing on events outside the sultan's campaigns endows *Ṭabaḳāt* with historiographical depth, richness of detail, and individual flair. For example, Muṣṭafā's accounts of his trip to Egypt in Ibrahim Pasha's retinue in 1524–1525, rebellions in Anatolia and Ibrahim's campaign against the rebels in 1527, or the trial of Molla Kabız during the same year provide the reader with previously uncirculated information.[63] Muṣṭafā narrates these events on his own authority and emphasizes the challenges posed by troubles in Egypt, rebellions in Anatolia, or religious dissent in the capital. The dramatic tone of each chapter culminates in a positive denouement, in which reason, hard work, careful management, detailed knowledge, and strong piety (represented by Ibrahim Pasha and Kemālpaşazāde Aḥmed) lead to an auspicious solution. Indeed, the figure of the meritorious administrator who solves problems through the use of his mental faculties is yet another addition that emerges in the third stage of Muṣṭafā's composition. Although he does not credit himself with any specific achievements, his message to his readers is quite transparent.

An Unfinished or Interminable Work?

The poets, historians, scribes, literati, and relatives who flocked to Muṣṭafā's home during his retirement likely were the first to read these additions. A consideration of three groups of manuscripts, identified by Petra Kappert in her edition of *Ṭabaḳāt* and discussed by Victor Ménage in a typically insightful review, establishes that Muṣṭafā gave the work its final form in the early 1560s. The extant copies are based on two copies made by his two sons, Hüseyin and Mahmud, in ca. 1560 and ca. 1580, respectively.[64] This history raises an important question: why does the work end with the construction of the Süleymaniye Mosque? The question becomes even more salient when one considers that Muṣṭafā found time to work on a number of other works during his retirement.

Kappert believes that the construction of the Süleymaniye constitutes the zenith of Süleyman's reign in Muṣṭafā's mind.[65] Ménage agrees but finds it significant that this event more or less coincides with Muṣṭafā's retirement. If the rumors about his dismissal by Rüstem Pasha were true, then he would have preferred not to dwell on the conditions of his retirement. A convenient ending would save Muṣṭafā from embarrassment and, even more importantly, from the pasha's anger. Ménage points to another potentially dangerous incident: the fight between princes Bayezid (d. 1561) and Selim (the future Selim II, r. 1567–1574) after 1558, Bayezid's escape to Iran, and his execution there by strangling at the hands of an executioner sent from Istanbul.[66]

It is obvious that, rather than dwelling on the fight between the princes or exploring the relatively uneventful last years of Süleyman, Muṣṭafā preferred to emphasize the mosque's construction as a potent symbol. The Bayezid affair could have had personal ramifications for Muṣṭafā and his family, as well. His brother Salih, through Muṣṭafā's intercession, had translated a collection of historical anecdotes and moral tales from Persian into Ottoman Turkish for Prince Bayezid. He had been appointed to a teaching post on the request of the prince in late 1558, a short time before the hostilities between the princes began.[67] Muṣṭafā was retired and had two sons who obviously expected to pursue successful careers, but their success depended on the approval of the heir apparent and his entourage.

Muṣṭafā's need to curry favor with Prince Selim is seen in his dedication of the *Cevāhirü'l-aḫbār* to the future sultan. This is his only work dedicated to any particular individual, and it is also his most pragmatic work in the sense that its primary objective is to curry favor. The work is a translation, from Arabic, of the story about Prophet Joseph and his brothers. By offering Selim the story of the innocent and handsome brother persecuted by his siblings, tormented, tortured, but finally reunited with his father, Muṣṭafā sought to emphasize, against any possible doubts, his allegiance to Selim. In this environment, the construction of the Süleymaniye is indeed the best ending note for Süleyman's reign, as it saves Muṣṭafā from wading into potentially dangerous waters.

Conclusion: Narrative, Empire, Identity

Hayden White argues that every narrative "has to do with the topics of law, legality, legitimacy, or, more generally, authority." A "historically self-conscious" author like Celālzāde Muṣṭafā, according to White, is particularly interested in "the question of the social system and the law that sustains it, the authority of this law and its justification, and threats to the law."[68] Muṣṭafā, as a deeply self-conscious bureaucrat and historian, indeed writes in order to propose and protect a particular social system, emphasizes the function of law and justice in promoting it, and also discusses the threats to this edifice at length. Among these threats are Habsburg dreams of universal monarchy and, more importantly, the Safavid "heresy." Ottoman subjects and officials themselves are under the constant threat of human fallibility, the absence of piety, the lack of reason, ambition, or disloyalty.

Already in the second half of the fifteenth century, such historians as ʿĀşıḳpaşazāde (d. after 1484), Neşrī (Mevlānā Meḥemmed, d. ca. 1520), or the compilers of the anonymous *Tevārīḫ* knew that history-writing was a way to intervene in ongoing debates about the nature of their polity. History established authority and either legitimized or criticized and denounced the present. Sixteenth-century Ottoman historians, dwelling in an expanded public and political space and addressing a larger number of readers, were acutely aware of this. Muṣṭafā believed that his career as a servant of the dynasty gave him authority over other historians who did not know the inner workings of the Ottoman administration. He was also convinced that he represented the correct historical and religious position vis-à-vis the Habsburgs, the Safavids, and other enemies or rivals of the Ottoman polity. This state-, Sunni-, and Ottoman-centric approach to Ottoman history has been repeated and expounded in modern Ottoman scholarship, and Muṣṭafā was one of the most prominent architects of this convenient fiction. Reading his works provides us, among other things, with clues about the origins of an Ottoman Sunni identity and a state- and dynasty-centric political ideology. There was an Ottoman imperialism before Muṣṭafā's age, but it found its language and arguments through the works of men like him.

Muṣṭafā enjoyed an exceptionally successful bureaucratic career, which had a considerable impact on the ways in which he viewed and interpreted various events. He lived in a world in which political and military tensions were always translated into the language of cultural competition and religious rivalry. He saw the sudden rise to prominence of scribes in the midst of newly centralizing early modern dynastic polities, just as he realized their vulnerability vis-à-vis the military class. He reacted to all of these issues with his works and hoped that they would contribute to the survival of the polity under the watchful eye of the sultan and through the rational and dedicated work of the scribes. Just as fifteenth-century Ottoman historiography is an ideological debate about the origins of the polity and the meaning of its past, sixteenth-century Ottoman historiography is a series of discussions about the definition of that polity and the meaning of its present. Muṣṭafā was well aware of this; especially toward the end of his life, joining this discussion and circulating his own opinions were, for him, at least as important as praising Süleyman's achievements.

Notes

This essay is an expanded and revised version of a paper presented at an Indiana University workshop in November 2009. I am grateful to Emine Fetvacı and Erdem Çıpa for organizing the workshop, carefully reading and commenting on different versions of the manuscript, and shouldering the considerable burden of preparing the present volume for publication. I thank Gottfried Hagen and the anonymous reviewer for Indiana University Press for their suggestions and comments. My discussions over the years with Cornell H. Fleischer and Snježana Buzov on Ottoman history and historiography considerably contributed to the formation of the arguments in this article, but actual and potential errors here and elsewhere are exclusively mine.

1. Celālzāde Muṣṭafā, *Geschichte Sultan Süleymān Ḳānūnīs von 1520 bis 1557, oder, Ṭabaḳāt ül-Memālik ve Derecāt ül-Mesālik / von Celālzāde Muṣṭafā genannt Ḳoca Nişāncı*, ed. Petra Kappert (Wiesbaden: Steiner, 1981), hereafter *Ṭabaḳāt*. In the endnotes below, Arabic numerals followed by a letter refer to the folio numbers of Celālzāde's original while Roman numerals refer to Kappert's introduction and notes.

2. For a discussion of Muṣṭafā's emphasis on the sixteenth century as an exceptional period, and the distance he puts between his and other works of history, see Kaya Şahin, "In the Service of the Ottoman Empire: Celālzāde Muṣṭafā, Bureaucrat and Historian" (PhD diss., University of Chicago, 2007), 327–335.

3. *Ṭabaḳāt*, XXXII–XXXV.

4. Joseph von Hammer-Purgstall, *Geschichte des Osmanischen Reiches* (Pest: C. A. Hartleben, 1828), vol. 3; İsmail Hakkı Uzunçarşılı, *Osmanlı Tarihi* (Ankara: Türk Tarih Kurumu, 1943), vol. 2; İsmail Hami Danişmend, *İzahlı Osmanlı Tarihi Kronolojisi* (Istanbul: Türkiye Basımevi, 1948), vol. 2; Fahrettin Kırzıoğlu, *Osmanlı'nın Kafkas-Elleri'ni Fethi (1451–1590)* (Ankara: Sevinç Matbaası, 1976); and Walter Posch, "Der Fall Alkâs Mîrzâ und der Persienfeldzug von 1548–1549: ein gescheitertes osmanisches Projekt zur Niederwerfung des safavidischen Persiens" (PhD diss., University of Bamberg, 1999).

5. *Ṭabaḳāt*, XXXVI–XL. The "elaborate" register is utilized for describing the sultan, various grandees, and battle scenes. The middle register is used for ceremonies and celebrations, while the simple register is for the narration of such mundane events as the progress of the campaigning army from one stop to the next.

6. *Ṭabaḳāt*, 132a–b: "Ḥażret-i pādişāh-ı encüm-ʿibād u sitāre-sipāh, ḫıdivv-i Cem-nijād u eḳālīm-penāh, ḫüsrev-i Dārā-derbān u Efrāsiyāb-çāker, ḳāān-ı İskender-ġulām u Sohrāb-nöker, sulṭān-ı ʿālem-gīr u cihān-tesḫīr, ḫāḳān-ı gītī-sitān u āfitāb-żamīr."

7. To give a few examples, Mamluks are said to be oppressors who stray from Islam and commit various sins (*Ṭabaḳāt*, 440b: "Çerākise-i nāḥise ki ẓulm u ḍalāl rāyātını ʿayyūḳa çıḳarub günāh u vebāl ṣaḥīfelerini memālik-i ʿArabistāna döşeyüb cihānda ẓulm u fesād ile meşhūrlardı"); in the account of the Belgrade campaign of 1521, armor-clad Hungarians are likened to wild animals and are referred to as infidels and polytheists destined to the fires of hell (*Ṭabaḳāt*, 47b–48a: "āteş-menzil,

ẓulmet-dil, şirk-pezīr, tārīk-żamīr, pūlād-beden, āhen-ser, çağāl-pūş u cevşen-zīver u dūzeḫī-hey'et, 'ifrīt-ṣūret müşrikler, kelbler, dūnlar, kāfirler, ḫınzīrlar, mel'ūnlar . . .").

8. *Ṭabaḳāt,* 29b–41a passim, 67b–68b.

9. *Ṭabaḳāt,* 174a–b, 197b–198a.

10. Piri Mehmed is the personification of reason, caution, and good government in these sections. For example, *Ṭabaḳāt,* 21b: "zihn-i pākı deryā-yı 'ulūm, 'akl-ı derrākı āyine-i sa'ādet-rüsūm idi. Ḥikmetde Büzürcmihr u Eflāṭūn, ḳavānīn-i firāsetde ḥakīm-i ẕū-fünūn idi"; and *Ṭabaḳāt,* 86a: "Pīr Muḥammed Paşa ki ol zamānıñ kemāl-i luṭf-i tab' u ḥüsn-i tedbīr-i dilpezīrī ile ferīdi, envā'-ı kemālāt u 'ulūm ile 'allāme-i 'aṣr olub eyyāmıñ vaḥīdi, kārdān u ṣāib-tedbīr, mahāret-i 'ulūm ile firāsetde Ārisṭō-naẓīr u Eflāṭūn-żamīr idi."

11. From his first appearance to his execution, he plays an important role in the narrative as the antithesis of Piri Mehmed (*Ṭabaḳāt,* 24b–115a).

12. For example, the narrative jumps from November 1527 to April 1529 and then from November 1543 to the spring of 1548. These gaps stem from the fact that the work focuses on those events that the author considers significant rather than providing a seamless chronological history.

13. For the text of the *berāt,* see *Ṭabaḳāt,* 179b–182b. Mehmet Şakir Yılmaz transliterated the text into Latin characters by comparing it with another version from Ferīdūn Beg's *Mecmū'a-i Münşe'āt,* vol. 1 (Istanbul: Dārü'ṭ-ṭıbā'ati'l-'āmire, 1848). See Yılmaz, "'Koca Nişancı' of Kanuni: Celalzade Mustafa Çelebi, Bureaucracy and 'Kanun' in the Reign of Süleyman the Magnificent (1520–1566)" (PhD diss., Bilkent University, 2006), 234–246.

14. *Ṭabaḳāt,* 459a–460b, 465b–470a.

15. Roland Barthes demonstrates the creation of the "effect of the Real" through the use of meticulous details, as discussed in Elizabeth A. Clark, *History, Theory, Text: Historians and the Linguistic Turn* (Cambridge: Harvard University Press, 2004), 96–97.

16. Cemal Kafadar, *Between Two Worlds: The Construction of the Ottoman State* (Berkeley: University of California Press, 1995), 60–117; and Cornell Fleischer, *Bureaucrat and Intellectual in the Ottoman Empire: The Historian Mustafa Âli (1541–1600)* (Princeton, N.J.: Princeton University Press, 1986), passim.

17. For Piterberg's description of Ottoman historiography from its beginnings to the first decades of the seventeenth century (together with relevant modern scholarly debates), see Gabriel Piterberg, *An Ottoman Tragedy: History and Historiography at Play* (Berkeley: University of California Press, 2003), 30–45. For his attempt at developing an "interpretive framework" that engages theoretical writings on the nature of text, discourse, narrative, and history, see ibid., 1–6, 50–68.

18. I find, like Piterberg, the following essays by Gabrielle M. Spiegel particularly useful: "History, Historicism, and the Social Logic of the Text," in *The Past as Text: The Theory and Practice of Medieval Historiography* (Baltimore: Johns Hopkins University Press, 1997), 3–28; and "Towards a Theory of the Middle Ground," in *The Past as Text,* 44–56. For a useful collection of relevant articles and excerpts from books that support Spiegel's approach to history and text, see Gabrielle M. Spiegel, ed., *Practicing History: New Directions in Historical Writing after the Linguistic Turn* (New York: Routledge, 2005).

19. See Frank N. Ankersmit, *Historical Representation* (La Jolla, Calif.: Stanford University Press, 2001), especially "The Linguistic Turn: Literary Theory and Historical Theory," 29–74.

20. Clark, *History, Theory, Text,* 170.

21. This biographical sketch is based on the following works: İ. H. Uzunçarşılı, "Onaltıncı Asır Ortalarında Yaşamış Olan İki Büyük Şahsiyet: Tosyalı Celâl zâde Mustafa ve Salih Çelebiler," *Belleten* 22, no. 87 (1958): 391–441; *Ṭabaḳāt,* III–X; Yılmaz, "'Koca Nişancı' of Kanuni," 26–164; and Şahin, "In the Service of the Ottoman Empire," 14–316.

22. Fleischer, *Bureaucrat and Intellectual,* 30–31; and 'Āşıḳ Çelebi, *Meşā'irü'ş-şu'arā,* ed. G. M. Meredith-Owens (London: Luzac, 1971), 135a, 228b.

23. ʿÂşıḳ Çelebi, for example, saw parts of his treatise on politics and morals, *Mevāhibü'l-ḫallāḳ fī merātibi'l-aḫlāḳ*.

24. Christine Woodhead, "After Celalzade: The Ottoman *Nişancı* c. 1560–1700," *Journal of Semitic Studies*, Supplement 23 (2007): 295–296.

25. There is now a consensus among Ottoman historians that the empire was an active participant in early modern history. See Daniel Goffman, *The Ottoman Empire and Early Modern Europe* (Cambridge: Cambridge University Press, 2002); and introduction to *The Early Modern Ottomans: Remapping the Empire*, ed. Virginia Aksan and Daniel Goffman (Cambridge: Cambridge University Press, 2007). For the near-simultaneous rise of imperial/dynastic entities that became major actors within a global, and not merely European, early modernity, see John Darwin, *After Tamerlane: The Global History of Empire since 1405* (London: Allen Lane, 2007), 50–99. For a very concise treatment of the features that unified early modern Eurasia, see Sanjay Subrahmanyam, "Connected Histories: Notes towards a Reconfiguration of Early Modern Eurasia," *Modern Asian Studies* 31, no. 3 (July 1997): 736–740. For further studies on the variants of new political theologies in the fifteenth and sixteenth centuries, see Subrahmanyam, "Sixteenth Century Millenarianism from the Tagus to the Ganges," *in Explorations in Connected History: From the Tagus to the Ganges* (New Delhi: Oxford University Press, 2007), 2:102–137; Tijana Krstić, "Illuminated by the Light of Islam and the Glory of the Ottoman Sultanate: Self-Narratives of Conversion to Islam in the Age of Confessionalization," *Comparative Studies in Society and History* 51, no. 1 (2009): 35–63; and Kaya Şahin, "Constantinople and the End Time: The Ottoman Conquest as a Portent of the Last Hour," *Journal of Early Modern History* 14, no. 4 (2010): 317–354.

26. Studies of these developments are too numerous to mention here. My understanding of the period is in line with a short but very poignant account by Snježana Buzov that emphasizes the particular challenges faced by Selim and Süleyman in the first decades of the sixteenth century: Snježana Buzov, "The Lawgiver and His Lawmakers: The Role of Legal Discourse in the Change of Ottoman Imperial Culture" (PhD diss., University of Chicago, 2005), 17–29.

27. Andrew J. Newman, *Safavid Iran: Rebirth of a Persian Empire* (London: I. B. Tauris, 2006), 13–20; and Faruk Sümer, *Safevi Devletinin Kuruluşu ve Gelişmesinde Anadolu Türklerinin Rolü* (Ankara: Güven Matbaası, 1976).

28. For the rise of Selim to power, see H. Erdem Çıpa, "The Centrality of the Periphery: The Rise to Power of Selīm I, 1481–1512" (PhD diss., Harvard University, 2007). For an account of Selim's reign, see Caroline Finkel, *Osman's Dream* (New York: Basic Books, 2006), 102–114; and Feridun M. Emecen, *Zamanın İskenderi, Şarkın Fatihi: Yavuz Sultan Selim* (Istanbul: Yitik Hazine Yayınları, 2010).

29. For a general account of Süleyman's reign, see Finkel, *Osman's Dream*, 115–151.

30. For the characteristics of the new Ottoman bureaucracy in the first half of the sixteenth century, see Josef Matuz, *Das Kanzleiwesen Sultan Süleymans des Prächtigen* (Wiesbaden: F. Steiner, 1974); İ. H. Uzunçarşılı, *Osmanlı Devletinin Merkez ve Bahriye Teşkilatı* (Ankara: Türk Tarih Kurumu, 1989); Cornell Fleischer, "Preliminaries to the Study of Ottoman Bureaucracy," *Journal of Turkish Studies* 10 (1986): 135–141; Fleischer, *Bureaucrat and Historian*, 214–224; and Yılmaz, "'Koca Nişancı' of Kanuni," 8–13. Buzov clearly demonstrates that the definition and redefinition of law and legality in terms of sharia and *ḳānūn* became a major preoccupation for Ottoman scribes and scholars in the first half of the sixteenth century. See Buzov, "The Lawgiver and His Lawmakers."

31. The ideological aspect of the Ottoman-Habsburg rivalry is tactfully demonstrated in Gülru Necipoğlu, "Süleyman the Magnificent and the Representation of Power in the Context of Ottoman-Hapsburg-Papal Rivalry," in *Süleymân the Second and His Time*, ed. Halil İnalcık and Cemal Kafadar (Istanbul: Isis Press, 1993), 163–194. The Ottoman-Habsburg struggle for universal sovereignty is analyzed in its various aspects in Ebru Turan, "The Sultan's Favorite: İbrahim Pasha and the Making of Ottoman Universal Sovereignty in the Reign of Sultan Süleyman (1516–1526)" (PhD diss., University of Chicago, 2007), 254–355. For Buzov's explanation of how the new ideological agenda devised by

Süleyman and Ibrahim went beyond the specific dynamics of the Ottoman-Habsburg struggle and offered a set of general principles on Ottoman sovereignty, see Buzov, "The Lawgiver and His Lawmakers," 29–45. For sixteenth-century debates on sovereignty, see Hüseyin Yılmaz, "The Sultan and the Sultanate: Envisioning Rulership in the Age of Süleyman the Lawgiver (1520–1566)" (PhD diss., Harvard University, 2004). For Ottoman messianism, see Cornell Fleischer, "The Lawgiver as Messiah: The Making of the Imperial Image in the Reign of Süleymân," in *Soliman le magnifique et son temps,* ed. Gilles Veinstein (Paris: La Documentation Française, 1992), 159–177; Fleischer, "Mahdi and Millenium: Messianic Dimensions in the Development of Ottoman Imperial Ideology," in *The Great Ottoman-Turkish Civilization,* ed. Kemal Çiçek (Ankara: Yeni Türkiye, 2000), 3:42–54; Fleischer, "Seer to the Sultan: Haydar-i Remmal and Sultan Süleyman," in *Cultural Horizons: Festschrift in Honor of Talat S. Halman,* ed. Jayne S. Warner (Syracuse, N.Y.: Syracuse University Press, 2001), 1:290–299; Fleischer, "Shadows of Shadows: Prophecy and Politics in 1530s Istanbul," *International Journal of Turkish Studies* 13, no. 1–2 (2007): 52–57; and Barbara Flemming, "Sāḥib-ḳırān und Mahdī: Türkische Endzeiterwartungen im ersten Jahrzehnt der Regierung Süleymāns," in *Between the Danube and the Caucasus,* ed. György Kara (Budapest: Akadémiai Kiadó, 1987), 43–62. Krstić demonstrates that the Ottomans and the Safavids actively participated in early modern debates on political theology and profoundly influenced each other (Krstić, "Illuminated by the Light of Islam," 35–63). The traditional approach to the Ottoman-Safavid conflict in modern Ottoman and Safavid historiographies, on the other hand, fails to recognize this critical issue, which still awaits the full-fledged treatment it deserves. For an early study whose lead has not been followed, see Elke Niewöhner-Eberhard, *Osmanische Polemik gegen die Safawiden im 16. Jahrhundert nach arabischen Handschriften* (Freiburg: Schwarz, 1970).

32. For a discussion of the change in Ottoman claims to universal sovereignty and the shift to a less dynamic and more conservative political theology, see Fleischer, "The Lawgiver as Messiah"; and Gülru Necipoğlu, "A Kânûn for the State, a Canon for the Arts: Conceptualizing the Classical Synthesis of Ottoman Arts and Architecture," in *Soliman le Magnifique et son temps,* 195–216. For a concise account of the ideological issues at stake during Süleyman's reign, see Cornell Fleischer and Kaya Şahin, "Süleyman the Magnificent," in *The Princeton Encyclopedia of Islamic Political Thought,* ed. Gerhard Bowering et al. (Princeton, N.J.: Princeton University Press, 2012).

33. Robert Mantran, "L'historiographie ottomane à l'époque de Soliman le Magnifique," in *Soliman le Magnifique et son temps,* 25–32.

34. Walter Andrews argues that new forms of patronage, authorship, and reading influenced poetic production in this period and that the politically charged atmosphere of the period led to the use of politicized metaphors in Ottoman Turkish poetry (see Andrews, "Literary Art of the Golden Age: The Age of Süleymân," in *Süleymân the Second and His Time,* 353–368) and provides a more detailed analysis of what he calls "the voice of power and authority." Walter G. Andrews, *Poetry's Voice, Society's Song: Ottoman Lyric Poetry* (Seattle: University of Washington Press, 1985), 89–108. Sooyong Kim offers a more nuanced picture of the relationship between court patronage and poetic production; see Kim, "Minding the Shop: Zati and the Making of Ottoman Poetry in the First Half of the Sixteenth Century" (PhD diss., University of Chicago, 2005), 6–55. His emphasis on the relative autonomy of literary activity and the increasing levels of linguistic and artistic consciousness in the first half of the sixteenth century is especially important for the arguments of the present article.

35. For the *şehnāme* literature, see Christine Woodhead, "An Experiment in Official Historiography: The Post of Şehnameci in the Ottoman Empire, c.1555–1605," *Wiener Zeitschrift für die Kunde des Morgenlandes* 75 (1983): 157–182; Woodhead, "Reading Ottoman Şehnames: Official Historiography in the Late Sixteenth Century," *Studia Islamica* 104–105 (2007): 67–80; and Emine Fetvacı, "The Office of the Ottoman Court Historian," in *Studies on Istanbul and Beyond,* ed. Robert G. Ousterhout (Philadelphia: University of Pennsylvania Museum of Archaeology and Anthropology, 2007), 7–21.

36. Christine Woodhead, "Perspectives on Süleyman," in *Süleyman the Magnificent and His Age,* ed. Metin Kunt and Christine Woodhead (London: Longman, 1995), 166–171.

37. Colin Imber, "Ideals and Legitimation in Early Ottoman History," in *Süleyman the Magnificent and His Age,* 147–153; J. R. Walsh, "The Historiography of Ottoman-Safavid Relations in the Sixteenth and Seventeenth Centuries," in *Historians of the Middle East,* ed. Bernard Lewis and Peter M. Holt (London: Oxford University Press, 1962), 197–211.

38. Concerning the production of independent works with historical content in highly politicized urban environments and their potential of political criticism, see Barbara Flemming, "Public Opinion under Sultan Süleymân," in *Süleymân the Second and His Time,* 59–67; Ebru Turan, "Voices of Opposition in the Reign of Sultan Süleyman: The Case of İbrahim Pasha (1523–36)," in *Studies on Istanbul and Beyond,* 23–35; and Ebru Turan, "Histories in Verse: Ottoman Imperialism and Its Supporters in Early Sixteenth-Century Istanbul" (paper presented at the annual meeting for the American Historical Association, Washington, D.C., January 3–6, 2008). For a discussion of the existence of a new public opinion in the sixteenth century, see Ebru Turan, "The Sultan's Favorite," passim; Ralph Hattox, *Coffee and Coffeehouses: The Origins of a Social Beverage in the Medieval Near East* (Seattle: University of Washington Press, 1985); and Nelly Hanna, *In Praise of Books: A Cultural History of Cairo's Middle Class, Sixteenth to the Eighteenth Century* (Syracuse, N.Y.: Syracuse University Press, 2003).

39. Gabrielle M. Spiegel, "Social Change and Literary Language," in *The Past as Text,* 183.

40. Studies of fifteenth-century Ottoman historiography are too numerous to mention here. The best account of its main concerns, which includes a summary of modern debates, is Kafadar, *Between Two Worlds,* 90–117.

41. On the basis of Douglas Howard's excellent study of Ottoman *naṣīḥatnāme* literature ("Genre and Myth in the Ottoman Advice for Kings Literature," in *The Early Modern Ottomans: Remapping the Empire,* ed. Virginia Aksan and Daniel Goffman [Cambridge: Cambridge University Press, 2007]), it can be argued that there are striking parallels among those sixteenth-century works of history and politics that were written by scribes: a preoccupation with language (150), an obsession with lists (153, 155–156), a concern with order and disorder (161–163).

42. For themes, tropes, genres, and linguistic registers in fifteenth-century Ottoman historiography, see Kaya Şahin, "Âşıkpaşa-zâde as Historian: An Analysis of the Tevârih-i Âl-i Osman [The History of the Ottoman House] of Âşıkpaşa-zâde" (MA thesis, Sabancı University, 2000).

43. For a comprehensive analysis of sixteenth-century Ottoman historiography, see Fleischer, *Bureaucrat and Intellectual,* 235–245. For a descriptive survey, see Abdülkadir Özcan, "Historiography in the Reign of Süleyman the Magnificent," in *The Ottoman Empire in the Reign of Süleyman the Magnificent,* ed. Tülay Duran (Istanbul: Historical Research Foundation, Istanbul Research Center, 1988), 165–222. For the creation of Süleyman's image through works of history, see Christine Woodhead, "Perspectives on Süleyman," in *Süleyman the Magnificent and His Age,* passim.

44. Constantin Fasolt demonstrates that, in the context of early modern Europe, history-writing and political activity were more closely intertwined than has been typically assumed (Fasolt, *The Limits of History* [Chicago: University of Chicago Press, 2004]). Unlike Fasolt's Hermann Conring, who used history-writing to develop an anti-imperialist stance, Muṣṭafā wrote his work to advocate for empire; the similarity between the two historians is that, while seeking to pursue particular political agendas, they created new historiographical idioms and approaches.

45. *Ṭabaḳāt,* 7a–b.

46. *Ṭabaḳāt,* 9a: "Bu pādişāh-ı memālik-sitān u ṣāḥib-ḳırān, şehinşāh-ı melā'ik-şān u ma'delet-nişānıñ zīr-i nigīn-i ḥükūmetlerinde rām olan ṭavā'if-i enāmdan zümre-i fużalā-yı kirām, fırḳa-yı ʿulemā'-yı ʿiẓām ile erbāb-ı fażl u ʿirfān, aṣḥāb-ı keşf u īḳān, eṣnāf-ı sipāh u ʿasker, envāʿ-ı cünūd u leşker, esbāb-ı fütūḥ u nuṣret, ālāt-ı ḥaşmet u şevket, gürūh-ı etbāʿ u enṣār, cümle-i ḥüddām-ı encüm-şiʿār, ʿamme-i reʿāyā u memleket, kāffe-i berāyā u vilāyet, memālik u eḳālīm-i maʿmūre, ḳılāʿ u biḥār-ı

mevfūre, ḫazāin u cihāz-ı nā-maḥdūd, cevāhir u emvāl u maʿādin-i nā-maʿdūd raḳam-ı tafṣīl ile merḳūm, ḳalem-i tavṣīf ile mersūm olunsa uʿcūbe-i zamān u nādire-i devrān olurdı."

47. *Ṭabaḳāt,* 8b–9a, 10a.

48. Uzunçarşılı, "Tosyalı Celâl zâde Mustafa ve Salih Çelebiler," 408–409; and Yılmaz, "'Koca Nişancı' of Kanuni," 105, 128. Cf. Ferīdūn Beg, *Mecmūʿa-i Münşeʾāt,* 546–551 (Mohacs), 602–604 (Moldavia), 604–606 (Van).

49. Although I see the same links between *fetḥnāmes* and some sections of *Ṭabaḳāt,* I disagree with Yılmaz's argument that the whole work is an expanded *fetḥnāme* (see Yılmaz, "'Koca Nişancı' of Kanuni," 189–192). As will be discussed below, Muṣṭafā not only expanded these shorter texts but also added new chapters that do not focus on the sultan's campaigns.

50. *Ṭabaḳāt,* 250b. Distiches by Tabriz literati praising the work are quoted in 251a–b.

51. For the close relationship between the language of bureaucratic practice and history-writing, and for the value attributed to *inşāʾ* in the sixteenth century, see Yılmaz, "'Koca Nişancı' of Kanuni," 174–182; Fleischer, *Bureaucrat and Intellectual,* 236; and Christine Woodhead, "From Scribe to Litterateur: The Career of a Sixteenth Century Ottoman *Kātib,*" *Bulletin of the British Society for Middle Eastern Studies* 9, no. 1 (1982): 55–74.

52. Sehī, *Tezkire-i Sehī,* 33; and Latīfī, *Tezkiretü'ş-şuʿarā,* 336.

53. *Ṭabaḳāt,* 10b–20a.

54. For a discussion of the table of contents as well the new ideas of system and order, see Şahin, "In the Service of the Ottoman Empire," 413–425. By neo-Platonism I understand the following definition by Oliver Leaman: "[Neoplatonism] does trace the production and reproduction of everything back to a source—and a single source at that—and it establishes a rational structure behind the universe" (Leaman, *A Brief Introduction to Islamic Philosophy* [Malden, Mass.: Blackwell, 1999], 5).

55. *Ṭabaḳāt,* XLI; V. L. Ménage, "Review," *Bulletin of the School of Oriental and African Studies* 47, no. 1 (1984): 156.

56. *Ṭabaḳāt,* 109b.

57. In the introduction to his *Selīmnāme,* a work that he finished toward the end of his life, Muṣṭafā states that he worked on *Ṭabaḳāt* during his retirement; he presents it as a truthful account and detailed panorama of Süleyman's reign (Celālzāde Muṣṭafā, *Selīmnāme,* ed. Ahmet Uğur and Mustafa Çuhadar [Istanbul: Milli Eğitim Bakanlığı, 1997], 46–77); and Celālzāde Muṣṭafā, *Selīmnāme,* London, British Museum Library, Add. 7848, 23a.

58. Patrick J. Geary, *Phantoms of Remembrance: Memory and Oblivion at the End of the First Millennium* (Princeton, N.J.: Princeton University Press, 1994), 11–12, 25–26.

59. For the march of the army and navy, see *Ṭabaḳāt,* 69b–84b, passim; for the news from the Hungarian front, see *Ṭabaḳāt,* 76a–b; and for the punitive expedition, see *Ṭabaḳāt,* 67b–68b, 77a–78a.

60. *Ṭabaḳāt,* 308a.

61. For the Belgrade campaign, the pashas' disagreement in the imperial council meeting, and the Rhodes campaign, see *Ṭabaḳāt,* 41a–65a, 46a–47a, and 65a–104a, respectively.

62. For the account of this campaign, see *Ṭabaḳāt,* 379b–411a.

63. For these accounts, see *Ṭabaḳāt,* 121a–130a, 157b–172a, and 172b–175b, respectively.

64. For Kappert's discussion and presentation of the three groups, see *Ṭabaḳāt,* XLI–LI. For Ménage's discussion of different manuscripts, as well as the sons' editorial strategies, see Ménage, "Review," 156–157.

65. *Ṭabaḳāt,* IX–X.

66. Ménage, "Review," 156.

67. Uzunçarşılı, "Tosyalı Celâl zâde Mustafa ve Salih Çelebiler," 425.

68. Hayden V. White, *The Content of the Form: Narrative Discourse and Historical Representation* (Baltimore: Johns Hopkins University Press, 1987), 13.

4 Conversion and Converts to Islam in Ottoman Historiography of the Fifteenth and Sixteenth Centuries

Tijana Krstić

Although the issue of conversion to Islam was at the core of one of the earliest historiographical debates on the origins of the Ottoman state, it subsequently became a subject that is almost universally treated in the context of Muslim–non-Muslim relations in the Ottoman Empire.[1] As a consequence, in current historiography conversion to Islam is framed as an issue that mattered primarily to non-Muslims, while the Ottoman Muslim community's experience of it is rarely questioned or problematized.

However, a closer look at narrative sources, beginning with the rise of Ottoman historiography in the fifteenth century, reveals not only that Muslim authors were concerned with the phenomenon of conversion to Islam but also that there were a variety of views on what the proper place and role of converts in Ottoman society should be. Not all genres were equally likely to feature discussions on conversion: especially rich sources include narratives dedicated to the striving of Muslim soldiers and holy men in encounters with "infidels," such as epics about Ottoman warrior-saints (*vilāyetnāmes*), spiritual biographies of holy men (*menāḳıbnāmes*), accounts of military campaigns (*ġazavātnāmes*), and the earliest Ottoman chronicles (*Tevārīḫ-i Āl-i ʿOsmān*) that blended genre elements from all of these with stories of early Ottoman rulers and their conquests. Additionally, later histories of the dynasty, narratives written by converts themselves, and various anonymous texts preserved in the miscellanies (*mecmūʿa*) that are omnipresent in Ottoman library collections and associated with all social strata of the Ottoman Muslim community also occasionally feature revealing comments. Collectively, these narratives point to a dynamic and constantly shifting debate about what comprised a good Muslim and a good subject of the House of Osman, as well as who defined religious and political "orthodoxy" in the Ottoman polity. They also remind us that the phenomenon of the earliest conversions to Islam and the transformation of the Ottoman polity into an empire were contemporaneous, mutually informing processes. This study explores portrayals of conversion and converts in fifteenth- and sixteenth-century Ottoman Muslim narratives in relation to the development of various religious, cultural, and political identities within the Ottoman polity during the same period.

Conversion and Identificatory Practices in the Early Modern Ottoman Polity

Recent historiography has brought into sharp focus the questions of whether we can discuss an "Ottoman" (*ʿOsmānlı*) identity in such a heterogeneous empire and who can rightfully be referred to as "Ottoman" beyond the members of the ruling dynasty and military-administrative elite. Such scholarship highlighted different Muslim identificatory practices[2] that existed in the early modern Ottoman Empire, based on criteria ranging from place of origin and profession to broader geo-cultural designations, such as *Rūmī, ʿArab,* and *ʿAcem.*[3] Of particular interest to this discussion is the category of *Rūmī,* which appears frequently in fifteenth- and sixteenth-century sources, most often as a term with which Muslims from the "Lands of *Rūm*" (i.e., Ottoman Rumelia and Anatolia) referred to themselves, as well as a term by which they were known to Muslims beyond this geographic area.[4] These categories do not, however, exhaust the various meanings and connotations of *Rūmī* (henceforth Rumi), which appears to have been a relational category that was shaped by society and evolved with the changing social and political conditions within and around the Ottoman Empire. So, in addition to being used in a purely geographical sense, "Rumi" could also denote a particular segment of society—"those who spoke Turkish (preferably a refined kind of Turkish, but not necessarily as their mother tongue) and acquired their social identity within or in proximity to urban settings, professions, institutions, education and cultural preferences."[5]

As a socio-cultural category, the term "Rumi" is differentiated from "Turk," a word that had primary associations of "ethnicity-not-transcended and attachment to tribal ways and cultural codes."[6] In that sense, both "Ottoman" and "Rumi" had social and cultural implications surpassing the "Turk." However, most frequently, the primary opposite of "Rumi" was not "Turk" but *ʿAcem* (another elusive category usually denoting "Persians" but with other connotations as well) and at times *ʿArab* (denoting any Arabic speaker, but also the Bedouin as well as other social groups).[7]

In his famous ode-like commentary on Rumis, the great Ottoman intellectual and historian Muṣṭafā ʿĀlī (d. 1600) provides an Ottoman view on the evolution of this geo-/socio-cultural category. According to ʿĀlī, one of the supreme characteristics of the Rumis is that they are "varied peoples," whether they lived in the "glorious days of the Ottoman dynasty," when they mixed with the "tribes of Turks and Tatars," or in his own time, when "most of the inhabitants of Rūm are of confused ethnic origins," among whose notables "there are few whose lineage does not go back to a convert to Islam."[8] For ʿĀlī, the Rumis, with their "piety, cleanliness, and faith," are the very essence of what is glorious about the Ottoman Empire, namely its ability to synthesize different cultures and ethnicities under the umbrella of Sunni Islam. The concepts featured prominently in ʿĀlī's commentary on Rumis are those of "mixing" and conversion ("either on their father's or their mother's side, the genealogy is traced to a filthy infidel"), which give rise to "purity" and "distinction" through the transformative power of the Muslim faith. Conversion is thus central to ʿĀlī's explanation of the evolution of Rumis as a group.

However, what did other Ottoman Muslims, both in ʿĀlī's time and before, think about conversion, the "mixing" of Muslims and non-Muslims, or Rumi-ness? Was there a unanimous endorsement of the religio-cultural synthesis that ʿĀlī seems to be describing? Since the early twentieth century, historiography of the Ottoman Empire has employed the term "syncretism" to capture the process of "mixing" and "blending" cultures, peoples, and religions brought together by Ottoman conquests and state-formation.[9] In recent years, however, scholars from various fields have come to challenge the uncritical usage of this term because it presupposes an orthodoxy (in this case, of Islam) that is "diluted" through contact with other religious traditions. In the context of Ottoman historiography, "syncretism" has been used both in this latter sense and imagined as a rather smooth and seamless incorporation of non-Muslims and converts into the Ottoman military, administration, and society.[10] What is overlooked in this narrative about the inclusive and "syncretic" Ottoman state is the challenge that the absorption of non-Muslims and converts posed to the Ottoman Muslim community, which was politically and religiously heterogeneous. Insistence on the language of smooth religio-cultural blending and inclusiveness has erased the plurality of voices for and against what was a conscious politics of religio-cultural synthesis promoted by Ottoman sultans. It has also obscured the competitive nature of sharing and coexistence through which an Ottoman Rumi socio-cultural category eventually emerged. This essay is an attempt to highlight some of those voices, suggest the ways in which they can be interpreted, and situate them in the context of the Ottoman polity's transformation into an empire between the mid-fifteenth and late sixteenth centuries.

Fifteenth- and Sixteenth-Century Ottoman Authors on Conversion and Converts

The rise of Ottoman historiography over the course of the fifteenth century coincided with a radical transformation of the Ottoman polity: from one that suffered near-destruction in the hands of Timur (d. 1405) and the subsequent Civil War (1402–1413), to one that struggled to digest the conquest of Constantinople and Mehmed II's (r. 1444–1446 and 1451–1481) centralizing and fiscal policies. It also paralleled the process of increased recruitment of non-Muslims and converts into the Ottoman military and political structures, reflecting the need for manpower and local know-how that the Ottoman sultans, with their dynamic expansion agenda, acknowledged and sought to remedy. It is therefore not a surprise that conversion and converts figure prominently in fifteenth-century *vilāyetnāmes*, *menāḳıbnāmes*, *ġazavātnāmes*, and, to a lesser extent, the earliest Ottoman chronicles of the *Tevārīḫ-i Āl-i ʿOs̱mān* genre, in which they invariably play an important symbolic role. Precisely because of the political climate in which they came into existence, wherein different religio-political factions within the Muslim community competed to set the agenda for the future of the Ottoman enterprise, these narratives do not represent a unified or one-dimensional corpus. With their mystically infused language and imagery, they continue to pose a methodological challenge to historians of the early Ottoman Empire, who have for the most part sought to distill some historical truth out of them. However, as Devin DeWeese suggests, rather than hoping to demythologize these narratives, both oral and literary, we must explore the ways in which their creators used the religiously charged language at their disposal to express their visions of human and communal truths.[11]

When it comes to depictions of conversion, perhaps the most fascinating fifteenth-century Ottoman narrative is *Ṣaltuḳnāme* (The Book of Ṣaltuḳ), a work of the *vilāyetnāme* genre that recounts the accomplishments of Sarı Saltuk, the archetypal missionary warrior-dervish who is credited with initiating the spread of Islam in Rumelia. In 1474, at the request of the Ottoman prince Cem Sultan (d. 1495), a man named Ebū'l-ḫayr-ı Rūmī (fl. 1480–1489) compiled this work from oral legends that had circulated for at least two centuries. The narrative of *Ṣaltuḳnāme* is particularly rich in scenes of Sarı Saltuk's duels with the flower of Christian knighthood and his overwhelming victories—upon which Christian warriors converted to Islam, awed by the saint's extraordinary military prowess. At the very beginning of Ebū'l-ḫayr-ı Rūmī's compilation, Sarı Saltuk fights Alyon-ı Rumi, a champion of the Pope and the Christian king. Upon defeat, Alyon embraces Islam as a sign of submission to Sarı Saltuk's overwhelming power. He receives a new name, Ilyas-ı Rumi, and becomes the saint's companion. Moreover, he volunteers immediately to fight the Christians in his stead.[12] Later in the text, Ilyas is courted by Christians to rejoin them. Besides killing the person sent to invite him back, he also asserts that when he was an infidel he did not have enough strength to kill fifty tied-up men, but now that he has become a Muslim his sword is sharper than those of the Christians.[13] Similar episodes in other narratives of the *vilāyetnāme* genre abound.[14]

Alyon-ı Rumi's transformation into Ilyas-ı Rumi nicely captures the process of development of a new Ottoman Rumi warrior and administrative elite in the fifteenth century. However, what is striking about this episode is the apparently quick integration of the warrior into the Ottoman military machine and his zeal against his former co-religionists. I have argued elsewhere that in the context of the fifteenth-century Ottoman polity, which abounded in troops of Christian and convert background, narratives like these served not only as a pastime by the campfire during campaigns but as scripts for desired behavior of those same troops.[15] The fact that *Baṭṭālnāme* (The Book of Battal, about the legendary warrior Battal Gazi), another Ottoman text of the *vilāyetnāme* genre that displayed a concern with conversion of Christian warriors similar to the *Ṣaltuḳnāme,* was used as a part of the Janissary curriculum suggests that narratives of this sort were deemed to possess a certain educational value and were expected to communicate the ideals of correct behavior to military converts.[16] Moreover, it is likely that converts—to the Ottoman cause and/or to Islam—themselves participated in the dissemination of these narratives as part of the process of fitting in and proving their loyalty to their comrades. Studies on religious conversion have long emphasized the importance of the "language of transformation," the necessity of adopting rhetoric specific to the religious or social group one is joining in the process of distancing oneself from the previous membership group.[17] For instance, one could imagine the famous prize-fighter (*deli*) from Grand Vizier Rüstem Pasha's (d. 1561) retinue whom Nicolas de Nicolay (d. 1583) met in Edirne in 1553 being such a disseminator. This warrior of Slavic background, who knew the Christian prayers and claimed to be a Christian at heart, nevertheless lived "with the Turks according to their law" and dressed in fierce-looking fighting clothes to frighten his enemies in battle, most of whom, one would imagine, were Christians.[18]

The conversion episodes from fifteenth-century Ottoman *vilāyetnāmes* and *ġazavātnāmes* therefore did not simply celebrate Muslim victories and Christian conversions or serve as entertainment, although these were undoubtedly important dimensions of their production and reception. They also performed the important social function of bringing cohesion to what must have appeared to some Ottoman Muslims as a dizzying, and not always appetizing, process of cultural and religious integration. In addition to the narratives promoting the image of the quickly integrated convert discussed above, other contemporaneous texts articulate a slightly more skeptical view and invite us to consider the difficulties and challenges that absorption of non-Muslims posed to the Ottoman Muslim community, which did not constitute a monolithic whole.

The conversion story of Köse Mihal, who has become the poster-child of Ottoman converts in modern historiography, provides an interesting opportunity to address some of these diverging views. The story of the process by which Mihal, the Christian Lord of Harmankaya (near Bursa), became a follower of Osman Beg (r. late 1290s–1324?) exists in several versions, most notably in the chronicles of ʿĀşıḳpaşazāde and Oruç, but is omitted from the anonymous *Tevārīḫ-i Āl-i ʿOs̱mān* (Chronicles of the House of Osman), the text that probably shared a common source with them until 1422.[19] Most historians have focused on ʿĀşıḳpaşazāde's account, in which Mihal and many infidels from Harmankaya joined Osman and fought alongside his army *before* converting to Islam—a phenomenon well attested to in fifteenth-century administrative sources as well.[20] According to ʿĀşıḳpaşazāde, Mihal was one of Osman's most important confidants, but—after a series of victories over Christians in Bithynia—Osman suggested to the warriors around him that they invite Mihal to embrace Islam. Were Mihal to refuse, Osman's followers would attack his lands. In the next scene, Mihal appears before Osman, kisses Osman's hand, and says: "My ruler! Make me a Muslim. I saw the Prophet in my dream and he asked me to come to the faith." He then professes articles of faith, becomes a Muslim, and is dressed in new clothes.[21]

Oruç provides a significantly different version of the story. In this account, Mihal's conversion immediately follows the Seljuk vizier Abdülaziz informing Osman that his father Ertuğrul had a dream, interpreted by Sheikh Edebali as foreshadowing the empire that Ertuğrul's offspring was to establish. In the narrative that clearly merges two extant historiographical versions of the famous dream, Osman marries Rabia, the daughter of Sheikh Edebali, thus uniting his own earthly power with the sheikh's spiritual legacy, embodied by his daughter. The morning after this crucial union takes place, while Osman and his men are entertaining themselves with hunting and jousting, they notice fire in the direction of *Rūm* (here, presumably Byzantine territories). Suddenly, out of this fire a lone horseman appears, approaches the group, and asks which of them is Osman. Facing Osman, the hero horseman, who is described as "one of the infidel notables" (*kāfir beglerinden*), falls to his knees, saying:

> "Osman Gazi! In my dream I saw your Prophet Muhammad Mustafa. He taught me the articles of Muslim religion, including the profession of faith (*şahada*), and the suras of *Fātiḥa* and *İḫlāṣ*. He said: 'Hey Abdallah! In the morning mount your horse. In such and such place there is a warrior for faith (*ġāzī*), his name is Osman and he is a warrior of such and such appearance. He embarked on the path of God with the intention of holy war, expecting nothing in return, and he is under the fold of my white banner. Get to him and become his follower.' My real name is Mihal. But the Holy Messenger gave me the name of Abdallah ['Slave of God'—a name typical of converts]. He said: 'Together with Osman make yourself bound to holy war (*ġazā*). Your offspring will fill the world. For generations they will engage in *ġazā*. By his side they will become famous. They will spread the faith by taking the banner of Islam all the way to Hungary.' When I woke up from my dream, I saw that my face was enlightened by the light of Islam." Saying this, he [Mihal] again professed faith in front of Osman and became a Muslim. Those Mihaloğulları who live in our times are his descendants.[22]

As the most detailed conversion episode in a whole family of fifteenth- and sixteenth-century Ottoman chronicles (especially those that use ʿĀşıḳpaşazāde as their main source for early Ottoman history), the story of Köse Mihal is of paramount importance to this discussion because of its paradigmatic value.[23] Köse Mihal personifies thousands of other (nameless) converted warriors from early Ottoman history—what kind of message(s) is his story supposed to relate? ʿĀşıḳpaşazāde's version has been cited frequently as proof that Osman's early followers included Christians. However, the role of Mihal in ʿĀşıḳpaşazāde's narrative has, I believe, further implications, which can be better understood in the context of the fifteenth-century political debate concerning the role of converts and non-Muslims in the Ottoman polity. After allowing Mihal to show his allegiance to Osman through a variety of battles waged together, ʿĀşıḳpaşazāde makes a point of briefly stopping the narrative to record Mihal's conversion. This can be read as the author's belief that the ultimate proof of loyalty to the Ottoman ruler—and the only way to become a true part of the Ottoman enterprise—is to embrace Islam. Nevertheless, ʿĀşıḳpaşazāde clearly emphasizes Mihal's faithful service over his conversion, which is described somewhat matter-of-factly rather than celebrated, as if to suggest that only those truly tested in their loyalty should be admitted into the closest circle around the Ottoman leader and into Islam.

Oruç's take on Köse Mihal's conversion is significantly different. By virtue of following the episode with arguably the greatest symbolism in all of Ottoman historiography—Osman's famous dream—Köse Mihal's conversion story appears both as an extension of the prophecy of the future greatness of the Ottoman enterprise and as an homage to the Mihaloğulları by an earnest admirer. Mihal's conversion is not only an immediate illustration of divine blessing for Osman Gazi's actions but also an exposition on the Mihaloğulları as the chosen instruments of God for the spread of *ġazā* and Islam. The message seems to be that without them, and those like them, Osman's mission would be impossible. Oruç embraces the notion that a sudden and untested convert can be a faithful servant of the Ottoman dynasty, perhaps, as a native of Edirne, reflecting more closely the logic of the Thracian frontier (*uc*) culture. Oruç's account also seems to echo the ideological program, apparently promoted by the Mihaloğulları themselves in the late fifteenth century, that aimed to glorify this frontier dynasty and its role in the establishment of the Ottoman state through sponsorship of various literary and architectural projects.[24] For instance, the same idea permeates the *Ġazavātnāme-i Miḫāloġlu ʿAlī Beg* (The Book of Mihaloğlu Ali Beg's Military Exploits), a fascinating versified homage to a descendant of Köse Mihal by Sūzī Çelebi of Prizren (d. 1524 or 1525).[25]

Although they draw on some of the same material, the chronicles by ʿĀşıḳpaşazāde and Oruç also diverge in significant ways both in the additional material they include and in the emphasis they give to that material. Elsewhere, I have analyzed in detail the divergences and possible meanings of the different versions of Osman's/Ertuğrul's dream.[26] At the center of these editorial choices apparently stood the authors' political allegiances and the ever-polarizing issue of how to define "real" *ġazā* and "true" *ġāzīs*, as well as how to approach the recruitment of both Muslims and non-Muslims for the Ottoman enterprise.

Several scholars have argued that, as a discourse, *ġazā*-centered narratives did not belong to one homogenous group, nor were the terms *ġazā* and *ġāzī* understood in the same way by all who appropriated them over time.[27] Although the meaning of *ġazā* as "holy war" has been analyzed by historians mainly in the context of its impact on Muslim-Christian relations, as a discourse that had a highly moral resonance, *ġazā* rhetoric was much more important for intra-Islamic polemics: as a vehicle for legitimization or de-legitimization and for support or critique of certain political agendas. The Rumelian raider commanders' understanding of *ġazā* and its objectives ran counter to Mehmed II's own, as well as to his experimentation with non-Muslim forms of political legitimacy, particularly the Roman and Byzantine imperial traditions that Mehmed sought to co-opt upon the conquest of Constantinople.[28] The converts socialized through central governmental structures (such as the *devşirme* recruits and sons of the Balkan nobility), and voluntary converts with high profiles (such as former

Byzantine and Balkan commanders) could and often did stand for vastly different agendas and interpretations of *ġazā*. These interpretations often carried more weight with the sultan and frustrated the goals of the "old *ġāzīs*," such as raider commanders and dervish communities.

It is often forgotten that the sultan was not the only individual with the opportunity to recruit converts and educate them in his own household. The history of the earliest conversions to Islam in the Ottoman realm and the absorption of non-Muslims into its political structures is also the history of early Ottoman state-building and its attendant struggles. During the fifteenth century the frontier raider commanders, who resisted the sultans' centralizing policies, also recruited converts into their households. Conversion thus played into the processes of ideological and religious differentiation already under way in the fifteenth-century Ottoman polity. Narrative sources from the period, such as the treatise by George of Hungary (d. 1502), indicate that the phenomenon of enslavement through warfare was at least as important to this process of recruitment for various interest groups as the voluntary crossovers of Rumelian Christians and the child levy (*devşirme*). George of Hungary describes throngs of merchants armed with chains marching alongside the Ottoman armies, ready to take the slaves off the soldiers' hands and transport them immediately to the closest slave market.[29] When one keeps in mind the Ottoman policy that those who did not surrender willingly to Muslim armies were subject to enslavement, and that many regions and fortresses around Rumelia refused to surrender without a fight, one begins to fathom the extent of the phenomenon. Frontier lords were in a particularly advantageous position to recruit the captured slaves to their households and armies.

For example, according to Mihaloğlu Ali Beg's endowment charter (dated 1496) for the mosque complex in Plevne (today Pleven, Bulgaria), the beneficiaries of his endowment—in the event his two sons should die—were to be his freed slaves (*'uteḳā'*), Hızır b. Abdullah and Yusuf b. Abdullah.[30] Incidentally, the same Hızır b. Abdullah also appears as the patron of an inscription at the tomb of Seyyid Gazi near Eskişehir in western Turkey, a shrine complex that attracts a wide variety of religious and political non-conformists and was also patronized by his master Mihaloğlu Ali Beg.[31] The second half of the fifteenth century witnessed a concerted effort on the part of the frontier lords to facilitate the creation of "alternative" religio-political communities, through the patronage of texts such as *vilāyetnāmes* and architectural complexes centered on holy men. In the texts about these venerated figures, including Otman Baba, Sarı Saltuk, Seyyid Ali, and even Sheikh Bedreddin (d. 1416), the Muslim conquest of Rumelia and further opening of the frontier was ascribed to such *ġāzīs* as Hacı Ilbegi (d. 1371?) and ancestors of Rumelian raider commanders, including Evrenos (d. 1417) and Mihal, while the role of the House of Osman was diminished. The cults of these holy men mobilized elements across Ottoman society that disagreed, more or less explicitly, with the politico-religious agenda of the Ottoman authorities.[32] Hızır b. Abdullah's actions suggest that he was socialized into a particular community that shared the ideals of the raider commanders and their spiritual advisers, who perceived themselves as the *true* "warriors for faith" (*ġāzīs*). Oruç himself appears to have adopted the same ethos.

The conquest of Constantinople in 1453 was an especially significant catalyst for the competing definitions of *ġazā*. Sultan Mehmed II's interest in and engagement with the religious and political traditions of Byzantine Constantinople are well attested to.[33] It was precisely this experimentation with "infidel" traditions, as well as practical measures taken to achieve the grandeur of a ruler in the mold of the Roman emperors, that distanced the sultan from groups who considered themselves the moral and historical core of the Ottoman Muslim enterprise. One of the greatest grudges these critics (many of whom stemmed from Rumelia) held against the sultan was his magnanimous policy toward non-Muslims during the repopulation of the conquered city, the forced resettlement of Muslim merchants and artisans from the provinces to Constantinople, and the subsequent decision to impose rent on houses that were initially granted as free-holding to the settlers. Different religious brotherhoods were also alienated because of the sultan's decision to confiscate pious endowment lands to finance military campaigns.[34]

Moreover, by the mid-fifteenth century debates about which direction the Ottoman polity should take began to reflect the importance of one's "tenure" in Islam. Thus, Çandarlı Halil Pasha (d. 1453), a member of an old Anatolian Muslim family that supplied viziers to the Ottoman throne, opposed the conquest of Constantinople, while Zağanos Pasha (d. 1461), a recent convert, encouraged it.[35] The fifteenth-century anonymous *Tevārīḫ-i Āl-i ʿOsmān,* one of the key sources on political and religious debates during this period, expresses the views of the "old *ġāzīs*," who saw Edirne, the Ottoman capital before the conquest of Constantinople, as their moral center. For the "old *ġāzīs*," as well as for many disaffected Sufi mystics, Constantinople was the city of polytheist idols that posed distinct danger to the integrity of a Muslim enterprise and, ideally, should be destroyed upon conquest—an event that was widely viewed as prefiguring the end of the world.[36] These ideas circulated in stories about the "Foundation of Constantinople and Hagia Sophia," which criticized Mehmed II's aspiration to appropriate the Byzantine imperial tradition embodied by the city of Constantinople and style himself an emperor in the image of infidel Byzantine rulers.[37]

"New *ġāzīs*," on the other hand, were most often former Christians who were focused around Mehmed II and aspired to make Constantinople, the city that was the center of their old world, the capital of the new empire. The new, elite converts surrounding Mehmed II, employed by the sultan in order to undercut the influence of native Muslim aristocracy, left their decisive imprint on post-conquest Constantinople, as the earliest available endowment charters for the city make clear. These also show a remarkable absence of religious scholars (*ʿulemā*ʾ) and dervish patrons of public works well into the time of Bayezid II (r. 1481–1512), who sought to reverse Mehmed II's policies.[38] It is noteworthy that ʿĀşıḳpaşazāde, whose own possessions in Istanbul were hit by Mehmed II's fiscal policies, expresses his resentment and criticism of the sultan by directing his rage at the vizier Rum Mehmed Pasha (d. ca. 1470), who is described as a "son of the infidel" still in touch with his Christian family and bent on retaking Istanbul from the "Turks" by imposing harsh fiscal demands on the Muslim settlers of the city. Rum Mehmed Pasha's identity as a supposedly new and untested convert, scheming with other "depraved, accursed infidels" who were Muslim only in name, is starkly highlighted in ʿĀşıḳpaşazāde's account.[39] Regardless of the fact that in other sections of his narrative ʿĀşıḳpaşazāde shows respect to Mehmed II's other convert viziers, such as Mahmud Pasha (d. 1474), the fact that he uses this rhetoric suggests that he expected it to resonate with some members of his audience. ʿĀşıḳpaşazāde clearly had his own understanding of where the boundary of Muslimness was, and, without criticizing the sultan directly, he implied that some of the latter's actions fell short of that boundary.

Although some of Mehmed II's more controversial policies were scaled back or reversed after his death by his son Bayezid II, who sought to restore good relations between the sultanic household and various religious circles, the policy of recruiting converts for key positions in the state, including the post of the grand vizier, continued unchanged. Likewise, both the controversial policy of marginalizing frontier lords and attempts to neutralize those among their followers who had Shiʿa affinities and tendencies for political dissent in Rumelia and Anatolia remained unchanged, executed through the institutionalization of Sufi orders under the watchful eye of the state. At the same time, Constantinople's position as the empire's capital solidified, as a local Muslim elite—which identified with the city but continued to negotiate its relationship with the Ottoman dynasty—gradually developed, starting in Bayezid II's time.[40] This new Muslim urban elite, which was coming into existence not only in Constantinople but throughout the "Lands of Rūm," fashioned its identity—in a selective and often competitive manner—upon the religious and cultural past of Constantinople's and the Ottoman polity's heterogeneous population, engaging with varied linguistic, political, religious, and cultural traditions of the medieval Islamic world. What was new about this stage in the evolution of "Rumi" as a social and cultural category was that it became explicitly cosmopolitan and reflected a peculiarly Ottoman imperial logic. Recent studies point to the fact that—contrary to the traditional narrative, according to which the Ottoman polity practically became an empire overnight upon the conquest of Constantinople—the process unfolded gradually in the period between the 1450s and 1550s, with Sultan Süleyman's (r. 1520–1566) reign representing not a culmination of a "classical" Ottoman system but an era of unprecedented experimentation and change in all spheres of Ottoman political life.[41] How did the Ottoman texts from this era represent and conceive of Rumi identity, conversion, and "mixing"?

Various Ottoman sources from the late fifteenth and early sixteenth centuries capture the process of raising and fashioning an ideal Ottoman Rumi. In the spiritual biography (*menāḳıbnāme*) of Sheikh Bedreddin, composed between 1455 and 1460, his grandson Ḥāfıẓ Ḫalīl tells of the famous Ottoman mystic's birth: to a *ġāzī* commander and the daughter of a local Christian nobleman in a church-turned-house at the Ottoman fortress of Simavna (today Kyprinos, Greece). Thanks to his mother, Bedreddin spoke Greek, which he used later in his life to preach to and convert Christians.[42] Similarly, in *Ġazavāt-ı Ḫayreddīn Paşa* (The Book of Hayreddin Pasha's Military Exploits, 1545), allegedly dictated by the great Ottoman pirate and admiral Barbaros Hayreddin Pasha (d. 1546) to his biographer Seyyid Mūrādī, the admiral tells of being born to an Ottoman cavalryman from Yenice-i Vardar (today Yannitsa, Greece) and a Greek Orthodox woman from the island of Mytilene, conquered by the Ottomans in 1462.[43] The admiral also spoke Greek and had knowledge of the Christian faith, which he used in polemics against various Christian enemies. Perhaps the most striking illustration of this Ottoman Rumi ability to synthesize the religious and cultural heritages of the "Lands of Rūm" and create something distinctly Ottoman is the story of Mehmed II's celebrated vizier Mahmud Pasha's recruitment into Ottoman service. According to the spiritual biography of Mahmud Pasha (*Menāḳıb-ı Maḥmūd Paşa-yı Velī*), which dates probably to the late fifteenth century, he was first spotted as a young monk from around Monastır (today Bitola, Macedonia) by an Ottoman official traversing Rumelia on the sultan's business. He is depicted as winning a competition in knowledge of Christian scriptures, besting three or four hundred other Orthodox monks. This knowledge apparently impressed the official and Sultan Murad II (r. 1421–1451), who, upon hearing the report of it, requested that the youth be brought to the court, where his intelligence could best be put to use. The narrative proceeds with the story of Mahmud Pasha's conversion, after seeing the Prophet in a dream, and his coming to the Ottoman court to be educated in Arabic language and Qur'anic sciences to an even higher degree of excellence.[44]

The interesting aspect of this last story is that there is nothing in the known biography of Mahmud Pasha (Angelović) that would indicate that he ever was a monk or that he possessed great knowledge of Christian scriptures.[45] However, the fact that the narrative places special importance on this aspect of his biography, in conjunction with the biographies of Sheikh Bedreddin and Barbaros Hayreddin Pasha, illustrates the belief that knowledge of the religious and cultural traditions of the "Lands of Rūm" enabled one to be a better Muslim and, potentially, a better Ottoman administrator because it allowed one to competently argue for Islamic and Ottoman superiority with reasons derived from the interlocutors' traditions—and potentially to bring others into the Muslim fold. The ideals of Mahmud Pasha's fictional biography were later realized in the recruitment and career of Sokollu Mehmed Pasha (d. 1579), one of the greatest Ottoman viziers, who, according to his biography, was taken by the *devşirme* recruiters precisely while receiving education in the Orthodox monastery of Mileševa (near Prijepolje, Serbia).[46]

The competitive nature of Ottoman Rumi identity is often overlooked, as are the finer points of episodes that appear in the sources labeled as "syncretic" and reflective of the supposedly "Christianized" nature of early Ottoman Islam. Such, for instance, is the famous episode from the *Ṣaltuḳnāme* in which Sarı Saltuk dresses as a priest to preach to Rumelian Christians from the Gospel (*Īncīl*). Only later in the text do we learn that this is not the Gospel known by Christians but the *true* Gospel that, according to the Muslim polemical tradition, came to Isa/Jesus. This text contains the announcement of Muhammad's prophecy, which Christians subsequently removed from their scriptures, thereby committing the sin of alteration of the scriptures (*taḥrīf*).[47] Other examples include the frequent episodes in various Ottoman *menāḳıbnāmes* in which Muslim saints walk on water (Sarı Saltuk, Imam Shafi'i) or resuscitate the dead (Bayezid-i Bistami, Sheikh Bedreddin)—apparent references to Jesus that, at face value, can be read as "Christianization" of Ottoman Islam. However, this is also a traditional Muslim polemical point against Jesus's divine status—if other Muslim saints can walk on water or resuscitate the dead, then Jesus is only one of the manifestations of sanctity that is embraced by Islam but cannot be equated with divinity, as Christians maintain. It is precisely in this "anti-syncretic" sense that such examples are used in sixteenth-century Ottoman sources, including the anonymous polemical work known as *Ġurbetnāme-i Cem Sulṭān* (The Book of Cem Sultan's Exile, after 1526); *Mecmū'atü'l-leṭā'if* (The Collection of Pleasantries, ca. 1540), by a certain Serrāc b. 'Abdullāh, himself apparently a convert; and *Kitāb tesviyetü't-teveccüh ilā'l-ḥaḳḳ* (The Book about One's Turning towards God, 1556–1557), by the convert and imperial interpreter Murād b. 'Abdullāh. These sources demonstrate that Ottoman converts to Islam took an active role in producing narratives, both anonymously and under their proper names, that negotiated the lines of separation between Islam and Christianity (or Judaism), ensuring that they were properly demarcated.[48]

In many ways, these three works were reacting to the peculiar religio-political atmosphere that characterized the reign of Sultan Süleyman. As much as this was a time of great cultural efflorescence and political prestige for the Ottomans, it was also a period of significant religious and political turmoil throughout the Mediterranean and an era of increasing inter-imperial competition—between the Ottomans and Habsburgs on one hand and the Ottomans and Safavids on the other. At stake in this imperial competition was not only political supremacy but religious supremacy as well. Informed by the apocalyptic currents of the day, Habsburg and Ottoman rulers competed for identification as a Universal Monarch who would unite the world under the banner of a single religion, prefiguring the Day of Judgment. At the same time, both Ottoman and Safavid rulers coveted the title of *mahdī,* the messianic figure of Islamic apocalyptic tradition who would combine the roles of a supreme military commander and renewer of religion.[49] In the early part of Süleyman's rule, his aspirations to Universal Monarchy were accompanied in some texts by an ecumenical, irenic, imperial vision of Islam as a religion that does not necessarily abrogate but perfects previous revelations.

Thus, in a text like *Ġurbetnāme-i Cem Sulṭān,* or the popular cycle of narratives on various aspects of Muslim-Christian polemics that is included in the much-copied *Mecmūʿatüʾl-leṭāʾif,* Islam is presented as a perfected version of Christianity and conversion to Islam as a natural evolution in the quest for spiritual perfection and religion that guarantees salvation.[50] Such portrayals of Islam went hand in hand with arguments about *translatio imperii,* in both political and religious senses, from the Roman emperors and Roman popes to Muhammad and eventually the Ottoman sultans, as was the case in Murād b. ʿAbdullāh's *Kitāb tesviyetu t-teveccüh ilāʾl-ḥaḳḳ* and Maḥmūd b. ʿAbdullāh's *Tārīḫ-i Ungurūs* (History of Hungary, ca. 1550). It is not surprising that many authors of texts relating the political supremacy of the Ottoman sultanate to the spiritual supremacy of Islam were converts to Islam, some of them of western European origin. Today, their narratives are either ignored or treated as oddities outside the framework of "mainstream" sixteenth-century Ottoman historiography, as their authors combined knowledge of Muslim and non-Muslim cultural and religious traditions with Ottoman imperial ideology within unique frameworks that were not readily accessible even to an educated Ottoman audience.[51] Nevertheless, these works are valuable period pieces, testifying not only to a particular moment in Ottoman imperial and religious ideology but also to the power of this ideology to appeal to converts. Indeed, quantitative studies show that in Rumelia the phenomenon of conversion was on a steady rise, while in Anatolia, where it had started much earlier, it entered its last phase.[52] Social mobility for converts of all backgrounds, as well as their integration into Ottoman society, is attested to also in contemporary Western sources.[53]

However, Süleyman's reign, especially in its later stages, also ushered in a new sensitivity toward both conversion and religion in general. As a consequence of military and ideological competition with the Safavid shah and his championing of Shiʿa Islam, which challenged both the unity of the Muslim community and the claim of the Ottoman sultan to be its universal leader, the concept of a religious orthodoxy, as well as heresy, began to be articulated in the Ottoman Empire.[54] Although this process had begun in the early sixteenth century, more consistent attempts to implement reforms ensuring stricter adherence of Ottoman Muslims to Sunni Islam came only in the late 1530s and 1540s, followed by a surge in the construction of *masjids*.[55] In this way, Süleyman initiated a Sunnitization and social disciplining project that would, despite various forms of resistance and fluctuations in religious trends under his successors, significantly change the religious landscape and sensibility of the empire. It would also constitute an important first phase in the Ottoman process of confessionalization that would culminate in the emergence of the Kadızadeli movement in the seventeenth century.[56]

Echoes of this new sensibility regarding religion, and a re-evaluation of state policies toward converts, can be found already in sources dating to Süleyman's time, although they became stronger in the later sixteenth century. In the context of rapidly changing social relations, bureaucratization, blurring of boundaries between the *ʿaskerī* and *re'āyā*, as well as increased competition for appointments—all legacies of Süleyman's reign—one-upmanship in religion became an important facet of Ottoman political life. For instance, in a letter submitted to Grand Vizier Rüstem Pasha sometime in 1555, a group of Janissaries complained that their recently appointed head officer (*aġa*) was an unjust, ignorant "Hungarian infidel who converted to Islam only yesterday and whose breath still reeks of pork." They argued that in the face of the Safavid challenge, the Ottoman army needed an officer with a proven record of religious integrity and service, rather than someone with a short tenure in Islam and a proclivity to distribute positions to newcomers.[57] These criticisms are echoed in the work entitled *Me'āṣir-i Selīm Ḫānī* (The Glorious Deeds of Selim Khan, also *Selīmnāme*), written by chancellor (*nişāncı*) Celālzāde Muṣṭafā (d. 1567), the paragon of faithful service to Süleyman's imperial bureaucracy, sometime around 1565. Among other things, Celālzāde, through a speech ascribed to Selim I, blames Sultan Bayezid II for initiating the practice of indiscriminate appointments of the sultan's slaves (*ḳuls*) over accomplished, deserving Muslims of either common or noble descent from the Balkans and Anatolia (*merdümzādeler*), even when those *ḳuls*' religious integrity, as well as intellectual and administrative capacity, was in question.[58] Celālzāde implies that the practice of promoting the undeserving *ḳuls* instead of opening the government to all pious, "genuine Muslims"—the qualities he associates with *merdümzādeler*—cost the Ottomans the support of the Anatolian Muslim notables who were thus incited to embrace the Safavid shah.[59] As both of these examples demonstrate, the Safavid challenge raised new questions about the religious, regional, and social identities of Ottoman Muslims, introducing a new dimension to the question of conversion and the state's unquestioning openness to and privileging of converts for leading positions in the military and government.

The prominent profile of converts in Mehmed II's administration, and the "concessions" made to non-Muslims during his reign, were also revisited by some authors. In a fascinating text from Murad III's (r. 1574–1595) reign, written probably in 1585, the author takes aim at the supposed "superficial" conversion of Bosnian Muslims.[60] He blames this phenomenon on Mesih Pasha (d. 1501), a prominent convert to Islam from the Byzantine Palailogos family, who began his rise to the rank of vizier in Mehmed II's time and later served as a grand vizier on two occasions under Bayezid II.[61] According to the text, soon after the conquest of Bosnia (1456), Mesih Pasha was appointed to carry out the land survey and found the Bosnian people in a state of suffering under heavy taxes and corvée.[62] In order to improve their condition, on the suggestion of local elders, Mesih Pasha requested from the Porte that the poll tax (*cizye*) levied on non-Muslims be abolished; when that was refused he devised a ruse that one man from each village should take a Muslim name in order to abolish the poll tax. This ploy supposedly allowed Bosnians to rebuild their villages but also sparked the process of conversion.

According to the author, Bosnians were divided into three groups: those who "guided by the divine light found salvation from the darkness of disbelief and staying true to their new names became Muslims"; those who settled in neighborhoods founded by their forefathers and, saying "my faith to me and yours to you," remained infidels and perished; and, finally, a group that remained in a state of helplessness and hesitation, neither accepting Islam nor remaining Christian, and lived like animals in the "wilderness of polytheism." These individuals were known as *Poturs*, from the "Christian" words "po" (meaning "half") and "Turčin" (meaning "Turk").[63] The author denigrates Poturs as creatures distinguished from animals only by their ability to learn good manners and who must constantly be managed in order to suppress their baser instincts. For this reason, the text asserts, Poturs are not allowed into the Janissary corps.[64] They are described as dirty individuals who are born in a pit, like swine, and who reek of garlic. However, the most significant problem the author has with Poturs seems to be the fact that they are of "two scripts," possibly meaning that they wear two amulets—one made of verses from the Qur'an and one with written Christian prayers and supplications.[65]

What was the author's motivation in producing this text? One possibility, as András Riedlmayer suggests, is that the text was authored by an elite Bosnian Muslim for a like-minded audience as a part of an elaborate in-group joke.[66] Other contemporary Ottoman sources feature similarly scathing humor regarding specific Muslim groups—one needs only look at Muṣṭafā ʿĀlī's description of the Egyptians, for instance.[67] Indeed, other stories in the same collection feature ribald humor with numerous words and passages in Bosnian that would be lost on an audience unfamiliar with the language. However, this elite Bosnian's criticism of the Poturs also suggests eagerness to distinguish himself from his compatriots (*hemşerīler*) with unsound reputations in an era when the issue of one's correct adherence to Islam began to draw more attention. Both as a consequence of heightened religious sensitivity in the empire and as a reflection of the fierce competition for patronage in the rapidly changing system of recruitment into the sultanic and other households, not only one's religious integrity but also one's ethno-regional origin (*cins*) gradually became a very important aspect of political networking, patronage, and social mobility. In the second half of the sixteenth and (especially) in the seventeenth centuries, Bosnian and Albanian clans were particularly apt in manipulating top spots in government and bureaucracy—a phenomenon that Muṣṭafā ʿĀlī fiercely criticized.[68]

So, while Muṣṭafā ʿĀlī celebrated the diverse and mixed character of Rumis as the essence of what was best about the empire, and some of his contemporaries, like the court historian Taʿlīḳīzāde (d. 1599), proclaimed the diversity of religious communities living peacefully within the Ottoman capital and the sultan's domains as bolstering the imperial and dynastic legitimacy of the Ottomans,[69] diversity and polarization along various lines within the Muslim community itself was becoming more prominent and worrisome. In addition to *cins*-based rivalries and Sunni/Shiʿa polarization, regional rivalries also began to be prominent during the same era. By the early seventeenth century the issue of recruitment for the imperial military and administration brought head to head the *Rūm ḳulları* (slaves, servants from Rūm) and the *evlād-ı ʿArab* (the descendants of "Arabs"), as well as the recruits from Rūm and those from the Caucasus.[70] Although converts by no means ceased to fill the government and military ranks in the sixteenth and seventeenth centuries, the infiltration of Muslims into the ranks of the Janissaries and other institutions previously closed to them, as well as the new preference for recruits from the Caucasus, led to the redefinition of the concept of the *ḳul* and the eventual discontinuation of the practice of *devşirme*. It also placed new importance on the length of one's "tenure" in Islam. The second half of the sixteenth century thus ushered in the struggle for power among various types of *ḳul* and ended the privileged status of the converts.

It would appear that these processes affected not only Ottoman authors' views on conversion and converts but also contemporary observers' views of the Ottomans. The statement of the Venetian special ambassador Lorenzo Bernardo (*bailo:* 1585–1587; special ambassador: 1591–1592) dated to 1592 suggests that he was aware of multiple tensions and distinctions within the Ottoman Muslim community already by the close of the sixteenth century. He writes that in "former times" the "Turks" were all of a single religion but that now they were split into three: the Persians, among the Turks like heretics among Christians; the Arabs, or Moors, who claimed that they alone had preserved the true religion; and the Turks from *Grecia* (i.e., Rūm), whom the former call "bastard Turks with a corrupted religion" because they mostly descend from "Christian renegades who did not understand Muslim religion."[71] From this and from other comments by seventeenth-century observers from Arab provinces—including the great Damascene Sufi ʿAbd al-Ghānī al-Nāblusī (d. 1731), who saw the Kadızadeli movement as a "Rumi" and "Turkish" folly out of place in Arab lands—it seems that Rumis among Muslims beyond the boundaries of Ottoman Rumelia and Anatolia could be associated, at least in some intellectual circles, with the notion of "upstartness" and a lack of credibility in matters of religion due to many Rumi converts' origins.[72] It would be interesting to examine how this image of Ottoman Rumis played into eighteenth-century debates over Islamic orthodoxy and the right to lead the Muslim community that effected Ottoman Arab provinces.[73]

Conclusion

Ottoman Muslim narrative sources from the fifteenth and sixteenth centuries present a variety of perspectives on conversion and converts, suggesting an ongoing and evolving debate on the issue throughout the period in question. These perspectives are embedded in and closely intertwined with particular literary genres and rhetorical constructions that must be carefully considered before one tries to discern the social realities behind them. Although recent scholarship in the field of Ottoman studies has done much to shed light on the variety of Ottoman narrative sources, their peculiar genre characteristics, and the dense web of patronage and social relations that underlie them, much work remains to be done before we can understand who various Ottoman authors were and why they wrote, the types of audiences they envisioned, and the responses they intended to elicit by choosing particular genres.[74] As is the case with other social phenomena, it is impossible to unearth the meanings various authors attached to conversion to Islam without understanding how they themselves fit into the social, religious, and political landscape of the time and how that landscape changed in response to the broader religio-political trends in the early modern Ottoman world and beyond. This means, as was argued in this essay, that references to conversion to Islam in various Ottoman narratives cannot be understood solely in the context of Muslim–non-Muslim relations. Rather, they are closely related to the social and economic transformation of Ottoman society, evolution in the definition of the Ottoman imperial idea and Rumi identity, and broader religio-political trends within and outside the Muslim world in the period between the early 1400s and early 1600s.

Notes

Parts of this essay draw on Tijana Krstić, *Contested Conversions to Islam: Confessionalization and Community in the Early Modern Ottoman Empire* (Palo Alto, Calif.: Stanford University Press, 2011).

1. First, Herbert Gibbons postulated that the Ottoman state was founded by a new "race" that came into existence through the comingling of Turks with Byzantine and Slavic converts to Islam, whose know-how of Byzantine institutional practices was crucial to the process of state formation, which the Turks did not have the wherewithal to execute themselves. See Herbert Gibbons, *The Foundation of the Ottoman Empire* (Oxford: Clarendon, 1916). In a forceful response to Gibbons, first in 1922 and then in 1934 in his *Origines de l'Empire Ottoman,* Mehmet F. Köprülü asserted that the Ottoman state was in fact a "purely" Turkish creation informed by Seljuk and Ilkhanid institutional experience. Subsequently, Turkish historians, like Ömer Lütfi Barkan, emphasized colonization from Anatolia rather than the local population's conversion to Islam as the key factor for the spread of Islam in Rumelia. For an overview of the Köprülü-Gibbons debate, see Cemal Kafadar, *Between Two Worlds* (Berkeley: University of California Press, 1995), 32–51; and Heath Lowry, *The Nature of the Early Ottoman State* (New York: State University of New York Press, 2003), 4–13. For a consideration of the colonization versus conversion debate, see Anton Minkov, *Conversion to Islam in the Balkans:* Kisve Bahası *Petitions and Ottoman Social Life, 1670–1730* (Brill: Leiden, 2004), 43–48; and Antonina Zhelyazkova, "Islamization in the Balkans as a Historiographical Problem: The Southeast-European Perspective," in *The Ottomans and the Balkans,* ed. Suraiya Faroqhi and Fikret Adanır (Leiden: Brill, 2002), 231–235.

2. In using the term "identificatory practices," I am building on Rogers Brubaker and Frederick Cooper's critique of the term "identity." See Rogers Brubaker and Frederick Cooper, "Beyond 'Identity,'" *Theory and Society* 29, no. 1 (2000): 1–47.

3. See Salih Özbaran, *Bir Osmanlı Kimliği: 14.-17. Yüzyıllarda Rûm/Rûmi Aidiyet ve İmgeleri* (Istanbul: Kitap Yayınevi, 2004); and Cemal Kafadar, "A Rome of One's Own: Reflections on Cultural Geography and Identity in the Lands of Rum," *Muqarnas* 24 (2007): 7–25.

4. In medieval Islamic Arabic and Persian literature, *Rūmī* designates the inhabitants of *Rūm* (Rome), or, more precisely, of the Eastern Roman or Byzantine Empire. Turkish-speaking Muslims who came to settle in Hellenic Asia Minor in the eleventh and twelfth centuries adopted the same term to refer to their Christian neighbors. However, the terms *Rūm* and *Rūmī* underwent change in the thirteenth and fourteenth centuries and came to be used also for Muslims inhabiting former Byzantine lands in Asia Minor. See *EI2,* s.v. "Rūm" (Nadia el-Cheikh and C. E. Bosworth). By the fifteenth century, the Ottomans came to use the phrase "Lands of Rūm" (*diyār-ı Rūm; bilād al-Rūm*)

to refer to their territories in both Anatolia and Rumelia. For the usage of *Rūmī* in fifteenth- and sixteenth-century sources, see Özbaran, *Bir Osmanlı Kimliği*, 89–120; Kafadar, "A Rome of One's Own"; and Giancarlo Casale, "The Ethnic Composition of Ottoman Ship Crews and the 'Rumi' Challenge to Portuguese Identity," *Medieval Encounters* 13 (2007): 122–144.

5. Kafadar, "A Rome of One's Own," 11.

6. Ibid. However, Kafadar points out that the term "Turk" did not have a universally negative meaning. "Turkish" was the name of the language that the elites spoke, and in certain cases the term "Türk" was used as self-reference in Ottoman sources.

7. Neither of these categories had an ethnic meaning. Although used most frequently to refer to the Iranians or Persians, *'Acem* could also designate a foreigner (as in *'Acemīoğlan*, the official term for *devşirme* recruits who were indeed "sons of foreigners" or non-Muslims), or even to a speaker of Eastern (Chagatay) Turkish. See Kafadar, "A Rome of One's Own," 15. At the same time, although in the Ottoman cultural discourse prior to the nineteenth century the term *'Arab* most often referred to the nomadic Bedouin, it could also denote speakers of Arabic regardless of ethnicity, including sub-Saharan Africans, or even contain the *'Acem* and *Özbek*, as seems to be implied in some usages of the designation *evlād-ı 'Arab* ("the sons of Arabs"). See Jane Hathaway, "The *Evlâd-i 'Arab* ('Sons of the Arabs') in Ottoman Egypt: A Rereading," in *Frontiers of Ottoman Studies*, ed. Colin Imber and Keiko Kiyotaki (London: I. B. Tauris, 2005), 1:203–216.

8. See Cornell Fleischer, *Bureaucrat and Intellectual in the Ottoman Empire: The Historian Mustafa Âli (1541–1600)* (Princeton, N.J.: Princeton University Press, 1986), 254.

9. For a more detailed consideration of the concept of "syncretism" in Ottoman historiography, see Tijana Krstić, introduction to *Contested Conversions to Islam;* and Krstić, "Narrating Conversions to Islam: The Dialogue of Texts and Practices in the Early Modern Ottoman Balkans" (PhD diss., University of Michigan, 2004), 85–99.

10. See Krstić, *Contested Conversions to Islam*, introduction.

11. See Devin DeWeese, *Islamization and Native Religion in the Golden Horde* (University Park: Pennsylvania State University Press, 1994), 159.

12. Ebū'l-ḫayr-ı Rūmī, *Salṭuḳnāme*, ed. A. H. Akalın (Ankara: Kültür ve Turizm Bakanlığı, 1987), 1:18–19.

13. Ibid., 1:145.

14. A nice parallel to Ilyas-ı Rumi's conversion in the *Salṭuḳnāme* is the conversion of Marko by Demir Baba in *Vilāyetnāme-i Demīr Baba*. See *Demir Baba Vilayetnamesi*, ed. Bedri Noyan (Istanbul: Can Yayınları, 1976), 105–108. Marko was the name of the greatest hero in Serbian and Bulgarian epic poetry.

15. See Krstić, *Contested Conversions*, chap. 2.

16. See Anonymous, *The Battalname, an Ottoman Turkish Frontier Epic Wondertale*, ed. and trans. Yorgos Dedes (Cambridge, Mass.: Harvard University, Department of Near Eastern Languages and Civilizations, 1996), part 1, 23. The oldest surviving manuscript of this work is dated to AH 840 (1436–1437).

17. See Lewis R. Rambo and Charles E. Farhadian, "Converting: Stages of Religious Change," in *Religious Conversion—Contemporary Practices and Controversies*, ed. Christopher Lamb and M. Darrol Bryant (New York: Cassell, 1999), 30.

18. See Nicolas de Nicolay, *The Nauigations into Turkie* (London: 1585; new ed., Amsterdam: Da Capo Press, 1968), 126.

19. On the relationship between these chronicles, see Halil İnalcık, "The Rise of Ottoman Historiography," in *Historians of the Middle East*, ed. Bernard Lewis and Peter M. Holt (London: Oxford University Press, 1962), 152–167. Colin Imber has argued that Oruç's version predates 'Āşıḳpaşazāde's and that Köse Mihal is an entirely fictitious character. He also asserted that 'Āşıḳpaşazāde invented Köse Mihal's curriculum vitae by projecting backward the biography of Mihaloğlu Ali Beg,

'Āşıķpaşazāde's contemporary who purchased the village of Harmankaya as a freehold in the late fifteenth century. See Colin Imber, "The Legend of Osman Gazi," in *Studies in Ottoman History and Law* (Istanbul: Isis Press, 1996), 323–324. However, Imber's theory has recently been challenged by Orlin Sabev, who warns against dismissing out of hand Köse Mihal's historicity. See Orlin Sabev, "The Legend of Köse Mihal—Additional Notes," *Turcica* 34 (2002): 241–252.

20. Halil İnalcık, "Stefan Duşan'dan Osmanlı İmparatorluğuna: XV. Asırda Rumeli'de Hıristiyan Sipâhiler ve Menşeleri," in *Fatih Devri Üzerinde Tetkikler ve Vesikalar* (Ankara: Türk Tarih Kurumu, 1954), 137–184; Lowry, *The Nature of the Early Ottoman State*, 55–94; and Melek Delilbaşı, "Christian *Sipahis* in the Tırhala Taxation Registers (15th and 16th centuries)," in *Provincial Elites in the Ottoman Empire*, ed. A. Anastasopoulos (Herakleion: Crete University Press, 2005), 87–95.

21. 'Āşıķpaşazāde [Dervīş Aḥmed], *Tevārīḫ-i Āl-i 'Oşmān*, ed. N. Atsız (Istanbul: Türkiye Yayınevi, 1947), 107; and 'Āşıķpaşazāde, *Osmanoğulları'nın Tarihi*, ed. K. Yavuz and M. A. Yekta Saraç (Istanbul: K Kitaplığı, 2003), 345–346.

22. Translation mine. For the passage from Oruç's chronicle, see *Die frühosmanischen Jahrbücher des Urudsch nach den Handschriften zu Oxford und Cambridge erstmals herausgegeben und eingeleitet*, ed. Franz Babinger (Hannover: H. Lafaire, 1925), 9–10.

23. Besides being discussed in the chronicles by Oruç, 'Āşıķpaşazāde, and Neşrī, the story of Köse Mihal's conversion continued to be recounted in sixteenth- and seventeenth-century chronicles as well. Moreover, his conversion is also visually depicted in the fourth volume of 'Ārif's *Shāhnāma-yi Āl-i 'Oşmān*, entitled *'Oşmānnāme* (finished around 1558), 45b. It is reproduced in Ernst J. Grube, *Islamic Paintings from the Eleventh to the Eighteenth Century in the Collection of Hans P. Kraus* (NewYork: H. P. Kraus, 1972), 223. I thank Sinem Eryılmaz for this reference.

24. See below, note 32.

25. For the text, see Agah Sırrı Levend, *Ġazavāt-nāmeler ve Mihaloğlu Ali Bey'in Ġazavāt-nāmesi*, 2nd ed. (Ankara: Türk Tarih Kurumu, 2000). The text was probably written in the first decade of the sixteenth century after the eponymous hero's death, possibly at the request of Mihaloğlu Ali Beg's brother Mehmed.

26. Krstić, "Who's Haunting the Ottomans?" (seminar paper, University of Michigan, 1999).

27. See especially Colin Imber, "What Does *ghazi* Actually Mean?" in *The Balance of Truth: Essays in Honour of Professor Geoffrey Lewis*, ed. Ç. Balım-Harding and Colin Imber (Istanbul: Isis Press, 2000), 165–178; Kafadar, *Between Two Worlds*, 91; and Linda Darling, "Contested Territory: Ottoman Holy War in Comparative Context," *Studia Islamica* 91 (2000): 134.

28. For more on this antagonism, see Stephane Yerasimos, *La fondation de Constantinople et de Sainte-Sophie* (Paris: Institute Français d'etudes anatoliennes d'Istanbul, 1990). See also Kafadar, *Between Two Worlds*, 138–150.

29. See Georgius de Hungaria, *Tractatus de moribus, condictionibus et nequicia turcorum. Traktat über die Sitten, die Lebensverhältnisse und die Arglist der Türken*, ed. and trans. Reihhard Klockow (Wien: Böhlau, 1994), 194–195.

30. For the endowment charter and its translation, see Zeynep Yürekli, "Legend and Architecture in the Ottoman Empire: The Shrine of Seyyid Gazi and Hacı Bektaş" (PhD diss., Harvard University, 2005), 134.

31. Ibid.

32. Yürekli argues that Mihaloğlu Ali Beg patronized those saintly cults that traditionally attracted discontents with the Ottoman regime. Thus, for example, we have traces of partnership between Mihaloğlu Ali Beg and Otman Baba in the latter's hagiography written in 1483. The same family also sponsored the rebuilding of the Seyyid Gazi temple between 1493 and 1512. Similarly, the descendants of Evrenos Gazi sponsored the remodeling of the shrine of Hacı Bektaş in approximately the same period. See ibid., 64, 128–129, 174–175. Yürekli even suggests that the characteristics of the *vilāyetnāme* genre, which combines elements of the warrior epic and hagiography, can be traced

to this partnership between the *uc begleri* and the dervishes affiliated with the cults of saints such as Sarı Saltuk, Otman Baba, Seyyid Ali, and Demir Baba, all of whom are chief protagonists of the known *vilāyetnāmes*. See also Mariya Kiprovska, "The Mihaloğlu Family: Gazi Warriors and Patrons of Dervish Hospices," *Osmanlı Araştırmaları* 32 (2008): 193–222.

33. See Tibor Halasi-Kun, "Gennadios' Turkish Confession of Faith," *Archivum Ottomanicum* 12 (1987–1992): 5–7; Julian Raby, "El Gran Turco, Mehmet the Conqueror as a Patron of the Arts of Christendom" (PhD diss., Oxford University, 1980); Julian Raby, "Mehmed the Conqueror's Greek Scriptorium," *Dumbarton Oaks* 37 (1983): 15–34; and Robert Osterhout, "The East, the West and the Appropriation of the Past in Early Ottoman Architecture," *Gesta* 43, no. 2 (2004): 165–176.

34. Halil İnalcık, "The Policy of Mehmed II toward the Greek Population of Istanbul and the Byzantine Buildings of the City," *Dumbarton Oaks Papers* 23 (1969–1970), 229–249.

35. Upon the conquest of Constantinople, Çandarlı Halil was executed because of his close relations with Byzantium and opposition to the idea of attack on the Byzantine capital. See Colin Imber, *The Ottoman Empire 1300–1481* (Istanbul: Isis Press, 1990), 161.

36. See A. Abel, "Un Ḥadīṯ sur la Prise de Rome dans la Tradition Eschatologique de l'Islam," *Arabica* 5, no. 1 (1958): 1–14; and Yerasimos, *La fondation de Constantinople et de Sainte-Sophie*, 183–199.

37. Yerasimos, *La fondation de Constantinople et de Sainte-Sophie*, 201–210.

38. See Çiğdem Kafescioğlu, *Constantinopolis/Istanbul—Cultural Encounters, Imperial Vision, and the Construction of the Imperial Capital* (University Park: Pennsylvania State University Press, 2009), 109–125.

39. "Pâdişâha bir vezîr geldi kim ol kâfirüñ oglıydı, pâdişâha gâyetde mukarreb oldı. Ve bu İstanbol'uñ eski kâfirleri bu vezîrüñ atası dostlarıdı, yanına girdiler kim: 'Hey ne'ylersin' didiler. . . . 'Cehd eyle kim bu halka bir re'y ü tedbîr-ile kim bu halk bu şehrüñ 'imâretinden el çekeler ve girü evvelki gibi bu şehir bizüm elümüzde kala' didiler. Vezîr dahı eydür . . . 'Bu halk dahı milkler yapmaktan el çekeler. Bu şehir ol sebeble girü harâba vara. Âhir girü bizüm tâ'ifemüz kala' didi. . . . Pâdişâhı râzı eyledi. . . . Bu mugvî mel'ûn kâfirlerüñ birisiyle bir adı Müsülmân dahı koşdılar ve ol mugvî kâfir ne didi-y-se yazdılar." 'Āşıḳpaşazāde, *Osmanoğulları'nın Tarihi*, ed. Yavuz and Saraç, 488–489 (excerpt as transliterated by Yavuz and Saraç). For 'Āşıḳpaşazāde's properties in Istanbul, see Halil İnalcık, "How to Read 'Āşık Paşa-zāde's History," in *Studies in Ottoman History in Honour of Professor V. L. Ménage*, ed. Colin Heywood and Colin Imber (Istanbul: Isis Press, 1994), 141–142, 145–146.

40. On this development, see Ebru Turan, "The Marriage of Ibrahim Pasha (ca. 1495–1536): The Rise of Sultan Süleyman's Favorite, Ibrahim Pasha, to the Grand Vizirate and the Politics of Elites in the Early Sixteenth-Century Ottoman Empire," *Turcica* 41 (2009): 3–36.

41. See Cornell Fleischer, "The Lawgiver as Messiah: The Making of the Imperial Image in the Reign of Süleyman," in *Soliman le magnifique et son temps*, ed. Gilles Veinstein (Paris: Galeries Nationales du Grand Palais, 1992), 159–177; Gülru Necipoğlu, "Süleyman the Magnificent and the Representation of Power in the Context of Ottoman-Hapsburg-Papal Rivalry," *Art Bulletin*, 71, no. 3 (1989): 401–427; and Necipoğlu, *The Age of Sinan* (Princeton, N.J.: Princeton University Press, 2005), 27–46.

42. See Ḫalīl b. İsmā'īl b. Şeyh Bedreddīn, *Menāḳıb-ı Şeyḫ Bedreddīn b. İsrā'īl*, ed. Abdülbaki Gölpınarlı and İsmet Sungurbey, in *Simavna Kadısıoğlu Şeyh Bedreddin Manakıbı* (Istanbul: Eti Yayınevi, 1967), 12–13, 89.

43. See Seyyid Mūrādī, *Ġazavāt-ı Ḫayreddīn Paşa*, in *Barbaros Hayreddin Paşa'nın Hatıraları*, ed. M. Ertuğrul Düzdağ (Istanbul: Tercüman, n.d.), 1:556–557.

44. Anonymous, *Menāḳıb-ı Maḥmūd Paşa-yı Velī*, Istanbul, Süleymaniye Kütüphanesi, Ayasofya 1940/2, 68b–71a.

45. See Theoharis Stavrides, *The Sultan of Vezirs: The Life and Times of the Ottoman Grand Vezir Mahmud Pasha Angelović (1453–1474)* (Leiden: Brill, 2001), 73–112.

46. See *EI2*, s.v. "Soḳollu Meḥmed Pasha" (Gilles Veinstein).

47. Ebū'l-ḫayr-ı Rūmī, *Salṭuḳnāme*, 1:35–38, 71–72.

48. See *Ġurbetnāme-i Cem Sulṭān,* ed. İsmail Hami Danişmend as "Gurbet-name-i Sultan Cem ibni Sultan Muhammed," in *Fatih ve İstanbul* 2, no. 12 (1954): 228–247; Serrāc b. ʿAbdullāh, *Mecmūʿatü'l-leṭāʾif,* Sofia, SS Cyril and Methodius National Library, Oriental Collection, Or. 2461, fourth *bāb;* and Murād b. ʿAbdullāh, *Kitāb tesviyetü't-teveccüh ilā'l-ḥaḳḳ,* London, British Library, Add. 19894, 126a–127a.

49. See Fleischer, "The Lawgiver as Messiah."

50. On this text, see Krstić, *Contested Conversions,* chap. 3.

51. On these texts, see Krstić, "Of Translation and Empire: Sixteenth-Century Ottoman Imperial Interpreters as Renaissance Go-Betweens," in *The Ottoman World,* ed. Christine Woodhead (Abingdon: Routledge, 2011), 130–142. See also Giancarlo Casale's contribution to this volume.

52. See Minkov, *Conversion to Islam in the Balkans,* 41–52, 19.

53. See, for instance, Stefan Gerlach, *Türkiye Günlüğü,* ed. Kemal Beydilli, trans. Türkis Noyan (Istanbul: Kitap Yayınevi, 2006), 2 vols.

54. See Ahmet Y. Ocak, *Osmanlı Toplumunda Zındıklar ve Mülhidler (15.–17. Yüzyıllar)* (Istanbul: Tarih Vakfı Yurt Yayınları, 1998), 203–239, 251–310; Markus Dressler, "Inventing Orthodoxy: Competing Claims for Authority and Legitimacy in the Ottoman Safavid Conflict," in *Legitimizing the Order: The Ottoman Rhetoric of State Power,* ed. H. Karateke and M. Reinkowski (Leiden: Brill, 2005), 151–176; and Krstić, "Illuminated by the Light of Islam and the Glory of the Ottoman Sultanate: Self-Narratives of Conversion to Islam in the Age of Confessionalization," *Comparative Studies in Society and History* 51, no. 1 (2009): 35–63.

55. See Necipoğlu, *The Age of Sinan,* 47–70.

56. For a more detailed discussion of the phenomena of confessionalization and social disciplining in the Ottoman Empire, see Krstić, *Contested Conversions.* See also Derin Terzioğlu, "Sufis in the Age of State Building and Confessionalization," in *The Ottoman World.*

57. T. M. Gökbilgin, "Rüstem Paşa ve Hakkındaki İthamlar," *Tarih Dergisi* 8 (1955): 48.

58. For a discussion of the concept of *merdümzāde* and its significance in both Celālzāde's work and in Selim I's bid for power, see H. Erdem Çıpa, "The Centrality of the Periphery: The Rise to Power of Selīm I, 1481–1512" (PhD diss., Harvard University, 2007), 156–163.

59. Celālzāde ascribes the following speech to Selim I: "ecdād-ı ʿiẓāmım devirlerinden berü āsitānemize ḫiḏmet idegelen merdümzādeleri ve yarar ve güzīde pehlevān ve nāmdār yigitleri ilerü getürmekden el çeküb dāyimā terbiyet-ü-iḥsanları ḳul ṭāʾifesine münḥaṣır olub ḳuldan gayrıya manṣıb virmedikleri içün vilayet-ü-memleketimiz ḫalḳınuñ yarārları Ḳızılbāş ṭāʾifesine meyl eyleyüb ol āsitāne ile buluşmaḳ üzre olmuşlardır deyü işitdüm." Celālzāde Muṣṭafā, *Meʾāṣir-i Selīm Ḫānī* (or *Selīmnāme*), London, British Museum Library, Add. 7848, 54b–55a, as cited in Çıpa, "The Centrality of the Periphery," 157. See also Celālzāde Muṣṭafā, *Selīmnāme,* ed. A. Uğur and M. Çuhadar (Ankara: Kültür Bakanlığı, 1990), 61. In another section of the same work, Celālzāde writes "Sulṭān Bāyezīd Ḫān zamānına gelince . . . ʿatabe-i ʿulyā-yı ʿOṣmāniyyeʾde ʿādet ve ḳānūn cümle-i şāhān-ı ʿāli-şānuñ ḳapuları mesūd olmayub mekşūf olub . . . erkān-ı devlet ve āʿyān-ı salṭanatları ol zemānenüñ merdümzādeleri kemal-i maʿārif-ü-feżāyil ile maʿmūr āzādeleri olub ḥaḳīḳaten müslümānlar pāk iʿtiḳādlar nisbet-u-taʿaṣṣubdan ʿārī ḥaḳḳ-şināslar merḥāmet-istināslar ṣāliḥ-ü-mütedeyyinler olurlardı . . ." Celālzāde, *Meʾāṣir-i Selīm Ḫānī,* 48b, as cited in Çıpa, "The Centrality of the Periphery," 160. See also Celālzāde, *Selīmnāme,* ed. Uğur and Çuhadar, 54.

60. I am grateful to András Riedlmayer, bibliographer for the Aga Khan Program for Islamic Art and Architecture at Harvard University and head of the Bosnian Manuscript Ingathering Project, for providing me with a copy of this manuscript (MS 4811/II), the original of which, from the Oriental Institute in Sarajevo, burned in 1992. He plans to publish the manuscript in the near future.

61. See *İA,* s.v. "Mesih Paşa" (Hedda Reindl), 309–310.

62. As Nenad Moačanin points out, Mesih Pasha would have been too young to be appointed to this duty, and his insertion into this text probably stems from his reputation as a scheming, pro-Venetian,

unsuccessful military and public servant of convert, Byzantine background, whose name (meaning "Messiah") was a convenient pun to depict the "savior" of the Bosnians. See Moačanin, "Mass Islamization of the Peasants in Bosnia: Demystifications," in *Melanges Professor Machiel Kiel* (Zaghouan: Fondation Temimi, 1999), 358. Moačanin discusses this text without having had access to the original manuscript but only to a partial transcription of it.

63. Anonymous, *Mecmū'a*, Oriental Institute in Sarajevo (Bosnian Manuscript Ingathering Project), MS 4811/II, 17b–18a: "Çün maṣlaḥat itmāma ve kār encāma irdi üç fırḳa oldılar. Anlarda ki şem'-i hidāyet-i ḥaḳḳ hādī olup żılām-ı żulmet-i küfrden rehā buldılar müsemmāların isimlerine tevfīḳ idüb Müselmān oldılar. Anlar ki 'innā wajadnā ābā'unā'l-awwalūn' semtine sālik oldılar 'lakum diynukum wa lī dīni' diyüb tehlike-i inkāra mülaḳī olub helāk oldılar. Ve ḳalanından bir fırḳası maḳām-i 'acz-ü-tereddüdde ḳaldılar ters-i bīm ü ḥām şerī'atdan ne mercū'ye mecāl ve ne āyīn-i ābā ve ecdādları üzere terk-i hiṣāl ḳıldılar. 'Aḳide-i nā-puḫtelerinde tereddüd ve teşekkük bāḳi ḳalub ne bellü āyīn-i İslāmı ḳabul ḳıldılar ve ne bellü Naṣarā oldılar. Ṣaḥra-yı şirkde hayvān gibi ḫayrān-ı muṭlaḳ ḳaldılar ki el-ān ol ṭā'ife-i kümāhe (or Kamā-hiya) Potur ıṭlaḳ olunur ki kelime-i Potur lafẓ-ı terkībidür 'po' ile 'Turçin' lafẓından muḥaffefdür. 'Po' dimek Naṣāra dilince yarım dimekdür ya'ni nıṣf, 'Turçin' lafẓından muraḫḫamdur ki 'Turçin' dimek Naṣāra dilince Müselmān dimekdür. Lafẓ-ı terkībisi 'Potur' olur ya'ni yarım Müselmān dimek olur . . ."

64. The author implies that the Poturs' lax religiosity was somehow known to the recruiters. This is an interesting assertion in light of the traditional view that Bosnian Muslims were allowed into the Janissary corps.

65. Anonymous, *Mecmū'a*, Oriental Institute in Sarajevo, MS 4811/II, 18a: "Aralarında ikişer nüsḥalu çoḳdur."

66. András Riedlmayer, personal communication, June 2, 2008.

67. See Andreas Tietze, *Mustafa 'Ālī's Description of Cairo of 1599: Text, Translation, Notes* (Wien: Verlag der Österreichischen Akademie der Wissenschaften, 1975), esp. 40.

68. Fleischer, *Bureaucrat and Intellectual*, 164–165, esp. note 72. See also Metin Kunt, "Ethnic-Regional (Cins) Solidarity in the Seventeenth-Century Ottoman Establishment," *International Journal of Middle East Studies* 5 (1974): 233–239.

69. See Necipoğlu, *The Age of Sinan*, 30.

70. See Hathaway, "The *Evlâd-i 'Arab*."

71. See James C. Davis, *Pursuit of Power: Venetian Ambassadors' Reports on Turkey, France, and Spain in the Age of Philip II, 1560–1600* (New York: Harper Torchbooks, 1970), 157.

72. In his response to the "ignorant Rumi" (*al-Rūmī al-jāhil*) who criticized Sufi *dhikr*, al-Nablūsī writes that the Rumi should remember that it was the Arabs who brought Islam to Anatolia, which Rumi must have forgotten because he "probably only recently left off eating pig, deifying Jesus and worshipping idols." See Barbara Rosenow von Schlegell, "Sufism in the Ottoman Arab World: Shaykh 'Abd al-Ganī al-Nāblusī (d. 1143/1731)" (PhD diss., University of California, Berkeley, 1997), 100.

73. See Dina Rizk Khoury, "Who Is a True Muslim? Exclusion and Inclusion among Polemicists of Reform in Nineteenth-Century Baghdad," in *The Early Modern Ottomans: Remapping the Empire*, ed. Virginia Aksan and Daniel Goffman (Cambridge: Cambridge University Press, 2007), 256–274.

74. Examples abound, but most pertinent for this study is Fleischer, *Bureaucrat and Intellectual;* Yerasimos, *La fondation de Constantinople et de Sainte-Sophie;* Kafadar, *Between Two Worlds;* Terzioğlu, "Man in the Image of God in the Image of the Times: Sufi Self-Narratives and the Diary of Niyāzī Mıṣrī (1618–94)," *Studia Islamica* 94 (2002): 139–165; Kafadar, "Self and Others: The Diary of a Dervish in Seventeenth Century Istanbul and First-Person Narratives in Ottoman Literature," *Studia Islamica* 69 (1989): 121–150; and Emine Fetvacı, "Viziers to Eunuchs: Transitions in Ottoman Manuscript Patronage, 1566–1617" (PhD diss., Harvard University, 2005).

5 Seeing the Past

Maps and Ottoman Historical Consciousness

Giancarlo Casale

THE WORLD MAP commonly known as the "Mappamundi of Tunuslu Hajji Ahmed" easily ranks among the most significant achievements of early modern cartography. Created as a woodcut in an unknown Venetian workshop in 1559, it is the earliest known Turkish-language work of any kind to be designed for publication and sale in the Ottoman market. With the exception of two earlier charts by the famous cartographer Pīrī Reʿīs (d. 1554), now extant only in fragmentary form, it also ranks as the oldest stand-alone Turcophone world map. Its copious companion text, intricately and painstakingly inscribed around the map's outer margins, is among the most extensive original Turkish-language geographical treatises to have survived from the sixteenth century.[1]

Yet for all of these singular qualities, Hajji Ahmed's map has attracted surprisingly little attention from Ottoman historians: no complete transcription or translation of its contents has ever been published; it is regularly omitted from catalogues and reference works devoted to Ottoman geography and cartography; and it has, to date, been studied by only a handful of scholars with the linguistic skills to read its contents. Even among these specialists, the main topic that seems to have generated genuine scholarly interest relates to the question of the "real" identity of its author, a subject first addressed by the philologist Victor L. Ménage in a seminal article published in 1958.[2]

According to a brief autobiographical sketch included in the map's marginal text, "Hajji Ahmed" was a Tunisian Muslim, trained in a Moroccan madrasa, who had the misfortune of being captured by pirates and sold as a slave to a Venetian nobleman, for whom he subsequently collaborated to create the map in exchange for the promise of freedom. Through a careful analysis of Hajji Ahmed's prose, however, Ménage was able to identify systematic—and in some cases egregious—errors of grammar, orthography, and usage, which, he argued, no madrasa-trained native speaker of Turkish or Arabic could have made. Ménage concluded: "The 'learned Moslem from Tunis,' *if he existed at all,* must have played at best no more than a very subordinate part in the preparation of the map which is ascribed to him."[3] Instead, he speculated, the true author of the text was most likely the chief Venetian dragoman Michele Membré (d. 1594), perhaps aided by his assistant Nicolò Cambi and financed by the entrepreneur and publisher Marc Antonio Giustiniani.

More than fifty years have passed since Ménage's article was published. In the intervening decades, a handful of scholars have questioned the categorical nature of Ménage's conclusions. But among the vast majority of Ottomanists, the map that bears Hajji Ahmed's name continues to be understood according to the terms outlined by Ménage: a forgery, written by an imposter, which as a result must be understood as having little or no relevance to the larger currents of Ottoman intellectual history.[4] Consequently, Ottoman historians have maintained an awkward silence in the midst of a recent explosion of interest in the map among museum curators, cartographers, and other specialists in the cultural history of early modern Europe.[5]

In the following pages, I would like to move beyond this narrow focus on the map's "authenticity" as an Ottoman source and turn instead to an analysis of what its author actually says about the world of the mid-sixteenth century and the Ottomans' place within it. While accepting the basic empirical validity of Ménage's thesis, I will argue that the map and its companion text should nevertheless be read as an original and remarkably compelling work of historical geography, presenting a picture of the Ottoman state that is defined both geographically and historically through its relationship to the twin legacies of ancient Rome and Alexander the Great. Moreover, through a comparison with several other examples of Ottoman cultural production from the mid-sixteenth century, I will suggest some ways in which the arguments put forward by "Hajji Ahmed"—and the specific visual form in which they are presented—might have resonated with the contemporary, learned Ottoman audience for which they were intended.

Hajji Ahmed's Mental Map

One important reason why Hajji Ahmed's map has inspired a recent wave of enthusiasm from non-Ottomanists—who, in the absence of a complete translation, have no access to its written content—is that it is so visually striking as a work of cartography (fig. 5.1). Its central image, a map of the world in the distinctive shape of a heart, is of a type known as a "cordiform projection," popular among European mapmakers of the mid-sixteenth century because it allowed both the eastern and western hemispheres to be represented in a single image with minimal distortion.[6] Below, along the bottom margin of the page, are three smaller images: a celestial sphere showing the earth ringed by the planets and two flanking star charts depicting the constellations of the winter and summer skies. Collectively, these four images comprise roughly half of the page, leaving the rest, with the exception of a title across the top and a stylized floral border around the other three edges, for the text. Appearing in very small script and completely filling the remaining space on the page, the text plays an important role in defining the overall visual impact of the map and parallels the physical organization of the map in a number of ways.

Like the map, the text is divided into several discrete sections. Parallel to the map's visual content, the text's longest component is a comprehensive overview of the world,

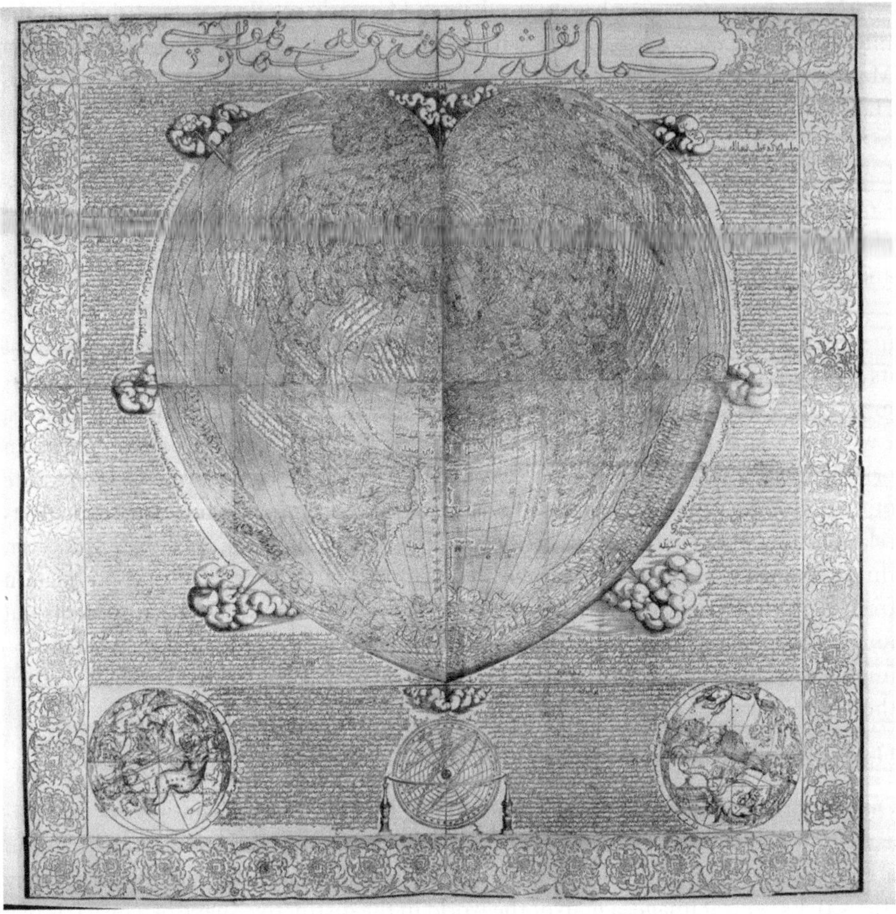

Figure 5.1. *Kemāl ile Naḳş Olınmış Cümle-i Cihān Nemūnesi,* or "Fully Illustrated Exposition of the World in Its Entirety," woodcut by Tunuslu Hajji Ahmed, Venice, 1559. All surviving copies are from a series of twenty-four impressions made in the late eighteenth century from the original sixteenth-century printing blocks.

which includes—as the author stresses repeatedly—descriptions of both the eastern hemisphere, well known to the ancients, and the newly discovered territories of the western hemisphere. This overview begins with a segment devoted to each of the world's "four continents" (Africa, Europe, Asia, and the New World), followed by passages dedicated to its seven most powerful rulers and twelve most important kingdoms. These subsections, while consisting of historical, geographic, and economic details about the lands in question, are woven together by an underlying organizational schema based on astrology, each of the seven rulers being associated with a planetary body and each of the twelve kingdoms with one of the twelve signs of the zodiac. In this way, the author neatly draws together his text, the accompanying "cordiform" world map, and the three smaller maps that depict the celestial as opposed to the terrestrial world. At the same time, the resulting set of associations among rulers, lands, and heavenly bodies serves a larger didactic purpose: through the interplay of astrology and geography, and of text and image, Hajji Ahmed uses his map to impose a hierarchical order on world history—one configured in such a way as to place the Ottoman sultan, because of his particular location in space and time, at the celestial apex of world rulership.

Admittedly, in making this assertion we are moving far from the interpretive framework that has until now been used to understand Hajji Ahmed and his map. Ménage, for example, insisted that the descriptions included in Hajji Ahmed's text were organized "according to no apparent logical sequence" and in general found the map's prose "so convoluted . . . that it is frequently difficult to establish a sequence of thought."[7] In this regard, however, it is important to remember that Ménage's primary interest was not analyzing Hajji Ahmed's "thought" so much as his language. And while the language is indeed riddled with mistakes and grammatically convoluted, a lack of native fluency in Turkish does not imply a lack of coherent ideas. With this in mind, let us return to the text itself and, by beginning where Ménage's analysis ended, briefly examine the passage in which Hajji Ahmed gives us his definition of "Europe":

> Europe: This is the part of the world that they also call "Frengistan" . . . This continent is special in that it is small compared to the others but at the same time more densely populated and intensively cultivated. The arts and sciences flourish there, and the fighting spirit of its people has served as a constant source of illumination, such that it is more beautiful and secure than other renowned and famous provinces. And furthermore it should be known that the greatest rulers of all ages have compared this land to the Sun, and most of them have ruled from here. These include the mighty Sultan Alexander the Great, who ruled nine hundred and eighteen years before the Prophet Muhammad Mustafa, and 284 years after him the Empire of the Romans [began its rule from here], and today in the year 967 of the Muslim calendar it is ruled by His Majesty Süleyman of the House of Osman, Sultan of Sultans and Refuge of the Rulers of the World, who is an even greater source for the illumination of humanity. And alongside of him the realms of the kings of France and of Spain are also included in this continent, which are comparable to the planets Jupiter and Mercury. And it also sparkles with the light of the famous and prosperous realms of Italy and Portugal and Germany and Sarmatia, which are all described in more detail below.[8]

Several elements of this passage are deserving of special attention, the most basic being its surprising invocation of "Europe" (*Avrūba*). This is, to say the least, an unexpected choice of terminology, for Europe as a concept was virtually unknown in the medieval Arab geographical tradition to which the Ottomans are generally considered heirs. Rather than referring to "continents," Arab geographers typically organized the world with reference to the seven "climes" (*aḳālīm*) that collectively encompassed the "inhabited quarter" (*rubʿ al-meskūn*), that portion of the earth considered suitable for human habitation. Hajji Ahmed is clearly well versed in this terminology, the term "clime" appearing at several points in his text. Nevertheless, he insists on using "the four continents" as his basic organizing principle and on giving pride of place to Europe as "the Sun."[9]

Equally unusual, but equally central to Hajji Ahmed's conceptual framework, is his insistence on defining "Europe" not only through its physical (and celestial) geography but also as a place that is unique in terms of its history and political traditions. Indeed, such an assertion would have come as a surprise not only to medieval Arab geographers but also to most Europeans of Hajji Ahmed's day. For even if the basic concept of organizing the physical world into "continents" was well established in European intellectual circles, it was only during the middle decades of the sixteenth century—precisely the time that Hajji Ahmed was writing—that a handful of European intellectuals first began to experiment with the idea of Europe as a concrete political and cultural space with an identity distinct from "Christendom."[10]

In other words, Hajji Ahmed composed his text at a historical moment during which "European identity," still in its earliest stages of development, had yet to be fully consolidated. And this, in turn, left him free to select criteria for defining Europe that differed in important ways from those that we, in the centuries since, have come to expect as de rigueur. Thus, in the passage above he makes no mention of Roman law, nor of Greco-Roman letters, nor, most strikingly, does he include any reference to Christianity. Instead, Hajji Ahmed keeps his emphasis on politics, ascribing Europe's greatness to its historical role as the birthplace of Alexander the Great and of the Roman Empire. And, crucially, in making this assertion he shows no hesitation in listing the Ottoman sultan alongside the kings of Spain and France as a European ruler—indeed, as the *most* European ruler—precisely because he has left aside the cultural and religious criteria of "Europeanness" according to which the Ottomans might otherwise be excluded.

Elsewhere, I have described the means by which Hajji Ahmed elaborates on this idea in subsequent sections of his text, as he devotes separate passages to each of the "European" countries on his list and systematically juxtaposes them with non-European states and rulers.[11] For our purposes, what is most important about his argument is the connection he draws between Europe, Rome, the legacy of Alexander the Great, and the imagery of the sun in establishing the Ottoman sultan as the greatest ruler of the ages. As Hajji Ahmed says explicitly, Alexander was a mighty world conqueror because he ruled *from Europe,* a place that in the hierarchy of continents "has been compared to the Sun . . . by the greatest rulers of all ages." Through his many subsequent conquests in the lands beyond Europe, Alexander established a precedent that would be copied in later centuries, first by the emperors of Rome and eventually by the Ottoman sultan, "an even greater source for the illumination of humanity." And this leads, climactically, to the following extended description of the rule of Süleyman the Magnificent, a passage that in many ways serves as the capstone of Hajji Ahmed's argument:

> His illustrious Majesty, the Great Ottoman Sultan, has been compared to the Sun. He first and foremost illuminates Europe, but the power from the rays [of his magnificence] also shine upon the lands of Asia and Africa, such that other rulers cannot even be compared to stars, either in terms of their brilliance or their greatness, for they are all obscured [beside his radiance]. This noble progeny, through its valor and bravery, is constantly victorious, ruling the provinces of Anatolia, Karaman, Diyarbakir, Erzurum, Baghdad, Damascus, Arabia, all of Egypt, the Balkans and Hungary, and has extended its borders as far as Germany, and to the borders of Arabia, and in Africa to the south as far as Ethiopia, and in the direction of the west, with the conquests of the lord of Algeria, as far as Morocco. In short, the glory and power and majesty of the House of Osman is immeasurable, and countless lords, both Muslim and Christian, have long paid tribute to it. And currently, from this illustrious house, the Sultan of Sultans who are the proof of rulership, Lord of the Conjunction of the time of Alexander of the Two Horns, His Majesty Sultan Süleyman rules from the Orient to Arabia with his bravery and power and glory and wisdom and justice and compassion. The majesty and wonder [of his rule] are such that they cannot be described by the tongue nor recorded and explained by the pen, although much has nevertheless been written in this regard.[12]

Thus, in the great constellation of peoples and rulers of the world, the Ottoman Empire and its sultan are the sun, "such that other rulers cannot even be compared to stars." And because Europe, in turn, is identified as the sun in the constellation of continents, the Ottoman sultan is confirmed as the physical embodiment of Europe. In consequence, the Ottoman sultan, and he alone, is the legitimate successor to Alexander the Great—his credentials being recognized precisely because, like Alexander, his conquests in the lands *beyond* the borders of Europe are so extensive.

A few additional anecdotes from other sections of the text, in which Hajji Ahmed discusses contemporary states *outside* of Europe in a comparative context, will serve to fill in the final missing pieces of his argument. For example, while giving an account of the native population of Peru, he remarks that, "these people once upon a time were all pagans, but now most of them have become Catholics . . . and have learned the Spanish language and customs, just as the people of Anatolia and Karaman have learned the language and customs of the Turks."[13] In this way, in a startling inversion of the standard narrative of Asia Minor's "Turkification," he suggests that the disappearance of Greek Orthodox hegemony in Anatolia was a symptom of *European* expansion in Asia, a repetition, in a modern guise, of the Alexandrian conquests and subsequent Hellenization of the East. This is also the reason Hajji Ahmed gives for writing his text in Turkish rather than Arabic (ostensibly his native language). In his words: "This translation, according to the orders of my master, I wrote in the Turkish tongue to the extent that I was able, since it is this language that rules the world."[14]

Finally, perhaps the most explicitly political section of Hajji Ahmed's text comes in the passage dedicated to Shah Tahmasp of Iran (r. 1525–1576), the Ottomans' most feared rival in the east. Here Hajji Ahmed describes the shah in glowing terms, noting that he "has great numbers of cavalry, and is an intelligent and powerful ruler, and once upon a time the province of Persia ruled all the lands of the east, and its borders extended all the way to the Roman Empire."[15] Having openly associated modern Safavids with the Persians of antiquity, however, he reminds his readers that the latter, for all of their greatness, "were unable to resist Alexander the Great, and were defeated and became subject to him." Presumably, Shah Tahmasp, too, "who has been compared to Mars, and illuminates Asia with his rays," was destined to be outshone by the rising European sun of Süleyman the Magnificent.[16]

Hajji Ahmed's Intellectual Circle

With the basic contours of Hajji Ahmed's argument established, our next task is to try to place it within a larger Ottoman intellectual context in order to understand its potential ramifications. Due to the enduring influence of Ménage, this is a subject that scholars have until now been reluctant to explore because of a conviction that, as a "forgery" composed by a non-Muslim, non-native Turkish speaker, Hajji Ahmed's map was not an authentically Ottoman text. However, even if we accept Ménage's basic premise—that the "real" Hajji Ahmed was a freely employed Italophone translator and not, as he claimed to be, a Muslim captive from Tunisia—the fact remains that he wrote, however imperfectly, in Turkish and clearly invested a great deal of intellectual effort in developing his arguments. Moreover, there is a good deal of evidence to suggest that he was a man firmly embedded within a particular Ottoman intellectual circle who shared his basic vision of the Ottoman Empire as a European state.

Let us begin with a slightly earlier period of Ottoman history: the grand vizierate of Ibrahim Pasha (1523–1536). As a significant body of recent research has shown, Ibrahim Pasha's years in office stand as the high-water mark of Ottoman investment in the *translatio imperii:* the project of developing an ideological, theological, and historiographical basis for establishing the Ottoman sultan as the legitimate heir of the Roman emperors. Ibrahim Pasha's own efforts in this regard were multifaceted and ambitious. In Istanbul, he oversaw the extensive rebuilding of the neighborhood around the Hippodrome—the old imperial city center that had been largely abandoned in the preconquest period—as a way of associating Ottoman rule over "the City of Constantine" with the revival of lost Roman greatness. Moreover, following the battle of Mohács in 1526, he decorated the garden of his own residence, itself prominently situated overlooking the Hippodrome, with classical statues from the palace of King Matthias Corvinus (r. 1469–1490) in Buda—thereby drawing an explicit link between himself, the Ottoman conquest of Hungary, and the rebirth of Istanbul as the "New Rome."[17]

Of all of the projects supported by Ibrahim Pasha in the service of the *translatio imperii,* however, by far the best known is the exorbitantly expensive piece of

Figure 5.2. *Portrait of Süleyman the Magnificent,* engraving by Agostino Veneziano, Venice, 1535. The four crowns, as interpreted by Gülru Necipoğlu, represent worldly rulership over "the four continents" and are amalgamated together in the form of the tiara of the Roman pontiff.

headgear that he commissioned for Sultan Süleyman in 1532 (fig. 5.2). Completed in the immediate aftermath of the first Ottoman siege of Vienna in 1529, the headdress was designed to be worn by the sultan as he marched on a second campaign to conquer the Austrian capital—a campaign that was intended to permanently extinguish the Habsburg dynasty's rival claim to being "Holy Roman Emperors" and to set the stage for the subsequent Ottoman invasion of Italy, the subjugation of the Pope in Rome, and, eventually, the unification of all of Christian Europe under the sultan's dominion. Accordingly, the headpiece itself was an extravagant, jewel-encrusted amalgamation of the Roman pontiff's tiara and of four separate imperial crowns, each representing rulership over one of the four corners of the world, or "the four continents."[18]

As an emphatic statement of Ottoman imperial claims, framed with reference to both classical antiquity and contemporary geography and completed against the backdrop of an ongoing rivalry with the Habsburgs for ownership of the Roman legacy, Süleyman's crown serves as an extremely useful point of comparison with Hajji Ahmed's map. Like the map, the crown was produced in a Venetian workshop, by Venetian artisans, using the most sophisticated techniques of Venetian craftsmanship. Also like the map, it employed a European visual and symbolic language (of tiaras and continents as opposed to turbans and climes) to elaborate a claim to universal sovereignty that was nevertheless unmistakably Ottoman. Finally, like the map, the crown was, until recently, understood by modern scholars to have no relationship to the cultural and political life of the contemporary Ottoman Empire and was instead dismissed as the product of "a purely speculative commercial enterprise by Venetian merchants and Venetian goldsmiths."[19]

How can we account for such a remarkable group of similarities? Fascinatingly, Ménage's thesis about the "real" identity of Hajji Ahmed can be of use in answering this question, as it hints at a personal connection between the creators of these two works. As mentioned earlier, Ménage proposed the chief Venetian dragoman Michele Membré as one likely candidate for authorship of the map, noting that Membré would have had the necessary linguistic skills, as well as contacts in the right publishing circles in Venice. His name also appears—alongside that of his assistant Nicolò Cambi and, suggestively, another individual by the name of "Cagi Acmet"—in a pair of Venetian archival documents related to a petition for a printing license for the map.[20]

Based on this documentation, the Italian scholar Antonio Fabris has argued that Ménage is too dismissive of the possibility that an actual person by the name of Hajji Ahmed played at least some part in preparing the map that bears his name.[21] Ménage's own view is that this possibility is simply not borne out by the Italianate idiosyncrasies of the text itself, indicating that "Hajji Ahmed," if in fact a real person, was merely used by the map's creators to accentuate its legitimacy—both for its future Ottoman readers and for the Venetian regulators who might otherwise have denied permission for its publication.

Whatever the specific role "Hajji Ahmed" played in preparing the map—which even Ménage admits is difficult to determine with certainty—it is clear that Michele Membré was also involved, and it is his role that allows us to draw a connection between the map and Süleyman's crown. For Membré, who was a native of the island of Cyprus and had received Venetian citizenship relatively late in life, had spent the years of Ibrahim Pasha's grand vizierate working as a junior interpreter for the Venetian *bailo* in Istanbul.[22] Furthermore, Ibrahim Pasha, who was himself originally a

Venetian colonial subject from the Adriatic coast of Greece, had commissioned the sultan's crown through the agency of several other Veneto-Ottoman intermediaries, including Alvise Gritti (d. 1534), the Istanbul-born illegitimate son of Venetian Doge Andrea Gritti (d. 1538), and Yunus Beg (d. 1551), an Ottoman dragoman originally from the Venetian Peloponnesus.[23] As a result, it is almost certain that Membré, too, as a young man, had been aware of, and probably personally involved in, negotiations surrounding the design and purchase of the crown.

This personal connection therefore provides a missing link that can explain the very close conceptual correlation between Hajji Ahmed's map and Ibrahim Pasha's crown, despite the twenty-five years that separate their dates of completion. Furthermore, it helps us to account for the numerous echoes in Hajji Ahmed's text of Ibrahim Pasha's wider universalist political program, as expressed through the official channels of the Ottoman state during his years in office. In 1527, for example, just after the Ottoman victory at Mohács, Süleyman's second vizier, Mustafa Pasha, had reminded the envoy of King Janos Szapolyai of Hungary (r. 1526–1540) that "just as there was only one sun on the horizon, so there was only one ruler of the world, his master [Süleyman the Magnificent]."[24] Rome, Universal Empire, the "Sun King": the resonance with Hajji Ahmed's text is too exact to be a coincidence.

To summarize: even if we accept Ménage's hypothesis that the "real" Hajji Ahmed was in fact Michele Membré (or, alternatively, a group of collaborators of which Membré was the leading member), there is no reason to understand his map as being, for this reason, in any way less authentically "Ottoman" than the famous crown commissioned by Ibrahim Pasha a generation earlier. Both were created in Venice, by Venetians, but nevertheless reflect a distinctly Ottoman cosmology of universal empire expressed through the concept of *translatio imperii.*

Of course, this is not to deny that there are also important differences between the two works. The crown was a stand-alone piece, paid for by a statesman and designed for a sovereign, that served a very specific political purpose: to project a particular image of Ottoman imperial authority to a European audience as a prelude to a military campaign. By contrast, the map, a printed work intended to be sold in the Ottoman market, was composed in Turkish and clearly intended for an Ottoman audience. So who actually composed this Ottoman audience, and how might they have responded to "Hajji Ahmed's" message?

At least a partial solution to this thorny but critically important question is found in the pages of yet another contemporary Ottoman work, known as *Tārīḫ-i Ungurūs* or "History of Hungary." Composed sometime in the 1550s by Maḥmūd Beg (d. 1575), a native of Vienna who fell captive to the Ottomans as a young man and later converted to Islam, the work is ostensibly a rendering into Ottoman Turkish of a Latin chronicle about the pre-conquest history of the Kingdom of Hungary. At the same time, it bears the subtitle of *İskendernāme,* or "Epic of Alexander," and is prefaced by a lengthy pseudo-historical narrative of Alexander the Great's conquests in classical antiquity. This introductory section is of particular interest because it describes Alexander as both “Roman Emperor” (*Rūm Pādişāhı*) and “Emperor of the Seven Climes” (*Pādişāh-ı heft-iḳlīm*) and combines a detailed narrative of his victory over Darius in Persia with a fictive account of the hero’s simultaneous conquests in Europe (which the historical Alexander never, of course, undertook). All of this material is interwoven, in subsequent sections, with chapters that deal with the more recent history of Hungary. The overall result is a narrative with clear prophetic overtones: through his conquest of Hungary, the Ottoman sultan has confirmed his inheritance of the legacy of Alexander the Great, ensuring, in turn, that he will vanquish “the Persians.” The authority of this message is, moreover, enhanced by its presentation as a “European” source in Turkish translation (despite the fact that, in reality, it is an entirely original work that is only loosely inspired by Western sources).[25]

Once again, we are confronted with a text that has too many obvious parallels with the work of Hajji Ahmed to be explained away as simple happenstance. And once again, we have evidence of a personal connection between the two authors. Given Maḥmūd Beg’s role as an interpreter for the Ottoman court throughout the 1550s and 1560s, it is virtually certain that he corresponded with Michele Membré, his counterpart in Venice, as part of his official duties. Maḥmūd is also known to have participated in several important diplomatic missions abroad during these years and to have visited several European capitals, including, notably, Venice—meaning that he must have met Membré on multiple occasions during his stay in *La Serenissima.* And because Maḥmūd seems to have originally entered Ottoman service much earlier, upon his capture by Ottoman forces at the battle of Mohács in 1526, in all likelihood he and Membré already enjoyed a personal relationship dating to the 1520s and 1530s, when both lived in Istanbul.[26]

With this information, we are now in a position to sketch out a rough socio-demographic profile of some of the key members of the intellectual circle in which “Hajji Ahmed” developed his thought: Yunus Beg, a Veneto-Ottoman from the Peloponnesus who served as a broker for Süleyman’s crown; Maḥmūd Beg, a Viennese renegade and author of *Tārīḫ-i Ungurūs;* and Michele Membré, the “real” Hajji Ahmed. All three men belonged to a group of translators who either worked for or regularly corresponded with the Ottoman court (and consequently with one another). All three, like a great many members of the Ottoman imperial elite of their day, were non-native Turkish speakers born as subjects of western European states. All three were literate but lacked the level of fluency in the high Ottoman style of Turkish that defined the madrasa-trained members of the Ottoman ulema. And all three men had lived in Istanbul during the grand vizierate of Ibrahim Pasha—who, as a native of the Venetian colony of Parga, could himself be included in this same general category.

Furthermore, this common socio-demographic profile hints at a shared set of political interests, as the years of Ibrahim Pasha’s grand vizierate coincide with the period during which individuals such as these—recent immigrants, *ḳuls,* first-generation

Muslims, and various other "new men" with ties to Christian Europe—were systematically favored by the Ottoman state to an extent rarely matched before or since. As a result, it was only natural for such individuals to favor a particular vision of the Ottoman Empire's past, and its place in the contemporary world, that would justify their privileged position and ensure that it would continue into the future.

The image of a "European Alexander" served this goal precisely. By presenting Alexander as a *European* ruler, who was associated with the Ottoman dynasty through the latter's inheritance of the legacy of ancient Rome, "European-ness" could thereby be understood as constituting an essential component of Ottoman identity—meaning that individual Europeans living in the empire could be considered, in a sense, the most Ottoman of all. Moreover, by accentuating Alexander's credentials as the vanquisher of the ancient Persians *from Europe,* his heritage could be used to argue that this European-ness remained vital for the continuing success of the Ottoman state even in an age, such as the 1550s, in which the empire's greatest rivals were no longer the Habsburgs of the Christian West but the Safavid Shiʿites to the east.

The Empire Strikes Back

Like all highly politicized interpretations of the past, the "European Alexander" thesis had detractors as well as proponents. Unsurprisingly, those who found it least convincing intellectually were those who had the most to gain politically by discrediting it. First among these were the highly literate, madrasa-trained, freeborn Muslims of the empire, who were especially well represented in the Ottoman chancery and legal system. For obvious reasons, such individuals had little interest in perpetuating an ideology of state that resulted in their systematic exclusion—in favor of palace slaves, renegades, and other outsiders—from some of the most important positions in the Ottoman establishment. Instead, they were eager to promote their own definition of imperial identity, which, rather than celebrating a historical link with Europe, was much more emphatically articulated through the language of Islam.[27]

In terms of the development of history as a distinct Ottoman literary genre, the contributions of this group are relatively well known. Their prose, written in a florid "high imperial style" of Ottoman Turkish, was steeped in the vocabulary, imagery, and literary traditions of Arabic and Persian. And their narratives, often directly inspired by Arabic and Persian precedents, placed the Ottoman dynasty firmly within a genealogy of "Islamic" history, beginning with Adam and the prophets and moving through the life of Muhammad, the history of the early Muslim community, the four "rightly guided Caliphs," the Umayyads, the Abbasids, and so forth.[28]

Nevertheless, within this narrative frame a prominent place was also reserved for Alexander the Great, albeit in his thoroughly Islamicized guise of *Ẕuʾl-Ḳarneyn,* or "of the Two Horns." This Alexander, far removed from the Hellenizing hero of Greco-Roman civilization, drew his prestige from having appeared in the verses of the Qurʾan, a status so exalted that he was sometimes included among the prophets of Islam. And while still recognized as a mighty conqueror, he was above all credited with having traveled to the ends of the earth, where, in order to protect civilization from the forces of darkness, he constructed a wall to keep out the barbarian hordes of "Gog and Magog."[29]

Thus, the figure of Alexander came to occupy a central battleground between two competing visions of Ottoman history: one that defined the empire as the "New Rome," destined to revive the lost glory of Greco-Roman antiquity, and another that defined it as a quintessentially Islamic state, entrusted by the ancients with the responsibility of preserving the integrity of the *ummah* from the pernicious influence of barbarian outsiders. Within each of these competing grand narratives was an infinite range of subcurrents and possible deviations, themselves worthy of a great deal more scholarly attention than they have received. What I would like to emphasize here is that these two divergent ways of representing the past, alongside their obvious political implications for the contemporary world, were also inextricably linked to a particular understanding of geographic space and its limits.

A good illustration of this relationship is provided by the Ottoman admiral and polymath Seydī ʿAlī Reʾīs (d. 1563) in his *Mirʾâtüʾl-Memālik*, or "Mirror of Countries," a first-person narrative of a voyage to India, composed upon his return to Istanbul in 1561. In what is easily the most famous passage of this work, the author recounts an exchange from his visit to the Mughal court in Delhi, during which the emperor Humayun (r. 1530–1540 and 1555–1556) asks whose empire Seydī ʿAlī believes to be more extensive—Humayun's own or that of the Ottoman sultan. Seydī ʿAlī's initial response is to say that "just as Alexander was ruler of the world and king of the seven climes, so is the Padishah of Rūm [i.e., the Ottoman Sultan]."[30] To demonstrate this point, he presents a list of Ottoman provinces that, collectively, represent each of the seven climes of the "inhabited quarter," beginning with Yemen in the south and ending with Hungary in the north. He concludes, however, by emphasizing that even outside of the borders of his own extensive dominion, Muslims around the world recognize their allegiance to the Ottoman sultan by spontaneously reading the *ḫuṭbe* in his name during their Friday prayers—including, according to what he has been told by the merchants he met during his travels, in the lands "of the great Khan of China." Duly impressed, Humayun exclaims: "Verily there is no sovereign worthy of the title 'padishah' other than the Padishah of Rūm!"[31]

One is naturally left to doubt that the real Humayun was as easily persuaded by these arguments as Seydī ʿAlī would have us believe. However, in interpreting the message that his story was designed to convey to an Ottoman readership after his return from India, it is worth taking into consideration the details of Seydī ʿAlī's own intellectual biography: as the madrasa-educated scion of a freeborn, old Muslim family with multigenerational ties to the Ottoman navy—a branch of the imperial establishment particularly densely populated with renegades and non-Muslims—Seydī ʿAlī was exactly the kind of author who had nothing to gain, and everything to lose, by embracing Hajji Ahmed's "European Alexander" thesis. This is clearly reflected in his own contrasting emphasis on the Ottoman sultans' credentials as defenders of Islam, recognized as such by Muslims everywhere.

Even so, we can also detect in his work—which is exactly contemporary with Hajji Ahmed's map—the same basic impulse to define the Ottoman state through a combination of world geography and historical narrative, with Alexander the Great as the central point of reference. So rather than a pair of authors who inhabit two entirely separate mental worlds, what we are dealing with here is something much more akin to a dialectic: two worldviews in direct competition with one another, which share a common vocabulary and point of departure even as they categorically deny the legitimacy of each other's positions.[32]

Equally significantly, these two competing worldviews were directly translatable into two distinct ways of representing the world visually, a point that Seydī ʿAlī addresses in a separate work, *Kitāb al-Muḥīṭ*, or "Book of the Ocean." Here, in a chapter dedicated to explaining the principles of cartography, he begins by identifying two basic types of world maps, *ḫarṭī* and *pāpāmūndī*. The former, which he claims to be derived from the Latin word "quarta," he defines as a map showing only the "inhabited quarter" of the world. In contrast, as he explains, "maps of the world in its entirety (*itmām-ı dünyā*) are called 'papamundi,' *papa* meaning the greatest of the Christians [the Pope], and *mundi* meaning the whole world."[33]

It matters little whether these etymologies are actually convincing by the standards of modern philological analysis (they are not). Instead, what interests us here is what these etymologies implied for Seydī ʿAlī. As a map showing only the world's inhabited "quarter," or *rubʿ al-meskūn*, a *ḫarṭī* was conceptually consistent with the standard representation of the world of pre-Ottoman Arabic geography: a Ptolemaic map showing the "seven climes over which the great Alexander had dominion." On the other hand, as maps that included areas (like the New World) unknown to the ancients—and that consequently divided the world by "continents" instead of "climes"—*pāpāmūndī* represented a disturbing departure from this tradition. By associating such maps, etymologically, with "the Pope," Seydī ʿAlī thus implies that their basic form constituted an explicitly Christian representation of geographic space and was therefore incommensurate with Ottoman Muslim identity.

Did Seydī ʿAlī have Hajji Ahmed specifically in mind when he wrote these words? Because we know virtually nothing about the circulation of Hajji Ahmed's map—or lack thereof—prior to its rediscovery in the eighteenth century, the safest answer is probably no. To return to an earlier discussion, however, it is worth remembering that an association between worldly rulership over "the four continents" and the universalist claims of the Roman pontiff not only emerges from Seydī ʿAlī's interpretation of European-style maps but is also explicitly conveyed by Süleyman the Magnificent's hat—in the latter case with the intent of assisting the sultan in appropriating both papal and imperial authority for himself. Nor is there any doubt that Hajji Ahmed's map, had Seydī 'Alī seen it, would not only have qualified as a *pāpāmūndī* according to Seydī 'Alī's criteria but was in fact intended to do so. So much can be surmised from its title, emblazoned proudly across the top in bold script: *Kemāl ile Naḳş Olınmış Cümle-i Cihān Nemūnesi,* or "Fully Illustrated Exposition of the World in its Entirety."

Maps and History

An appreciation of the fundamental, antagonistic dichotomy between those who insisted on mapping the world *in its entirety* and those who insisted on *not* mapping the world in such a way can help us find answers to a number of critical and still unresolved questions about the consolidation of a canonical Ottoman historiographical tradition during the middle decades of the sixteenth century. Why, for example, did authors like Muṣṭafā 'Ālī (d. 1600) or Celālzāde Muṣṭafā (d. 1567), when constructing the grand narratives that would leave a definitive mark on later generations of Ottoman historians, consistently place the Ottoman Empire within a narrative framework that included space for India, sub-Saharan Africa, central Asia, sometimes even China, but only very rarely Europe, and never the New World?[34] Why, when they chose to illustrate these narratives with world maps, did the illustrations typically take the form of Ptolemaic world maps, often copied directly from medieval Arabic geographies, and never Western-style *mappaemundi*?[35] And why did such narratives, which could find space in the pre-Ottoman past for the pharaohs of Egypt, the ancient Iranian kings, the Mongols, and many other pre-Islamic dynasties (including, of course, Alexander the Great), never reserve any significant space for the Roman Empire? From a modern perspective, these apparent blind spots can seem so cavernous, so insistent, and so baffling that it is all too easy to dismiss them as the result of simple ignorance—the product of a timeless "Islamic" perspective that made it impossible for the Ottomans of the late sixteenth century to comprehend a world in the process of rapid change. Instead, what I would like to suggest is that such authors as Celālzāde and Muṣṭafā 'Ālī were motivated to develop their distinctive worldviews not out of ignorance of any alternative but rather by a willful desire to suppress those alternatives whose political implications were directly contrary to their own collective interests.[36] By denying a physical space to Europe and the New World in the mental map upon which they constructed Ottoman history, these members of the Ottoman scribal class hoped to deny a legitimate space within the Ottoman elite to a social group that, until that time, had constituted their most dangerous rivals for patronage, prestige, and imperial favor.[37] In the end, their efforts were so successful that, today, we have difficulty even imagining "the Ottomans" according to any terms other than those that the members of this freeborn, Muslim, madrasa-trained scribal class defined during this critical moment in history.

Herein lies the tragedy of Hajji Ahmed, whose own ambiguous and contradictory status as an author can be explained through this definitive mid-sixteenth-century shift in the construction of "Ottoman-ness." A generation earlier, in the 1520s and 1530s, it was still perfectly possible for a non-Muslim, Italian-trained, humanist intellectual to come to Istanbul and find himself showered with official favor, his very presence in the city confirming the rebirth of Istanbul as the "New Rome."[38] But by the 1550s, although there were still those who defended a vision of the Ottoman Empire as a "European" state, such individuals could no longer make their case on their own terms. Deprived of a scribal education and native fluency in Turkish, "Hajji Ahmed" could now hope to speak with authority only by adopting the guise of a Tunisian Muslim, held in captivity by the "Franks" and longing to be redeemed to the "land of the Muslims." Yet, ironically, in so doing, he accepted the very premise upon which his adversaries based their arguments. Four and a half centuries later, he has yet to recover his voice.

But let us not conclude on such a bleak and uncompromising note, and end instead with another question: Might there have been ways in which the members of this newly consolidated scribal class, in their enthusiasm for stifling the opposition, internalized some of the very ideas that they hoped to discredit? Certainly, the name that this group adopted for the Ottoman imperial elite's collective identity—"Rūmī" meaning "Roman"—suggests one way in which this was indeed so.[39] But we have other, more self-conscious, indications as well. Muṣṭafā ʿĀlī, for example, in his celebrated political treatise *The Counsel for Sultans,* includes the following extended description of Alexander the Great as the ultimate model of a powerful and just ruler:

> Alexander of the Two Horns within the shortest time, namely within a period of dates which are given as fourteen years, assembled the expanse of the East and the West under the sun of his dominion. As is well known, he reached the high honor of prophethood and, by being mentioned in the Qur'an, the position of being God's envoy, as some have asserted. Being the emperor of the world and the sovereign over all mighty kings, he had completed all the requirements of the Caliphate and obtained all the necessities of the emirate and government. Nevertheless, he appointed Plato as his representative and always held priceless consultations with Aristotle. The power of his throne was resplendent at all times through the hold of the Greek thinkers, and his government over East and West excelled through the assistance of the philosophers of his time.[40]

Here we see Alexander "of the Two Horns," a Qur'anic prophet ruling over "the Caliphate," but also as Alexander "the Great," patron of Greek philosophers and ruler of "the Kingdom of the Sun." The echoes of Hajji Ahmed are still recognizable even in defeat. And in their ensemble, they serve as a cogent reminder that Hajji Ahmed's failure by no means marks the end of a story but merely the end of one chapter—and the beginning of another.

Notes

1. Several copies of the map are accessible in public library collections, including the Library of Congress, Washington, D.C.; the William Clements Library, University of Michigan; the John Carter Brown Library, Brown University; and the Biblioteca Marciana, Venice. However, all known copies of

the map date from a series of twenty-four impressions made in the late eighteenth century from the original woodcut blocks, which are today in Venice's Museo Correr. For this essay, I have consulted the copy at Chicago's Newberry Library, Novacco 8F 11. A facsimile of the copy from the William Clements Library, unfortunately with no accompanying transcription or translation, is also available. See George Kish, *The Suppressed Turkish Map of 1560* (Ann Arbor, Mich.: William Clements Library, 1957).

2. See V. L. Ménage, "The Map of Hajji Ahmed and Its Makers," *Bulletin of the School of Oriental and African Studies* 21 (1958): 291–314. Since the appearance of Ménage's article, I am aware of only two other studies of the map's contents published by Ottomanists. The first is a redaction of a text from an anonymous manuscript at Oxford's Bodleian Library that is almost identical to the companion text from Hajji Ahmed's map, published by Bedi Şehsuvaroğlu under the title "Kanuni Devrinde Yazılmış ve Şimdiye Bilinmeyen bir Coğrafya Kitabı," in *Kanuni Armağanı* (Ankara: Türk Tarih Kurumu, 1970), 207–225. Şehsuvaroğlu, however, makes no mention of the map in this article, and was apparently unaware of the connection between it and the text he edited. More recently, Giampiero Bellingeri included a transcription and Italian translation of several passages of the text as an appendix to his important article, "Fascie 'altaiche' del mappamondo turco-veneziano," in G. Bellingeri, *Turco-Veneta* (Istanbul: Isis Press, 2003), 61–81.

3. Ménage, "The Map of Hajji Ahmed and Its Makers," 307. Emphasis is from Ménage's original text.

4. The most significant exception is the previously cited article by Bellingeri. Since Ménage, he is the only scholar to have subjected Hajji Ahmed's text to serious philological study, uncovering many linguistic and cultural layers that Ménage's approach dismissed.

5. Recent studies of the map by Europeanists include Pascale Barthe, "An Uncommon Map for a Common World: Hajji Ahmed's Cordiform Map of 1559," *L'Esprit Créateur* 48, no. 1 (2008): 32–44; Benjamin Arbel, "Maps of the World for Ottoman Princes? Further Evidence and Questions Concerning 'The Mappamondo' of Hajji Ahmed," *Imago Mundi* 54 (2002): 19–29; and Antonio Fabris, "The Ottoman Mappa Mundi of Hajji Ahmed of Tunis," *Arab Historical Review for Ottoman Studies* 7–8 (1993): 31–37. In addition, an impressive number of recent museum exhibits have featured the map. See Stefano Carboni, ed.,*Venice and the Islamic World, 828–1797* (New Haven, Conn.: Yale University Press, 2007); Jay A. Levenson, ed., *Encompassing the Globe: Portugal and the World in the 16th and 17th Centuries* (Washington, D.C.: Smithsonian, 2007); Ian Manners, ed., *European Cartographers and the Ottoman World, 1500–1750: Maps from the Collection of O. J. Sopranos* (Chicago: Oriental Institute, 2007); and Peter Noever, ed., *Global Lab: Art as a Message, Asia and Europe 1500–1700* (Wien: MAK/Hatje Cantz 2009).

6. On cordiform maps, see George Kish, "The Cosmographic Heart: Cordiform Maps of the 16th Century," *Imago Mundi* 19 (1965): 13–21.

7. Ménage, "The Map of Hajji Ahmed and Its Makers," 294, 299.

8. In the transcription below (and those that follow in subsequent notes), I have sought to preserve, to the extent possible, the idiosyncratic orthography and usage of the text's original prose. Thus, I have chosen neither to "correct" obvious errors of spelling and grammar nor to flag such errors and comment on them individually (to do so adequately would require far more space than is available here). I refer curious readers to Ménage's previously cited article, which discusses many of these questions in detail. "Avrūba: Ol ʿālemüñ ḥiṣṣesidür ki Frengistān dirler . . . bu ʿālemüñ olan ḥiṣṣesi ḫuṣūṣā ki ġayrlerine göre küçük olur liʾenne ḥiṣṣe-i mezbūrede olan şehrleri ġayrı ḥiṣṣelerden ziyāde sıḳ ve [???] ve maʿmūr olmaġın ve anda dāʾimā ṣanʿatları ve ʿilmleri keṣret üzre ve ʿavām ġāzīleri [?] tamām vāḳiʿ olduġı sebebden her zamān özgelerinden eżʿāf mużāʿaf [?] tenvirlenüb ve benām ve meşhūr vilāyetlerden ziyāde güzel [ve] muḫtārdur ve bu illerden maʿlūm olunan budur ki dāʾimā dünyāda ẓ[ā]hır ve vāḳiʿ olan muʿaẓẓam pādişāhları güneşe beñzetmişlerdür ve taḫt-ı serīrlerinüñ ẕikr olunan ḥiṣṣede ekṣer-i zamānda anda olurlar idi zirā zamān-ı evāʾilde Ḥażret-i Resūl Muḥammed el-Muṣṭafādan aḳdem sene ṭoḳuz yüz on sekizinde el-Sulṭān Muʿaẓẓam Pādişāh

Skender begledi ve ba'dehu iki yüz seksen dört yılından ṣoñra Rūm Mülūkānı begledi ve ḥāliyā tārīḫ-i Müslümānuñ sene ṭoḳuz yüz altmış yedi yılında Ḥażret-i Pādişāh-ı Nesl-i 'Oṣmān Sulṭānü'l-Selāṭīn-i Cihān ve Melce'-i Ḫavāḳīn-i Devir an-Devirü'l-Sulṭān Süleymān ki ġayrilerinden ziyāde nūr-ı 'ālemiyāndur begleyub ve bundan ġayrı mezbūr ḥiṣṣeye dāḫilinde İspānya Pādişāhı ve Françа Pādişāhı beglik iderler. Bunlar Müşteriye ve 'Utāride teşābüh iderler. Ve daḫi İṭālyā ve Būrṭūġāl ve Almān ve Sārmaçay nām mu'aẓẓam ve ma'mūr memleketlerinden tābān ve direhşān olunub nice ki mezbūrları içün aşaġada beyān ve şerḥ olunur." Right column, lines 63–82.

9. It is also interesting to note that while "continent" has no direct equivalent in medieval Arabic geography, Hajji Ahmed translates it as "*ḥiṣṣe*"—a term firmly entrenched in the technical vocabulary of Arabic astronomy, denoting the coordinates and elliptical arcs of stars and planets.

10. See Denys Hay, *Europe: The Emergence of an Idea* (Edinburgh: Edinburgh University Press, 1968), as well as the recent collection of essays in Anthony Pagden, ed., *The Idea of Europe: From Antiquity to the European Union* (Cambridge: Cambridge University Press, 2002).

11. See Giancarlo Casale, "16. Yüzyıla Ait Türkçe Dünya Haritasında Avrupa Düşüncesi," in *Harp ve Sulh: Avrupa ve Osmanlılar*, ed. Dejanirah Couto, trans. Şirin Tekeli (Istanbul: Kitap Yayınevi, 2010), 56–81.

12. "Nevāb-i celālet-me'āb-i 'aẓamet-niṣāb ḥażret-i 'alī 'Oṣmān ki sulṭān-ı 'aẓamdur güneşe beñzenildi ibtidā Avrūba ṭarāfı münevver ider ḫuṣūṣā şu'lelerinden olan ḳudret A'ziye ve A'friḳye nām ṭarāfları ya'nī aylar ve ġayrı pādişāhlara kevākibler beñzetilmez eger aydınluḳlarıdur ve eger 'aẓimetlük[leri]dür bi'l-külliyā seter ve ḳarañlıḳ ider ve bu nesli mükerrem secā'at ve merdānlıḳ ile dā'imā manṣūr olub bu bābda külliyā Ānāṭūlī ve Ḳaramān ve Diyārbekir ve Arż-ı Rūm ve Baġdād ve Şām memleketleri ve 'Arabistān ve külliyā Mıṣr memleketleri ve Rūm-ili ve Ungurūs ve bundan ġayrı niçe vilāyetler fetḥ ve żabṭ eylemişdür ve Alāmāna degin sınūr ḳodı ve 'Arabistān ṭarāfına nihāyet yirlerine degin sınūr ḳoyub ve A'frīḳada ki ḳıble ṭarāfındadur Ḥabeş ile sınūr ḳodı ve Maġrib ṭarāfına şerīf begi żabṭ eylediği yirlerine degin sınūr ḳonuldı muḥaṣṣalā neslī ḥażret-i 'alī 'Oṣmānuñ olan salṭanatı ve 'aẓīmeti ve ḳudreti ve ġanīliġi ḥaddi [ve] ḥesābı yoḳdur ve niçe müselmān ve naṣrānī begleri ḳapusına ḫarāc virürler ḥāliyā daḫī 'alī neslinden sulṭān-ı selāṭīn būrhān ul-ḫavāḳīn ṣāḥib-ḳırānü'l-zamān ki İskender ẕü'l-ḳarneyne mis̱l olan Sulṭān Süleymān Şāh kendinün şecā'atı ve ḳudret 'aẓamet ve ḥikmet ve 'adālet ve şefaḳat birle şarḳdan ġarba degin ḥükmi geçer el-ḥaṣıl el-kelām 'aẓametliġin ve 'acā'ibliġi ve salṭanatı dīl ile vaṣf idüb ve ḳalem ile yazub beyān ve taḳrīr eylemesine ḳadīr ve ḳābil degildür bu ḫuṣūṣı içün ḥadīşelerün muḳtaṣır üzre yazıldı." Left column, lines 16–34.

13. "Bundan evvel bu vilāyetüñ ḫalḳı cem'isi pūtperestler idiler. Lākin ḥāliyā İspānyol ṭā'ifesi bu vilāyetleri fetḥ eyledüklerinden soñra ehlisi ekşeri Frenk meẕhebine dönmiş . . . İspānyoldan dil ve ḳā'ide ve ġayrı ṭariḳler ögrendiler . . . nice ki Anaṭolunuñ ve Ḳaramanuñ ḫalḳı daḫi Türk ṭā'ifesinden hemçünān dil ve ḳā'ide ögrendiler." Right column, lines 114–116.

14. "Ve bu tercüme ḳadīr olduġım ḳadar aġamuñ emr ile Türk diline yazdum zirā kīm bu dil dünyāda ġayetile ḥükm ider." Left column, lines 150–151.

15. "Ve atlu 'askerden mübālaġa 'askeri var el-ḥaṣıl fehmlü ve ḳuvvetlü pādişāhdur. Ve ẕikr olan Fars vilāyeti ḳadīm zamāndan dükelli maşrıḳ ḫalḳa bir müddet ḥükm eylemişler imiş sınūrları daḫi 'Arab ṭarāfına Rūm-iline degin ta'īn eylediler lākin mu'aẓẓam İskenderüñ ḳuvvetinden muḳābelesine mecālleri ve ḳudretleri olunmadı ecilden maġlūb olub iṭa'aṭlarına gelmişler idi." Left column, lines 122–124.

16. "Merīḫe beñzenildi ki şu'lesile Adīyāyı münevver ider." Left column, line 120.

17. For an in-depth discussion of these efforts, and the policies that motivated them, see Ebru Turan, "The Sultan's Favorite: Ibrahim Pasha and the Making of Ottoman Universal Sovereignty in the Reign of Süleyman the Magnificent" (PhD diss., University of Chicago, 2007), esp. 170–172 and 195–196.

18. See Gülru Necipoğlu, "Süleyman the Magnificent and the Representation of Power in the Context of Ottoman-Hapsburg-Papal Rivalry," *Art Bulletin* 71, no. 3 (1989): 401–427.

19. Ibid., 402.

20. Ménage, "The Map of Hajji Ahmed and Its Makers," 308.

21. Fabris, "The Ottoman Mappa Mundi," 31–37.

22. For a brief biography of Membré, see N. Mahmoud Helmy, "Membré, Michele," in *Dizionario Biografico degli Italiani*, http://www.treccani.it/enciclopedia/michele-membre_(Dizionario-Biografico)/.

23. Necipoğlu, "Süleyman the Magnificent," 402.

24. Gábor Ágoston, "Information, Ideology, and the Limits of Imperial Policy: Ottoman Grand Strategy in the Context of Ottoman-Habsburg Rivalry," in *The Early Modern Ottomans: Remapping the Empire*, ed. Virginia Aksan and Daniel Goffman (Cambridge: Cambridge University Press), 100.

25. For a related discussion of this text, see the contribution of Tijana Krstić in the present volume, as well as a more detailed analysis in Krstić, "Of Translation and Empire: Sixteenth-Century Ottoman Imperial Interpreters as Renaissance Go-Betweens," in *The Ottoman World*, ed. Christine Woodhead (Abingdon: Routledge, 2011). I thank Tijana for sharing her work with me before publication. See also István Borzsák, "A 'Hungarian History' through Turkish Eyes and the Alexander the Great Tradition," in *Occident and Orient: A Tribute to the Memory of Alexander Scheiber*, ed. R. Dán (Budapest: Akadémiai Kiadó, 1998), 31–38.

26. On Maḥmūd Beg's career, see Pál Ács, "Tarjumans Mahmud and Murad: Austrian and Hungarian Renegades as Sultan's Interpreters," in *Europe und die Türken in der Renaissance*, ed. B. Guthmüller and W. Kühlmann (Tübingen: Max Niemeyer Verlag, 2000), 307–316.

27. On this question, see Cornell Fleischer, "The Lawgiver as Messiah: The Making of the Imperial Image in the Reign of Süleyman," in *Soliman le Magnifique et son temps*, ed. Gilles Veinstein (Paris: Galeries Nationales du Grand Palais, 1992), 163–179. For a general discussion of the politics of Ottoman history-writing during the late sixteenth century, see also Baki Tezcan, "The Politics of Early Modern Ottoman Historiography," in *The Early Modern Ottomans: Remapping the Empire*, 167–198.

28. The best-studied example of this type of author is of course Muṣṭafā ʿĀlī. See Cornell Fleischer, *Bureaucrat and Intellectual in the Ottoman Empire: The Historian Mustafa Âli (1541–1600)* (Princeton, N.J.: Princeton University Press, 1986); and Jan Schmidt, *Pure Water for Thirsty Muslims: Muṣṭafā ʿĀlī of Gallipoli's Künhü'l-Aḫbār* (Leiden: Het Oosters Instituut, 1991).

29. For a comparative discussion of the figure of Alexander in the historiography of Mughal India, Safavid Iran, and early modern southeast Asia, see Sanjay Subrahmanyam, "Connected Histories: Notes towards a Reconfiguration of Early Modern Eurasia," *Modern Asian Studies* 31, no. 3 (1997): 735–762. See also Su Fang Ng, "Alexander the Great and Early Modern Classicism from the British Isles to the Malay Archipelago," *Comparative Literature* 58, no. 4 (2006): 293–312.

30. "İskender dünyaya ḥükm idüb yedi iḳlīme mālik olması ġālibā Pādişāh-ı Rūm olduġı gibidür." Seydī ʿAlī Reʾīs, *Mirʾātü'l-Memālik*, in *Mirʾâtü'l-Memâlik: İnceleme, Metin, İndeks*, ed. Mehmet Kiremit (Ankara: Atatürk Kültür Dil ve Tarih Yüksek Kurumu, 1999), 115.

31. "Ḥaḳ budur ki rū-yi zemīnde pādişāhlıḳ nāmı devletlü ḫündigāruñ ḥaḳḳıdur özgenün degüldür." Seydī ʿAlī Reʾīs, *Mirʾātü'l-Memālik*, 116–117.

32. In this respect, the relationship between Seydī ʿAlī Reʾīs and "Hajji Ahmed" can be compared with the development of Portuguese historiography in the Indian Ocean in relationship to the historiographical traditions of Iran and southeast Asia. See Sanjay Subrahmanyam, "Crónica and Tārīkh in the Sixteenth-Century Indian Ocean World," *History and Theory* 49 (2010): 118–145.

33. Quoted in Pınar Emiralioğlu, "Cognizance of the Ottoman World: Visual and Textual Representations in the Sixteenth-Century Ottoman Empire, 1514–1596" (PhD diss., University of Chicago, 2005), 247.

34. On Muṣṭafā ʿĀlī's discussion of Ottoman history in the comparative context of other contemporary empires, see Jan Schmidt, *Mustafa Âli's Künhül-Ahbar and Its Preface According to the Leiden Manuscript* (Leiden: Nederlands Instituut voor het Nabije Oosten, 1987), 50–51. On the life and works

of Celālzāde, see İbrahim Kaya Şahin, "In the Service of the Ottoman Empire: Celālzāde Muṣṭafā, Bureaucrat and Historian" (PhD diss., University of Chicago, 2007).

35. See, for example, two examples of such world maps from copies of Muṣṭafā 'Ālī's *Künhü'l-Aḫbār* in the Topkapı Palace Library, displayed online as part of the recent museum exhibit Piri Reis'ten Katip Çelebi'ye: http://tarihvemedeniyet.org/2009/08/harita-sergisi-piri-reisten-katip-celebiye/.

36. On this question, see H. Erdem Çıpa's discussion of the apposition of *merdümzādes*—the loyal, freeborn Muslim servants of the sultan—and the unfairly privileged *ḳuls* in Celālzāde's *Selīmnāme*. H. Erdem Çıpa, "The Centrality of the Periphery: The Rise to Power of Selīm I, 1487–1512" (PhD diss., Harvard University, 2007), 157–163.

37. For a related discussion of the politicization of science in the late sixteenth century, see Baki Tezcan, "Some Thoughts on the Politicization of Early Modern Science," *Journal of Ottoman Studies* 36 (2010): 135–156.

38. During the grand vizierate of Ibrahim Pasha, for example, the palace of Ibrahim Pasha's boon companion Alvise Gritti in Pera was a well-known center for the patronage of humanist scholars such as Tranquillo Andronico (d. 1571) and Pietro della Valle (d. 1562). See Ebru Turan, "The Sultan's Favorite," 295–296.

39. On this question, see Salih Özbaran, *Bir Osmanlı Kimliği: 14.-17. Yüzyıllarda Rûm/Rûmi Aidiyet ve İmgeleri* (Istanbul: Kitap Yayınevi, 2004); and Cemal Kafadar, "A Rome of One's Own: Reflections on Cultural Geography and Identity in the Lands of Rum," *Muqarnas* 24 (2007): 7–25.

40. Muṣṭafā 'Ālī, *Naṣīḥatü'l-Selāṭīn*, in *Muṣṭafā 'Ālī's Counsel for Sultans of 1581*, ed. and trans. Andreas Tietze (Vienna: Verlag der Österreichischen Akademie der Wissenschaften, 1978), 1:52.

6 From Adam to Süleyman
Visual Representations of Authority in ʿĀrif's Shāhnāma-yi Āl-i ʿOsmān

Fatma Sinem Eryılmaz

In the spring of 1558, the court eulogist ʿĀrif was ready to present the first complete volume of his dynastic literary project *Shāhnāma-yi Āl-i ʿOsmān* (The Shāhnāma of the House of ʿOsmān) to his patron and king Süleyman (r. 1520–1566), the tenth sultan in the dynastic line of Osman.[1] ʿĀrif's was a universal history project consisting of five volumes.[2] The first volume, entitled *Anbiyānāma* (The Book of Prophets), narrates in Persian verse a selection of stories of the biblical antediluvian prophets, including Adam (*Ādam*), Seth (*Shīsh*), Enosh (*Anūsh*), Cainan (*Kanʿān*), Mahalaleel (*Mahlāʾīl*), Jared (*Barad*), Enoch (*Idrīs*), and Noah (*Nūḥ*).[3] The narrative also mentions leading figures from Iranian mythic history, such as kings Kayumars (*Kayūmarṣ*), Zahhak (*Ḍaḥḥāk*), and (especially) Jamshid (*Jamshīd*).[4]

In fact, as the title of ʿĀrif's project indicates, the literary and, to a lesser extent, visual program of *Shāhnāma-yi Āl-i ʿOsmān* adopted the Persian poet Firdawsī's (d. 1020) classic rendering of Iranian mythic history in his *Shāhnāma* written at the beginning of the eleventh century. In *Anbiyānāma,* two of the ten miniatures depict selected moments from the reign of the great Iranian King Jamshid: Jamshid with the old lady and Jamshid being slain in two.[5] Aspiring to write a second *Shāhnāma,* the great classic of the Islamicate cultural world, more than five hundred years later was a rather daring—if not arrogant—feat for a writer. Adapting an epic that chronicles the mythic past of a rivaling eastern neighbor in order to glorify Ottoman lineage and its contemporaneous descendants could have been considered downright haughty.

Leaving the possible judgment of their Safavid contemporaries aside, what concerns us here is the visual and literary descriptions of the ideal ruler in *Anbiyānāma.* I have argued elsewhere that the Ottoman *Shāhnāma* of ʿĀrif portrays Sultan Süleyman as an ideal ruler, divinely selected and favored to lead, guide, and legislate humanity, over whom he also had the right to exercise jurisdiction.[6] In this essay, I argue that the foundations for the image of Süleyman as a quasi-prophet-king were established in word and image in the first volume of ʿĀrif's *Anbiyānāma.*

Adam's Authority

If *Anbiyānāma* has a primary hero, it is certainly Adam. After the twelve introductory folios, fifteen of the remaining thirty-five explain the story of Adam from God's blowing of his soul into Adam's body to his death. Three of the ten miniatures in the visual program of the book were also dedicated to moments in Adam's life. They depict Adam giving the first sermon,[7] Eve giving Adam the grain of Paradise,[8] and the sacrifice of his sons Cain and Abel.[9] The visual representation of Adam's leadership in the first two of these three images in *Anbiyānāma* will be the first analytical focus of this essay.

In the second chapter (*sūra*) of the Qur'an it is written that God announced to the angels his intention to create a viceroy. When the angels showed their dismay by questioning his decision to create a human being who would cause war and bloodshed on earth and to place him over the angels—who have always glorified and adored him—God reminded them that surely he knew things that the angels did not. God then taught Adam the names of all things and ordered him to teach these names to the angels.[10] The knowledge of names—given to him by God—provided Adam a higher status than the angels, who had not been shown the same divine favor; Adam's act of teaching these names to the angels, thereby sharing the knowledge given to him by the divine source, confirmed this supremacy. The first miniature of Adam in *Anbiyānāma* is a representation of this supremacy (fig. 6.1).

In the miniature, a flying angel brings an already crowned Adam a bunch of grapes on a tray while the other angels are standing or kneeling before him respectfully. Adam is depicted standing in a pulpit (*minbar*), wearing a stately robe and a crown. The pulpit is the only architectonic element in the representation. The contrast between the angels sitting or standing in a spatially ambiguous state and Adam looking down at them from the enclosure of the pulpit adds an iconic quality to Adam's figure.

This iconic quality becomes even stronger due to the extension of the image of Adam in the pulpit beyond the page. It is worthwhile to pause a moment to imagine how this book would be viewed and preserved: ordinarily, one would fold the oversized part of the page as he or she closed the book. However, once the page is folded, the pulpit cannot be seen. Thus, when the reader/viewer opened the double folios in which the image is laid on the recto, he would encounter a group of angels looking toward the left in anticipation. Only upon opening the folded part would one see the object of the angels' gaze: the crowned Adam addressing them from a pulpit in gold. The unveiling of Adam's image in the pulpit must have enhanced its impact.

As for the angels who constitute Adam's audience, most of them are seated on bent knees, resembling respectful madrasa students, while a few are standing. A more accurate description would be that most are kneeling in the posture of the Islamic community in a mosque, with those at the back standing due to the lack of space.

The extraordinary aspect of this image results from its thematic choice. To my knowledge, *Anbiyānāma* is singular in representing Adam's first sermon to the angels.

Figure 6.1. Adam's first sermon, ʿĀrif, *Anbiyānāma*, 1558. Bruschettini Foundation for Islamic and Asian Art, 15a.

In manuscripts on the life stories of the prophets, the scene that is usually chosen for representation at this point in the narrative is the angels' reverence toward Adam. Adam's divinely bestowed superior position, juxtaposed with the angels' subjugated posture before him, invites clear associations with the relationship between an absolute ruler and his subjects. In the visual idiom, this association has most often been delivered by the symbols of universal earthly authority, such as the hexagonal throne and the crown. Below are two examples belonging to the same genre and period as 'Ārif's *Anbiyānāma*.

In a copy of a book thematically similar to *Anbiyānāma*, al-Tha'labī's (Aḥmad b. Muḥammad b. Ibrāhīm Abū Isḥāḳ al-Nīsābūrī, d. 1035) *Qiṣaṣ al-Anbiyā'* (The Stories of the Prophets), we encounter an example of this popular scene.[11] In this representation, the scene is depicted indoors in a courtly atmosphere; the view with trees to Adam's right indicates the Garden of Paradise (fig. 6.2).

Adam is represented sitting in a royal cross-legged position on a hexagonal throne. He is wearing the helmet-like crown typical in depictions of heavenly figures and pre-Islamic Iranian kings. Here, however, the angels are bareheaded, with their hair tied at the top rather than hidden under a crown. The angels' hairstyle—hair collected on top of their heads—is not an unusual detail per se; in fact, it is common in such compositions. At the same time, the contrasting depiction of angels with helmet-like crowns in all of the other images in the manuscript strongly suggests that in this scene the absence of the angels' crowns is intentional. In this image, the prophet's unique crown appears to indicate his kingly status—and hence his political authority.

In another copy of al-Tha'labī's popular work we encounter the representation of the same event: the reverence of the angels before Adam.[12] In this miniature, Adam is depicted sitting on a hexagonal throne wearing both a crown and a fiery nimbus to which an angel is adding more fire (fig. 6.3).

In the top left corner of the image, another angel is waiting with a tray of additional fire behind a hill. Some of the angels are depicted wearing crowns while others are bareheaded.

To Adam's right another angel is bringing a crown. The representation of the first crown (with the fiery nimbus) in an image in which Adam is bestowed with two crowns suggests that the first crown, the one that he is already wearing, represents his spiritual authority, while the crown that is being brought to him by an angel indicates his political authority. In this way, earthly and spiritual authorities are represented separately, by two crowns, one with and the other without the nimbus. Furthermore, according to the chronology represented in this image, God had bestowed spiritual authority on Adam prior to political authority. Hence, the reverence of the angels becomes part of Adam's political coronation ceremony.

Both manuscripts mentioned above were produced probably in the second half of the sixteenth century, like 'Ārif's *Anbiyānāma*, and all three belong to the same royal collection. In the first example, the scene of the angels' reverence to Adam narrates his

Figure 6.2. The reverence of the angels, al-Thaʿlābī, *Qiṣaṣ al-Anbiyāʾ*, probably sixteenth century. TPML, Istanbul, E.H. 1430, 8a.

Figure 6.3. The reverence of the angels, al-Thaʿlābī, *Qiṣaṣ al-Anbiyāʾ*, probably sixteenth century. TPML, Istanbul, H. 1226, 8b.

supremacy over the angels as the viceroy-king of God. While the spiritual dimensions of the scene would always be obvious to the viewer (i.e., the incident takes place in Paradise with the first Islamic prophet and angels), in this image it was not the aspect that was emphasized.

In the second image, two separate forms of Adam's authority over the angels, one spiritual and the other political, are indicated. These two forms are interrelated, as both stem from divine will and favor. Moreover, the image points to a certain temporal order in the bestowal of these authorities: Adam's spiritual authority precedes his political authority over the heavenly inhabitants of Paradise.

As in the second example, *Anbiyānāma*'s Adam, too, is granted two crowns and hence two forms of authority. Furthermore, the order of the crowns is repeated: first he receives the crown of spiritual authority and only then the crown of political authority. We read:

When the angels saw God apparent on his face
They threw themselves in prostration with much pomp
To the prayer niche (*miḥrāb*) of the curved eyebrow of that heart-soothing one
The angels positioned themselves for prayer one by one
By chance that day marked by auspicious light
Was a Friday of the week according to that time
When Adam was honored that Friday
He was glorified by the Almighty with the angels' reverent prostration[13]

The text relates the reverence of the angels and Adam's role as the "imam" of the Islamic community, which was at this point composed of angels. The text continues by stating that the incident took place on a Friday of the week within the temporal concept of Paradise, suggesting parallels between the images of the angels' reverential position before Adam and the Islamic community's following their imam in Friday prayers as he guides them through the steps of prayer, alternating between standing, kneeling, and prostrating positions according to the various stations in the prayer scheme.[14]

After the explanation that Friday was given as holiday to Adam's descendants as a result of the angels' honoring him on a Friday, the text continues:

When God bestowed Adam with such guidance
He adorned the crown of his head with the Crown of Salvation
With the hand of His intrinsic divine power
He invested his body with the robes of Paradise
He taught him all names
He subjugated all things to him
He then ordered a throne of divine light (*nūr*)
The angels placed it due to their disposition and joy
On the select path, God's Pure One
Climbed up the throne with the Crown of Magnanimity[15]

We should note here that the position of Adam as the imam of his community does not limit his status to merely that of a guide in Friday prayers for the Islamic congregation. Instead, according to *Anbiyānāma,* Adam becomes the first imam who has the spiritual authority to lead the community of believers on the path to salvation. Hence the first of the two crowns that he was granted by God is the Crown of Salvation.

According to the text of *Anbiyānāma,* he is then invested with the royal robe that is depicted in the image of him giving the first sermon. When God teaches him the names of all things, the divine knowledge passed to Adam makes him sovereign to everything he knows as such. After God orders Adam a throne of divine light, Adam walks up the steps toward his throne with the second crown granted to him: the Crown of Magnanimity.

The narrative continues with the angels lifting the throne on their shoulders and circumambulating the heavens. This act of glorification becomes further confirmation of Adam's suzerainty over the heavens as God's viceroy, for he names all of the angels he sees on his tour and thereby confirms his dominion over them. Following the circumambulation, God orders the archangel Gabriel to announce that the heavenly residents are to gather in rows to listen to Adam's sermon.[16]

ʿĀrif then continues to describe the royal appearance of Adam, adorned with glittering precious stones, gold, and pearls. On his finger is a royal seal of ruby and pearls; his two tresses are likewise ornamented with star-like gems.[17] In a royal robe adorned with precious jewels and gold, wearing the Crown of Magnanimity as well as a seal ring and possessing a throne of divine light, Adam is described as the sovereign of Paradise only after God himself.[18]

As we have noted, Adam's political authority was also represented in paintings of the reverence of the angels in both copies of al-Thaʿlābī's *Qiṣaṣ al-Anbiyāʾ*. Furthermore, ʿĀrif's differentiation between two types of authority is similar to the one made in the second example discussed above. In contrast to these two manuscripts, however, in *Anbiyānāma* the reverence of the angels is not represented visually. Instead, the textual descriptions stand as a prelude to Adam's first sermon, which is depicted with a miniature. The double representation—literary and visual—of Adam's delivering his divine knowledge as a sermon underlines its importance. At the same time, it pushes the conventionally preferred scene of the reverence of the angels to a secondary position.

Here a phenomenological clarification is needed: authority derived from knowledge does not comprise an overriding power; angels possessed many powers that the human Adam did not. Furthermore, authority based on knowledge does not guarantee political power. In both the Judeo-Christian and Islamic traditions, God appointed Adam as his viceroy over the angels and put this decision into practice by sharing his knowledge and appointing him as a teacher. Hence, Adam's authority comes, first, through God's will, second, through God's favoring him in his act of sharing knowledge, and, finally, through Adam's acquired knowledge. In other words, while knowledge is empowering, as is demonstrated in the story of Adam in the Qur'an, in *Anbiyānāma*, and in Islamicate and Judeo-Christian literature in general, power is not contingent upon knowledge.

Instead, Adam's divinely bestowed sacred knowledge confirms his spiritual authority as the first imam to lead the Muslim community on the right path to salvation. At the same time, it confirms his political authority. *Anbiyānāma* states openly what is implied in the Qur'an: the angels suffer embarrassment remembering their initial doubt in accepting Adam as God's viceroy. They realize his superior knowledge as he explains the process of Creation in his sermon. In other words, Adam not only delivers the names of all things but also has a further knowledge of events only known to God as the Creator. Bearing in mind the association of the deliverance of the Friday sermon first as a declaration and then as a confirmation of political authority in Islamic political history, we should note that *Anbiyānāma* depicts the first sermon of its kind.

Anbiyānāma's second depiction of Adam's legacy concerns the well-known topic of his sinning by eating the forbidden fruit of Paradise. The particularity of this scene stems once again from its thematic choice, which contrasts discretely but nevertheless clearly with the convention as we know it.

Adam Loses His Kingdom

The *Anbiyānāma* scene depicts the moment shortly before the sinning of Adam. In the Garden, Eve is seen offering her partner a cluster of wheat (fig. 6.4).

Both image and text draw a clear parallel between Adam's fall from grace and his losing his kingship. Off of his centrally placed hexagonal throne, he is seen accepting the wheat from Eve. The presence of the peacock and a figure that seems to be Satan, along with the serpent, confirms that among the volumes in the current royal Ottoman collection on the lives of the prophets, *Anbiyānāma*'s version of the story of the original sin as described in this miniature corresponds only to the version in the *Qiṣaṣ* of al-Kisā'ī (fl. ca. 1100). To my knowledge, only in *Qiṣaṣ* and *Anbiyānāma* are each of the three figures conspiring against Adam and Eve present, Satan unhidden.[19]

In the version narrated in al-Kisā'ī's *Qiṣaṣ* and 'Ārif's *Anbiyānāma*, Satan promises that he will teach the peacock, the most beautiful bird of Paradise, the three words that can save him from old age, illness, and death; thus, he convinces the peacock to help him enter Paradise. The peacock, being afraid of the Guard of Paradise (*Riḍwān*), fetches the serpent, the mistress of the beasts of Paradise, to help Satan. Seduced by the same promise, the serpent agrees to take Satan between her fangs to Paradise. There, Satan carries out his plan of temptation by approaching Eve. He talks to her first through the mouth of the serpent and then outside of the serpent's body, pretending to be a slave who had eaten from the Forbidden Tree and hence gained eternal life.[20]

Like the story of the angels' reverence toward Adam, the sinning of Adam and Eve is a theme commonly illustrated in manuscripts of the prophets' life stories. As is noted

Figure 6.4. Adam and Eve about to eat the forbidden fruit, ʿĀrif, *Anbiyānāma*, 1558. Bruschettini Foundation for Islamic and Asian Art, 20a.

above, once again the moment depicted in the *Anbiyānāma* miniature differs clearly from the moment typically represented in the narration of the sinning of Adam and Eve in Paradise.

In contrast to the image in *Anbiyānāma*, in many of the miniatures from the Ottoman palace collection the two protagonists of the scene are depicted in exodus, after they have sinned.[21] They are conventionally drawn mounted on or standing by a fearsome dragon and a beautifully executed peacock (fig. 6.5).

Artists' preference for representing these animals in such fabulous fashion suggests that the scene owes much of its allure to the exoticism that the image of the peacock and the serpent in the Garden of Paradise promises.

The *Anbiyānāma* miniature treats these two animals much more literally. Here, the awe-inspiring images of the two animals are reduced in size and importance to de facto participants in the incident. The peacock looks more like a humble goose than its majestic self and the snake is merely a snake and not a dragon. The two animals are pushed aside to the bottom right of the image, along with the dwarfed Satan. In this way, the composition highlights the importance of Adam and Eve, who are the largest figures.

Moreover, as in the manuscripts in the Ottoman royal collection mentioned above, the convention has Adam and Eve half-naked, each with only a skirt made of leaves. In the *Anbiyānāma* depiction, however, both figures are dressed in royal outfits, hence stealing further from the exoticism of the scene.

The verses on the page do not describe Adam becoming aware of his nakedness, nor do they narrate the actual moment depicted in the image; instead, they describe its aftermath. The text explains that Adam was literally stripped of his garments and the insignia of kingship: he loses his throne, crown, and seal ring. In this way, his nakedness becomes a metaphor for his descending to a baser state after losing the supremacy and glory God bestowed upon him earlier:

> His crown flew off his head because of that sin
> His hand became empty of its ring, his head bare of its crown
> His belt fell from his waist onto the ground
> The seal ring dropped down from his fingers
> His body became bare of crown and garment
> Just like a branch in autumn is made to suffer by a strong wind[22]

The message that Adam loses his kingdom after he sins is further underlined in the *Anbiyānāma* miniature by the presence of his community, watching the events unfold from under a portico. This community becomes audience to the most decisive event in human history as it was conceived in the Judeo-Christian and Islamic traditions. At the same time, its existence confirms Adam's political stance as a ruler. After all, a ruler, by definition, needs subjects to rule.

Although each of the angels is depicted with a standard hairstyle—their head crowned either by an elegant knot of their long hair or by a golden helmet-crown—here they are represented, curiously, without visible wings. Without their characteristic

Figure 6.5. Expulsion of Adam and Eve, al-Tha'labī, *Qiṣaṣ al-Anbiyā'*, probably sixteenth century. TPML, Istanbul, H. 1225, 14b.

multicolored wings, this elegantly dressed and mostly crowned group of figures also resembles a royal crowd.

The presence in *Anbiyānāma* of a relatively long section and two miniatures on the reputed Iranian king Jamshid's fall from divine grace and loss of his throne evokes an association with Adam's story. It also suggests that, among other functions, *Anbiyānāma* might have been intended as advice literature, with examples of even prophets and legendary kings sinning and losing their divine favor. If so, it is possible that the resemblance of the group under the portico to a royal assembly is intended to create self-consciousness among the royal readers/viewers who would see in the group their look-alikes.

Whether they are merely angels whose wings are hidden behind them or they stand in for a royal assembly in order to teach a lesson to *Anbiyānāma*'s royal readers, at least a part of their function is clear. Along with the architecturally organized space, they stress the political and "worldly" kingship of Adam at this stage, ironically in the "heavenly" Garden. Indeed, with her crown and courtly dress, Eve, too, looks like a queen.

Let us take a moment to recapitulate what we have observed thus far in the version of Adam's story represented in *Anbiyānāma*. We have seen that God granted Adam two forms of authority, spiritual and political. The existence of these separate forms is made clear in the text by the representation of each form through a specifically named crown: the Crown of Salvation for spiritual and the Crown of Magnanimity for political authority. Later, when Adam eats the forbidden fruit of Paradise, he is stripped of his political authority. The next time he is represented visually in *Anbiyānāma,* in the image of his sons' sacrificial offerings to God, Adam is depicted bareheaded but with a nimbus: he is no longer a king, but he is still a prophet. We have also seen that both the political and spiritual natures of his authority are confirmed by his teaching the sacred knowledge he received from God to the rest of the Muslim community in Paradise.

The Science of the Prophets

While Adam's spiritual and especially his political authority are represented in manuscripts other than *Anbiyānāma,* the emphasis on the science of the prophets appears particular to this volume. Considered from this perspective, Adam's not only teaching the names of things but also delivering a sermon on God's creating power is an interpolation on his sacred knowledge that is formally delimited in the Qur'an and Islamic literature to "the names of all things."

The emphasis on the science of the prophets is embellished by the regular repetition of its transmission through his descendants. Indeed, the passing of the authority-confirming divine knowledge to Adam's chosen line of descendants is articulated clearly in ʿĀrif's text. Time after time we read that the arriving prophet is equipped with divine light (designated often by an adjectival or nominal compound that includes the word *farr,* such as *farrahī* or *farrukh*) and wisdom based on knowledge (*dānish*), such as in the case of Jared or Enoch.

The volume's visual program further underlines the significance of the science of the prophets. Three of *Anbiyānāma*'s ten miniatures represent the relevant prophets exercising their teaching capacities. Aside from the representation of Adam's sermon, there are two other representations of this theme. The depictions of Adam's last son and rightful heir Seth teaching tailoring and his descendant Enoch teaching writing deliver the message that the capacity of each of the *Anbiyānāma* prophets to teach the science (*'ilm*) that he had received from God is one of the most important themes explored in the manuscript.

Nevertheless, just as the construct of Adam's separate political and spiritual authorities is not an invention in 'Ārif's book, neither are the themes of the empowering and authority-confirming wisdom of the prophets and their capacity as teachers. These themes are extended variations of the references in the Qur'an concerning prophets.

In the Sura of the Prophets (*al-Anbiyā'*) it is stated that God gave Lot ruling authority (or jurisdiction) (*ḥukm*) and science (*'ilm*).[23] Shortly after, when referring to Solomon and David, the same phrase is reiterated: God gave them all ruling authority (or jurisdiction) and science.[24] In other words, the spiritual guidance that is included in the meaning of Islamic prophethood was accompanied by two other qualities, political authority and sacred knowledge, both of which were bestowed as graces by God.

It is no coincidence that the same terminology—involving the grammatical roots of the words for ruling authority and science in Arabic—is used by the angels in reference to God. In the second chapter of the Qur'an, in the section on his appointment of Adam as his viceroy, after teaching Adam all names, God asks the angels to name things.[25] The angels appear to have only partial knowledge of the names and say that they only know what God has taught them. They conclude their reply with the submissive and glorifying words, "You are the possessor of science (*al-'alīm*) and ruling authority (*al-ḥakīm*)."[26]

The use of the same vocabulary in the Qur'an's second chapter and in the twenty-first chapter on prophets indicates that a relationship mimicking that between God and the angels is envisioned between God's appointed prophets, who were also anointed with sacred knowledge, and the Islamic community. Naturally, the latter relationship conforms to a much humbler scale, for in Islam prophets were human agents appointed by God and did not possess divine knowledge in its entirety.

Returning to 'Ārif's text, we can state that, rather than pure creativity, it is, first, the persistent and consistent exploitation of these themes and, second, its unique choice of thematic emphasis in both literary and visual programs that mark a difference between *Anbiyānāma* and other books on the prophets' life stories. Could we, or should we, however, classify 'Ārif's volume as an example of the genre of *Qiṣaṣ al-Anbiyā'*? How can we justify the inclusion of a significant section with two miniatures on the Persian king Jamshid and shorter references to other well-known names of Persian mythic history, such as the kings Kayumars, Zahhak, and Merdas (*Merdās*), Zahhak's father? What does an "Ottoman *Shāhnāma*" mean when we consider 'Ārif's work?

The Question of Genre

Although thematically *Anbiyānāma* approaches the genre of stories of the prophets, it cannot be properly classified as such. Aside from the selective inclusion of Iranian mythic history, we should not disregard the fact that *Anbiyānāma* was not conceived as an independent work. It was the first of a five-volume universal history project. A comparison with another Ottoman *Shāhnāma* project that ʿĀrif began, the giant Imperial Scroll (*Ṭomār-ı Hümayun*), allows us to suggest a probable organizational scheme.[27]

After an introductory section and two disk-maps, the narrative of the Scroll is delivered in the form of a genealogical tree. Despite its very different format, the Scroll also tells its version of universal history from Adam, originally, to Sultan Süleyman.[28] As in the five-volume history project, in the Scroll information is organized in five consecutive sections demarcated by the visual contrast between them.

The Scroll's first section corresponds to *Anbiyānāma* and comes to an end with the Flood in Noah's time: the Flood is represented by the visual effect of a rushing flood of interwoven words[29] (fig. 6.6).

Hence, the second section of human history begins with the aftermath of the Flood and continues until the arrival of Prophet Muhammad. While the third runs through Islamic history and finds its conclusion with the appearance of Osman, the eponymous founder of the Ottoman dynasty, on the historical stage, the fourth section of the Scroll is marked by the history of the Ottoman state until Sultan Süleyman, who lifts the curtain for the fifth, and originally last, act.

If we follow the same scheme for ʿĀrif's history in book format, the currently extinct second volume of the project must have continued chronologically, narrating the stories of the Islamic prophets and Iranian mythic kings after the time of Noah, most probably until Prophet Muhammad. The likewise extinct third volume would then narrate principally Islamic history until the debut of the Ottoman dynasty.

ʿOsmānnāma, the extant fourth volume of ʿĀrif's *Shāhnāma,* continues the narration from the time of Osman Beg and provides a chronological account of Ottoman history.[30] It arrives at an immature break in the immediate aftermath of the death of Bayezid I (r. 1389–1402) in captivity in 1402. In the fourth volume, the relatively haphazard placement of the colophon, which appears to have been added later, strongly suggests that the text was meant to continue. The originally planned end must have been the death of Selim I (r. 1512–1520), for the fifth and final volume is dedicated to the time of the reigning sultan Süleyman, the son of Selim.

As the first volume of a universal history project that includes religious, mythic, and political history as well as a propagandist emphasis on the Ottoman Empire and its contemporaneous sultan, to which genre does *Anbiyānāma* belong? I suggest that we start seeking the answer by exploring the present inventory of the royal collection to which it belonged, in order to see the relevant works prepared before and around the time that ʿĀrif and his team were producing their work.

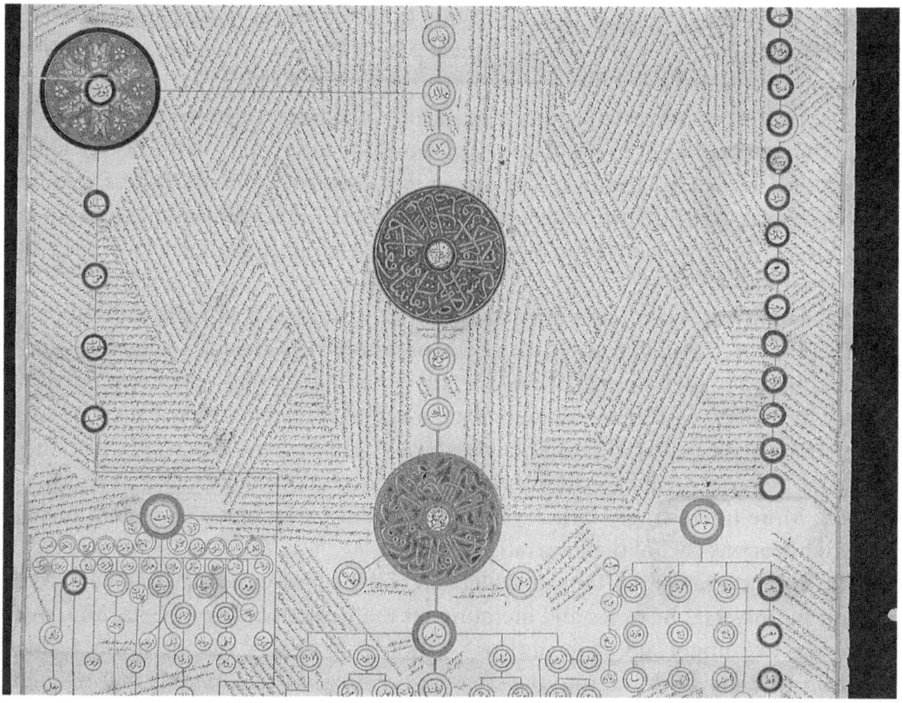

Figure 6.6. Visual representation of the Flood in Noah's time. *Ṭomār-Hümāyūn,* 'Ārif/Eflāṭūn, around 1560, TPML, Istanbul, A. 3599.

The Stories of the Prophets and Universal Histories in the Topkapı Collection

There are eleven volumes in Persian on the histories of the prophets in Topkapı Palace Museum's manuscript library. Eight are sixteenth-century copies of al-Tha'lābī's *Qiṣaṣ al-Anbiyā*[31] and one is the work of Muḥammad b. al-Ḥasan al-Daydūzamī (d. 13th c.).[32] We have already discussed some of the visual representations in these copies. The authors of the other two *Qiṣaṣ* are anonymous.[33] Among the Arabic manuscripts in this genre, at least fourteen were prepared before the seventeenth century[34] and at least five of the copies in Arabic are of al-Kisā'ī's work from the same period.[35] As we have seen above, some narrative details of the textual and visual depictions of Adam and Eve eating the forbidden wheat in *Anbiyānāma* closely correspond to the narration of the same story in al-Kisā'ī's collection.

Among Topkapı Palace Museum's Arabic manuscripts are also two copies of al-Tha'lābī's *Qiṣaṣ al-Anbiyā',*[36] one of which (A. 2964) was prepared in 1556, about two years before *Anbiyānāma*'s date of completion. Furthermore, the Topkapı collection includes six volumes of what seem to belong to the same set of Muḥammad b. Jarīr al-Ṭabarī's (d. 923) universal history in Arabic.[37] In its Persian collection presently there is only one translated copy of this work (E.H. 1390) from the eighteenth century.[38]

The interest in universal history that includes the histories of the prophets is visible in the other holdings of the library, which include nine copies of the universal history of Muḥammad b. Mirkhwand (d. 1497–1498), *Rawżat al-ṣafā*.[39] Of these volumes, seven were prepared after the sixteenth century. Of the sixteenth-century copies, however, one (A. 2916) was copied in 1553, when 'Ārif's own universal history project was in preparation.

Şükrullāh's (d. 1459–1460) *Bahjat al-Tawārīkh* (R. 1538) is present with two copies. The Topkapı catalogue also lists a copy of *Tawārīkh-i ʿālam* (A. 2935) by Aḥmad b. Muḥammad b. Muḥammad al-Bukhārī (d. 13th c.). Another well-known universal history in the current Persian manuscript collection is Rashīd al-Dīn's (d. 1318) *Jāmiʿ al-Tawārīkh,* represented with three copies: H. 1653, H. 1654, and R. 1518.[40] Each of these universal histories treats the life stories of the prophets, though often in summary fashion. More interestingly, Ṭabarī's history and Bukhārī's *Tawārīkh-i ʿālam* include Iranian history as part of their narrative program.

The brief survey of the Topkapı collection sketched above demonstrates a marked interest in universal histories and literature on the stories of the prophets. Moreover, it displays two important characteristics of universal history-writing in the Islamic tradition that survived well into the sixteenth century. First, it reveals that religious and political histories were conceived as integral parts of the same story of human civilization. While the non-division between the sacred and secular should not be surprising in a pre-modern universal history, it is still worthwhile to revise it as we seek to understand the cultural origins of ʿĀrif's work.

The second significant trait of the Topkapı collection is the acceptance of mythic history outside of the domain of the three Religions of the Book—Judaism, Christianity, and Islam—but within the domain of universal history. In the case of Islamic historiography, the principal reference was Iranian mythology brought to a comprehensive written form by Firdawsī in his *Shāhnāma* at the very beginning of the eleventh century. Although the inclusion of mythic history does not appear to be obligatory, as we have seen in the examples included in the Topkapı collection, it certainly presents itself as a valid option.

For the purposes of this essay, it suffices to note that the inclusion of Iranian mythic history in Ṭabarī and Bukhārī's histories provides precedence for *Anbiyānāma* and places it within a certain line of tradition in universal history-writing. Consequently, narrating the life story of the Iranian mythic king Jamshid in the first volume of ʿĀrif's universal history is not an anomaly. As a result, notwithstanding its thematic proximity to the genre of stories of the prophets, we can formally classify *Anbiyānāma* as the first chapter of a pre-modern universal history project that combined Islamicate religious, political, and mythical history in its special amalgam.

Nevertheless, I argue that, for ʿĀrif, writing linear history was only a means to an end. I contend that ʿĀrif and his team, while maintaining the outer shell of a universal history, are telling a further story, that of Sultan Süleyman's special role in history, as it begins from Creation. The hints of this story can be found in what has been defined as the two characteristics that mark *Anbiyānāma*'s differences from similar books: its persistent and consistent exploitation of the themes of the nature of authority and the science of the prophets and its singular thematic choices, which are emphasized in its visual program. In order to investigate the particular treatment of these issues in *Anbiyānāma,* let us revisit the genre to which it is thematically, if not conceptually, most related.

The Literature on the Prophets' Life Stories and *Anbiyānāma:* A Comparison of Interests

Whether as individual works or as parts of larger histories, the stories of the lives of the prophets owed their popularity among the various social classes of medieval and pre-modern Near Eastern society not only to the religious significance of their subject matter but also to the curious details they explained. These stories narrated events of a distant past with different norms. People lived for many hundreds of years. God communicated much more directly with humans. Even if they were not the order of the day, miracles were not uncommon. Although their intrinsic truth was not doubted by the faithful, the prophets' life stories certainly shared much with folkloric fairy tales and mythology in their frequent inclusion of extraordinary and exotic details. These curious details provided material for the illustrations of the books of the genre. The representations of Paradise, prophets, elegant and colorful angels, and other extraordinary creatures added further attraction to the written texts.

In the case of *Anbiyānāma,* however, we observe that the typical allure of the genre of prophets' life stories was not effectively exploited visually. Instead of Adam and Eve in exodus on wondrous animals, for example, we see them more statically placed as the king and queen of Paradise just before their losing their kingdom. The obvious choice for Noah's story, his ark loaded with pairs of animals, is rejected in favor of a range of calamities possibly suffered by the disobedient and the unfaithful. It is not the intrinsically sinister representation of the crow teaching Cain how to bury his brother, whose corpse Cain is typically depicted carrying and that we see in *Anbiyānāma.* Instead, God's choice of the brothers' sacrificial offerings is represented.

Unfortunately, many of the manuscripts that represent the stories of the prophets in word and image are not dated properly. Among those that are dated, the books produced earlier than *Anbiyānāma* are not illustrated. It seems that the illustration of books of this genre began in or around the sixteenth century.[41] Hence, we are not in a position to state that ʿĀrif and his team of artists stepped out of an already existing artistic convention with the scenes that are depicted and the moments that are emphasized in *Anbiyānāma.* Still, this should not hinder us from insisting on *Anbiyānāma*'s diversity. Even if all of the extant illustrated manuscripts in the genre were dated after it, we can say that *Anbiyānāma*'s thematic choices were not aesthetically convincing enough to establish a tradition for books of this genre produced for the Ottoman palace in the 1570s.[42] While the *Anbiyānāma* depictions maintain their own beauty, they do not whet the viewer's appetite for curiosity.

Aesthetic criticism is not what is intended here. Instead, I argue that the thematic and compositional choices made in *Anbiyānāma* point toward other priorities, which were dictated to a large degree by the tastes and needs of the sultan and his court. In other words, the wonderful images of an illustrated book on the prophets' lives produced during the reign of Murad III (r. 1574–1595) might not have found the same favorable reception in the court of the older and ailing Süleyman.

In the case of *Anbiyānāma*, we have images that are not mere illustrations to add color and wonder to the text: they add aesthetic value, but they are not only decorative. Rather, they form an integral part of the narrative. They tell the stories of prophets and kings acquiring and at times losing political or spiritual authority and divine favor.[43] They demonstrate the disobedience of the first humans and prophets against God's rules and that, ultimately, they were always punished.[44]

In addition, we have seen that *Anbiyānāma*'s visual program presents teaching and civilizing the Islamic community as essential parts of the nature of prophethood.[45] Consequently, if we take the images in *Anbiyānāma* of Adam giving a sermon and Seth and Enoch teaching as representations of exemplary actions, we conclude that it is a responsibility of the prophets to share with their community the knowledge granted to them by God and transferred to them through the genealogy of Adam.

Interestingly, despite the book's title *Anbiyānāma* (The Book of Prophets), ʿĀrif rarely uses the term for prophet either in its singular or plural form—that is, *nabī* or *anbiyāʾ*. Thus, he also avoids engaging directly in the controversy among Islamic scholars concerning who among Adam's descendants until Noah was a prophet (*nabī*) and who was merely a deputy (*khalīfa*). Still, in the chapter headings, only after the names of Adam, Seth, Enoch, and Noah does ʿĀrif use the respectful phrase "peace be upon him," designating these men as Islamic prophets. Likewise, the name of Jamshid, who is one of the most important protagonists of the volume, does not appear even once in the chapter headings. In this way ʿĀrif acknowledges that Jamshid is not an actual Islamic prophet or a saint. With these measures, ʿĀrif carefully remains within the parameters of Islamic orthodoxy. Without crossing these boundaries, he tells his own "dynastic story."

All of the messages, the exemplary qualities and human errors of *Anbiyānāma* prophets and kings are described in word and image with what we can call "dynastic vocabulary." Although most of the same stories are included—albeit often in much shorter versions—in other world histories and stories of the prophets, in *Anbiyānāma* they are narrated with a "dynastic" perspective. From such a perspective, whether or not the protagonists of these stories are considered "prophets" (*anbiyāʾ*) is only of secondary importance: all of the biblical figures are God's deputies (*khalīfa*), or viceroys, on earth. They all inherit divine light (*farr*) and sacred knowledge (*dānish*). In this way, 'Ārif's storytelling in *Anbiyānāma* approximates the succession of prophets to dynastic succession.

Anbiyānāma's protagonists leave their "thrones" to their heirs. There are rightful heirs, like Seth, and those who try to usurp authority, like Cain. In filial relationships, the father is always in the right. In contrast, we read of both obedient (Abel, Seth, Enoch, Mahalaleel, Kayumars) and disobedient (Cain, Noah's son, Zahhak) sons.

Fraternal relationships are mentioned only in cases of inherent tension. Cain, disobeying God's rule, kills his brother Abel to marry his own twin sister, who was to be the rightful wife of Abel. Later, Seth kills his unbelieving, murdering brother Cain. Mahalaleel holds an assembly composed of dignitaries and his brother Kayumars after his father, Cainan's, death. They are both capable sons, but their father had declared Mahalaleel his rightful heir. The tension is resolved by Kayumars's unconditional obedience to his brother: now that their father was dead, leaving Mahalaleel as his rightful heir, Kayumars was obliged to see his brother as father and king.

Significantly, this meeting invites a nearly one-to-one correspondence with the imagined meeting between Osman's sons Orhan (r. 1324–1361) and Alaüddin (d. 1331) in *'Oṣmānnāma,* the fourth volume of 'Ārif's Ottoman *Shāhnāma.* Due to Alaüddin's compliancy, Orhan's meeting with his brother also ends in a similar, peaceful fashion. After reading the detailed descriptions of these invented meetings in *Anbiyānāma* and *'Oṣmānnāma,* one cannot help but wonder: Were these meetings conjured in order to set examples to Sultan Süleyman's two remaining sons, Bayezid (d. 1561) and Selim (r. 1566–1574)?

As a matter of fact, the issue of dynastic succession had been an open wound for the Ottoman dynasty since its days as a budding principality at the beginning of the fourteenth century. Sultan Süleyman's great-grandfather Mehmed II (r. 1444–1446 and 1451–1481) had even legalized fraternal bloodshed with a law code declaring that it was acceptable for the prince upon whom sovereignty was bestowed by God to kill his brothers for the sake of public order.[46] However, it was Süleyman's father Selim I who had raised the level of violence to a level never seen before. In his late teens, then-prince Süleyman witnessed his father's massacre of his uncles, nephews, and probably his grandfather in order to seize the Ottoman throne. Needless to say, for a prince, murdering his own father was never deemed acceptable, by law or by custom.

As he started aging, Sultan Süleyman himself became convinced that there were threats to his own throne and possibly his well-being by his first-born, Mustafa (d. 1553). Merely five years after having his widely popular son Mustafa killed—and his own reputation of justice ruined by this action—around 1558, when *Anbiyānāma* was produced, the tension between his remaining two sons was on the rise. It would not come as surprise that 'Ārif's Ottoman *Shāhnāma* reflected anxiety and fear of bloodshed and even offered solutions approved by the sultan. In fact, the concern for the imminent problems of succession would explain well the noticeable emphasis on father-son stories and Cain's "over"-representation, as well as the imagined meeting between Mahalaleel, the Hebrew prophet, and Kayumars, the ancient Persian king, as brothers.

Whether or not ʿĀrif's *Shāhnāma* offered solutions for a peaceful resolution of dynastic succession, the first volume, with its dynastic tone and its selection of highlighted themes, reminisces rather suggestively of contemporaneous concerns. Pertaining to filial and fraternal behavior, it presents both idealized examples to emulate and unmistakably bad ones from which to learn. At the same time, *Anbiyānāma* confirms the constant good will of the father. Moreover, the emphasized stories of human error and sins (Adam, Cain, Jamshid, Zahhak, Noah's son); disobedience and punishment (Cain, Jamshid, Noah's son); seduction by the devil and the harm it causes (Adam and Eve, Cain, Jamshid); as well as fatherly affection, disillusionment, despair, anger, and suffering (Adam, Noah, and, though less elaborated, Zahhak's father, Merdas) invite the reader/viewer to empathize with the early prophets as if they were fellow humans from one's own century. The discernable similarities between the concerns of *Anbiyānāma*'s prophet-kings and those of the Ottoman "king" Süleyman approach the projection of the personae of the prophet-kings onto Süleyman.

However, if one wished to promote the image of the sultan as a prophet-king, it would not have sufficed to drag down the divinely chosen prophet-kings to the human level of an elderly sultan whose legacy was in danger. The image of the sultan should be elevated toward the level of prophet-kings.

The Nature of Sultan Süleyman's Authority

> While he is not a prophet, to that distinguished creature
> The Creator gave all moral qualities of the prophets
> All saints recognized his saintly power
> If that shah is called "holy," that suits the notion of holiness.
> Especially necessary and important are the attributes of the earlier kings who were adornment of the rank of world-rulers and personification of the imperial position such as subjects-nourishing endeavors and justice-spreading affairs. The rays of light that are marks (of holiness) were manifest and visible, evident and clear like lights in his noble character, on his face that resembles the shining sun.[47]

With these words, Celālzāde Muṣṭafā Çelebi (d. 1567), one of the most prominent Ottoman statesmen of the sixteenth century, described the young sultan Süleyman in the preamble to the law code of Egypt. If we believe his words, they indicate clearly that this well-respected statesman, who served as chancellor to Süleyman between 1534 and 1555, considered himself before a saintly universal emperor. The sultan he served, "while not a prophet," was bestowed by God the moral qualities of a prophet as well as saintly power.

The fact that Celālzāde wrote these words in the introduction to a highly important public and legal document—and that they were not the outcome of mere eccentricity, as both the writer and his preamble remained in position—leaves no doubt that his views were accepted and approved. The prominent bureaucratic position of Celālzāde and the public quality of the document also make it more than likely that he was not the only person who envisioned and/or described his sultan in these terms. The image of the sultan as the saintly king must have had currency at least among other high statesmen as well as among the lower officials who had to pay them lip service.

In fact, Süleyman's own interest in acquiring a special crown from Venice around 1532, less than ten years after the preamble was written, demonstrates that a version of Celālzāde's claim of political authority and spiritual guidance for the sultan was shared by Süleyman himself. Furthermore, it was shared by his Grand Vizier Ibrahim Pasha (d. 1536) and Treasurer Iskender Çelebi (d. 1534), both of whom encouraged and mediated the order and the purchase.[48]

This crown of four tiers was richly encrusted with jewels and decorated with a plumed aigrette (fig. 5.2). Visually, it resembled the outcome of the superimposition of two crowns: the imperial crown that formed the base and the papal crown of three tiers. The structure of the plumed helmet-crown also made allusions to similar helmet-crowns in the images of Near Eastern kings and especially of Alexander the Great in Ottoman miniatures.[49] Unlike the tiered form of the crown, the plume as a decoration belonged, in fact, to the conventional ceremonial headgear of the sultan. In all, the image of Süleyman with this extraordinarily high crown of four tiaras was a powerful and rather haughty symbolic declaration of his leadership in both the temporal and the spiritual realms.

The existence of such a crown, which repeatedly appeared in contemporaneous engravings and pamphlets by western European artists, also signified that in the early 1530s the idea of Süleyman's joint universal political and spiritual authority was still publicly claimed. Whereas Celālzāde's words were directed to an Ottoman audience composed mainly of the judiciary branch of the pre-modern Ottoman state, the symbolism of the crown was directed toward a western European audience in general and to the Pope and the Habsburg emperor Charles V (d. 1556) in particular.

Indeed, the crown was ordered for the occasion of Süleyman's military campaign toward Vienna, where he hoped to meet Charles as the commander of the Habsburg troops. Charles V had been crowned Holy Roman Emperor by the Pope in February 1530. In September 1529, a few months prior to the coronation, in his famous discourse in Madrid, he had stated his desire to be the universal ruler "as it is established in the Sacred Kingdom of the Heavens."[50] To the disappointment of the Ottoman sultan, however, the Holy Roman Emperor withheld the order for a decisive battle with the Ottoman army. In 1533, without an encounter with his rival Ottoman emperor, Charles retreated to Spain.

The crown of four tiers represented Süleyman's claim over the universalist ambitions not only of Charles V but also of the Pope. We do not know whether the Ottoman sultan investigated the symbolic meaning of the tri-level papal crown, although such curiosity on his part should be regarded as a logical possibility. It would be interesting to know if Süleyman was aware that one of the common interpretations of the three tiaras made direct reference to the three-fold office of Christ: as priest, prophet, and king. Another popular interpretation explains the symbolism of the crown in terms of the three-fold authority of the Supreme Pontiff: as Universal Pastor, Universal Ecclesiastical Jurisdiction, and Temporal Power. Still another interpretation associates the three tiaras with the Pope's role as lawgiver, judge, and teacher. The terminological and ideological similarities between the ambitions of the Pope and Süleyman "the Lawgiver"[51] are clear and numerous.

In this political environment of contention in the first half of the sixteenth century, Süleyman's crown also revealed that, in the Mediterranean basin, expectations of politically and spiritually unified governance were shared.[52] As for the symbolic language used to express them, it was easily translatable. The idea of charging each level of a crown with a different authority that we have seen in both Süleyman's superimposed double crown and the papal crown of three tiaras reflects a mentality akin to the one behind the descriptions of Adam's authority in *Anbiyānāma*. The associations with temporal and spiritual authority, as well as educational guidance, that figure repeatedly among interpretations of the symbolic meaning of the papal crown echo the themes salient in *Anbiyānāma*'s literary and visual program, a section of which we have examined previously.

While direct importation from one example to another does not seem likely, it is also difficult to deny the existence of a common cultural denominator at least in the pre-modern Mediterranean context in which the crown was used as a prominent instrument in representing authority and in which authority was seen as the exercise of power in several realms.[53]

Furthermore, in both the Christian and Muslim cultural domains the ideal and most legitimate base of authority, may it be temporal or sacred, was the Divine.[54] We can consider the words of Celālzāde and Charles V as two of many formulations of this ancient base of authority. It is also in this context that the representations of authority in *Anbiyānāma* become relevant to the Ottoman political culture in Süleyman's time.

Conclusion: The Significance of *Anbiyānāma* in Constructing Süleyman's Image

We have seen that in the first volume of the first dynastic history project of Süleyman's reign, the two miniatures on Adam's legacy demonstrate that God created a kingdom to be ruled by a human in the Garden before Adam and Eve's expulsion. In fact, as it appears in the miniatures, in the original and ideal scheme of things God willed only one human to rule all creatures, the way Adam did. In a sense, the image Sultan

Süleyman's artists were painting in the sinning scene of Adam was merely a version of the "Sacred Kingdom of the Heavens" to which Charles V was referring in his imperial speech in Madrid as he supported his universalist claims on a religious basis.

In contrast to the crown of four tiers, however, the Persian verse of 'Ārif's Ottoman *Shāhnāma* and its Persianate miniatures did not address a western European audience. To be exact, *Anbiyānāma* and the other four volumes of his universal history belonged to a specific group of books prepared for the literary and visual consumption of the sultan and his court. Unlike Celālzāde's preamble to the law code and Süleyman's crown of four tiaras, which were prepared for an external public of varying composition and size, 'Ārif's *Shāhnāma* was manufactured for the eyes, ears, and minds of an audience within the palace. Its refined language; persistent yet subtle dealing with taboos (such as the defeat of the Ottoman sultan Bayezid I by Timur in the fourth volume and Prince Mustafa's execution by his father Süleyman's order in the fifth); and the presence of historical, literary, and visual references to incidents, works, and people easily recognizable by the court elite but perhaps not by the common literate subject (such as Grand Vizier Rüstem Pasha's [d. 1561] physical particularities and the reputed soldier-poet Yaḥyā Beg's [d. 1578] poem after Mustafa's execution in the fifth volume) reveal that the project was directed toward an inner audience limited in number but not in stature.[55]

As such, 'Ārif's *Shāhnāma-yi Āl-i 'Os̱mān* had not only a propagandist but also an instructive quality. This quality previously has been mentioned in relation to the lessons the reader/viewer could derive by "reading" the literary and pictorial narration of the sins represented in *Anbiyānāma*. Other indicators of the instructive function of 'Ārif's project include the attention shown and the space given in *Sulaymānnāma*, the fifth volume of the project, to the workings of and the ranks forming the Ottoman order. This care also reflects an instructive mindset that aims to present and conserve the correct parameters of an established and idealized order. The same mindset can be observed in the organization of the figures in the depictions of the same fifth volume, in groups according to their duties and ranks (fig. 6.7).

Aside from reflecting an inherent obsession with hierarchy and order, these and other details make it highly likely that, like the many books circulating in the court, one important function of 'Ārif's *Shāhnāma* was "to create a common culture and a shared imperial identity."[56] As is often the case with history-writing, in the hands of 'Ārif and his team of artists narrative history became a vehicle to construct a certain identity. In the case of *Shāhnāma-yi Āl-i 'Os̱mān,* the identity referred to is principally dynastic. It is also exceptionally ambitious.

In effect, 'Ārif's *Shāhnāma* bends not only the Persian literary language but also Iranian iconography to elevate the history of the Ottoman dynasty to mythic levels. By commencing the fourth volume—and hence the fourth epoch of human history—with the arrival of Osman, it implants the relatively new and hybrid seeds of the dynasty into a historically privileged terrain irrigated simultaneously by Iranian mythology

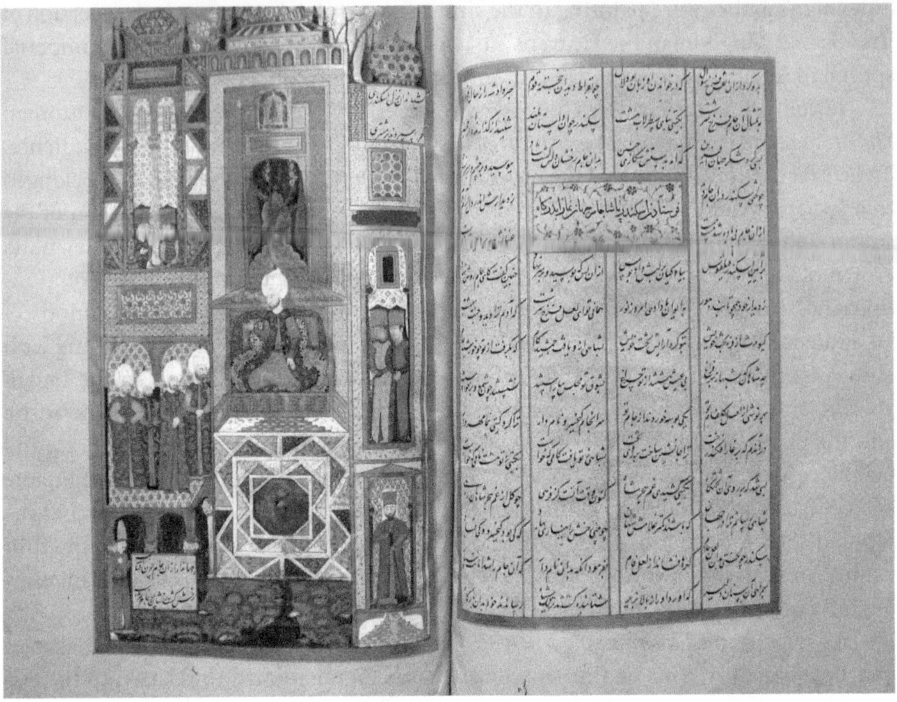

Figure 6.7. Süleyman presented with the ruby cup, ʿĀrif, *Sulaymānnāma*, 1558. TPML, H. 1517, 557a.

and Islamicate legacy. As the age of the prophets does not end with the closing of the first volume of *Anbiyānāma,* the Ottoman age begun by the arrival of Osman does not end with the fourth volume. On the contrary, the following volume brings the glad tidings of a new Ottoman epoch, that of Süleyman. In this last volume, the qualifications for the prophet-kings presented in *Anbiyānāma* find their realization once more after an entire journey of world history. It is also here that the sultan is raised toward the level of *Anbiyānāma*'s prophet-kings, the narration of whose human suffering, I had argued previously, brought them close to Süleyman.

According to the introductory pages of *Sulaymānnāma,* no other person joined royal glory and religious leadership in his person like Sultan Süleyman, who ruled over the world in a century equally extraordinary. ʿĀrif writes that both the century, the tenth after the Hijra, and its child and lord—the tenth in the Ottoman dynasty, Sultan Süleyman—were far more different than anyone could have imagined.[57] Moreover, in the cosmology described in the introductory folios of this volume ʿĀrif declares that the Ottoman ruler was the last reformer of (the true) religion (*mujaddid*)[58] and the seal indicating the end of "credence and kingship" (*kīsh-u-shāhī*).[59] In other words,

Süleyman was the last mythic-king of the "new *Shāhnāma*" as well as the last person who combined prophetic authority with the political in human history and educated and guided humanity toward the right path. As Adam began the first era of human history, Sultan Süleyman marked the last.

Notes

1. This essay would not have been possible without the kind help and generosity of Dr. Alessandro Bruschettini of the Bruschettini Foundation of Islamic and Asian Art in allowing me to work on *Anbiyānāma*. I also owe many thanks to İlber Ortaylı, the director of the Topkapı Palace Museum, and Zeynep Çelik Atbaş from its manuscript library for permission to use their images. All of the manuscripts are preserved in the Topkapı Palace Museum manuscript library, except *Anbiyānāma* and *ʿOṣmānnāma*, which are in the Bruschettini collection. Catalogue numbers of manuscripts consulted at the Topkapı Palace Museum Library (TPML) are as follows: A. 2861, A. 2862, A. 2863/1, A. 2863/2, A. 2863/4, A. 2864, A. 2865/1, A. 2865/2, A. 2866, A. 2867, A. 2868, A. 2964, A.2965, A. 3006, A. 3599, B. 41, B. 249, E.H. 1430, H. 1224, H. 1225, H. 1226, H. 1227, H. 1228, H. 1517, H. 1570, H. 1653, H. 1654, H.S. 578, R. 1518, R. 1536, R. 1540 mükerrer. All of the translations are mine unless otherwise noted. Only the excerpts from the text are transcribed fully. The Persian transcriptions follow the spelling of the original text as much as possible and hence diverge from the modern spelling at certain points.

2. ʿĀrif was the penname of Fetḥullāh Çelebi, who acted as the first official *şehnāmeci* (or *shāhnāma-gūy*, Ottoman *shāhnāma* narrator) during the reign of Sultan Süleyman. For ʿĀrif's career and the Ottoman *shāhnāmas* of Süleyman's reign, see Fatma Sinem Eryılmaz, "The Shehnamecis of Sultan Süleymān: ʿĀrif and Eflatun and Their Dynastic Project" (PhD diss., University of Chicago, 2010). For other evaluations of the Ottoman *shāhnāmas*, see Christine Woodhead, "Reading Ottoman Şehnames: Official Historiography in the Late Sixteenth Century," *Studia Islamica* 104/105 (2007): 67–80; and Baki Tezcan, "The Politics of Early Modern Ottoman Historiography," in *The Early Modern Ottomans: Remapping the Empire*, ed. Virginia Aksan and Daniel Goffman (Cambridge: Cambridge University Press, 2007).

3. ʿĀrif does not explain the stories of Enoch's descendants until Noah. Instead of the legacies of Methuselah (*Matūshālaḥ*) and Lamech (*Amak*), he includes a section with no chapter headings on the mythic Iranian king Jamshid. In the text we also encounter curious spellings for Jared and Seth: "Barad" and "Shīsh," respectively.

4. Kayumars is the first mythical Iranian king. Zahhak is the son of Merdas, who was believed to descend from an Arabic tribe. Seduced by the evil source Ahriman, Prince Zahhak kills his father and usurps the throne. As a result of his pact with Ahriman, a snake that needs to be fed a human head each day appears on each of his shoulders. Thus, Zahhak becomes a doomed and demonized figure. He is also the one who takes over the reign of Jamshid after the latter falls from divine favor, and Zahhak orders Jamshid to be slain in two.

5. The remaining images represent incidents from the legacies of the prophets Muhammad (the miraculous ascension), Adam (Adam's first sermon, Adam and Eve [*Ḥawwā*] about to eat the forbidden fruit, the sacrifice of Cain [*Qābīl*] and Abel [*Hābīl*]), Seth (Seth teaching tailoring, the battle of Seth and Cain), Enoch (teaching writing), and Noah (the Deluge).

6. Eryılmaz, "The Shehnamecis of Sultan Süleymān."

7. *Anbiyānāma*, 15a.

8. Ibid., 20a.
9. Ibid., 25b.
10. Qur'an, 2: 30–33.
11. TPML, H. 1226, 8b.
12. TPML, E.H. 1430, 8a.
13. *Anbiyānāma,* 14a.
14. There is, however, an important distinction between the two situations. The angels are prostrating in adoration of the vision of God on Adam's face. Adam is the first imam, but he also, in a sense, embodies, or at least reflects, the divine essence. In contrast, Muslims do not prostrate before the imam but before God and behind the imam. The imam is an ordinary member of the Muslim community with a special temporary assignment in Islamic religious practice. Adam, however, is not an equal member of the community of the faithful. He is raised above the angels—and closer to God.
15. *Anbiyānāma,* 14a.
16. Ibid.
17. Ibid., 14b.
18. The quality of the image does not allow us to determine whether Adam is wearing a double-tiered crown, which would include both his Crown of Salvation and his Crown of Magnanimity.
19. All translations from al-Kisā'ī are from *The Tales of the Prophets of al-Kisa'i,* trans. Wheeler M. Thackston, Jr. (Boston: Twayne, 1978), 36–42. In the versions related in al-Ṭabarī, for example, Satan talks to Eve either through a serpent or openly as an angel. The peacock does not appear in any of the versions, and in those in which Satan does not hide there is no mention of the snake. See *The History of al-Ṭabarī (Ta'rīkh al-rusul wa'l-mulūk),* trans. Franz Rosenthal (Albany: State University of New York Press, 1989), 1:274–282. In *Bahjat al-Tawārīkh,* Satan talks to Adam and Eve through the snake, telling them that in order to stay in Paradise eternally they must eat from the cluster of grain. TPML, R. 1538, 49a.
20. For various versions of the story of the original scene and general references, see *EI2,* s.v. "Ādam" (Johannes Pedersen).
21. From the royal Ottoman collection in the Topkapı Palace Museum manuscript library we can give as examples several copies of al-Tha'lābī's *Qiṣaṣ al-Anbiyā',* including H. 1225 (14b, fig. 5), H. 1228 (8a), and R. 1536 (16b). From the same collection, B. 250 (36a), a copy of Muḥammad b. al-Ḥasan al-Daydūzamī's *Qiṣaṣ al-Anbiyā'* offers another similar example.
22. *Anbiyānāma,* 20a, published in Esin Atıl, *Süleymanname: The Illustrated History of Süleyman the Magnificent* (New York: Harry N. Abrams, Inc., 1986), 59.
23. Qur'an, 21: 74.
24. Qur'an, 21: 79.
25. Qur'an, 2: 31, 32.
26. Qur'an, 2: 32.
27. On the Imperial Scroll and its authorship, see Eryılmaz, "The Shehnamecis of Sultan Süleymān."
28. With later additions, the Scroll's text extends to the beginning of the reign of Mehmed III (r. 1595–1603).
29. TPML, A. 3599.
30. This manuscript is preserved in the collection of the Bruschettini Foundation of Islamic and Asian Art.
31. TPML, B. 249, H. 1224, H. 1225, H. 1226, H. 1227, H. 1228, R. 1536, E.H. 1430.
32. TPML, B. 250; Fehmi Edhem Karatay, *Topkapı Sarayı Müzesi Kütüphanesi Farsça Yazmalar Kataloğu* (Istanbul: Topkapı Sarayı Müzesi, 1961), 47.
33. TPML, R. 1534, H. 1236; Karatay, *Farsça Yazmalar Kataloğu.*

34. TPML, R. 1584, R. 1585, A.2964, A. 2965, A. 2861, A. 2862, A. 2863/1, A. 2863/4, 2865/2, A. 2866, A. 2867, A. 2868, A. 3006, and B. 41. An additional four (A. 2863/2, A. 2864, A. 2865/1, H.S. 578) are not dated. A. 2863/2 formally resembles the Mamluk copies and must date from the late fifteenth century. The calligraphy of A. 2864 and A. 2865/1 also suggests that they originate from the same source and hence are likely to date from late fifteenth or early sixteenth centuries.

35. TPML, A. 2861, A. 2862, A. 2863/1, A. 2863/4, A. 2865/2. The undated copies A. 2863/2, A. 2864, A. 2865/1 are also copies of the same work, most probably from the same period.

36. TPML, A. 2964, A.2965; Fehmi Edhem Karatay, *Topkapı Sarayı Müzesi Kütüphanesi Arapça Yazmalar Kataloğu* (Istanbul: Topkapı Sarayı Müzesi, 1966), 3:406–407.

37. TPML, A. 2929/1, A. 2929/9, A. 2929/11, A. 2929/12, A. 2929/13, R. 1555; Karatay, *Arapça Yazmalar Kataloğu*, 3:339–341.

38. Karatay, *Farsça Yazmalar Kataloğu*, 37.

39. Ibid., 39–42.

40. Ibid., 38, 53, 329. For this essay I examined H. 1653.

41. Although sixteenth-century interest in the visual representation of the prophets' life stories calls for examination in itself, such an investigation falls outside the scope of this article.

42. For examples of the visual programs of books on the stories of the prophets, see Rachel Milstein, Karin Rührdanz, and Barbara Schmitz, *Stories of the Prophets: Illustrated Manuscripts of the Qiṣaṣ al-Anbiyā'* (Costa Mesa: Mazda Publishers, 1999), especially 185–217.

43. For example, the images of the sinning of Adam and Eve, Jamshid with the old lady, and Jamshid slain in two.

44. For example, the images of the sinning of Adam and Eve, the sacrifice of Cain and Abel, the battle of Seth and Cain, Jamshid with the old lady, Jamshid slain in two, and the Deluge.

45. For example, the images of Adam giving the first sermon, Seth teaching tailoring, and Enoch teaching writing.

46. "Ve her kimesneye evlādumdan salṭanat müyesser ola ḳarındaşların niẓām-ı 'ālem içün ḳatl itmek münāsibdir ekṣer 'ulemā daḫī tecvīz itmişdür anuñla 'āmil ola." *Ḳānūnnāme-i Āl-i 'Oṣmān* (Istanbul: Aḥmed İḥṣān ve Şürekāsı, 1330/1914), 27.

47. From the translation of the preamble to the law code of Egypt by Snježana Buzov. Snježana Buzov, "The Lawgiver and His Lawmakers: The Role of Legal Discourse in the Change of Ottoman Imperial Culture" (PhD diss., University of Chicago, 2005), appendix A, 209. I thank Buzov for sending her unpublished thesis.

48. Gülru Necipoglu, "Suleyman the Magnificent and the Representation of Power in the Context of Ottoman-Hapsburg-Papal Rivalry," *Art Bulletin* 71, no. 3 (1989): 401–427.

49. Ibid., 411.

50. Translation mine. The complete quotation is "nuestro deseo y voluntad es que no haya muchos señores, sino uno solo, como está constituido el Santo Reino de los Cielos." Series directed by John Lynch, *Monarquía e Imperio: El Reinado de Carlos V*, 194. For a general overview of Charles's imperial project in English, see John Lynch, *Spain 1516–1598: From Nation to World Empire* (Oxford: Blackwell, 1994), especially 95–116.

51. We do not know if Süleyman was given the epithet of "Lawgiver"—or "*Ḳānūnī*" in Turkish—during his reign. However, he cultivated justice as one of the pillars of his reputation and is credited for the standardization of law to an extent that was exceptional for a pre-modern state of such vast territorial domain.

52. Indeed, the Ottoman-Habsburg contention had the effect of uniting apocalyptic expectations with the universalist ambitions of the rivaling rulers. In this respect, we should note Mevlānā 'Īsā's (d. 1543) third rescension (1543) of his Ottoman history *Cāmi'ü'l-Meknūnāt* (The Compendium of Hidden Things), in which he argued that Sultan Süleyman had a special role as the temporal and

spiritual leader who would guide humans to the new millennium in his capacity as the Master of the Conjunction (*ṣāḥib-ḳırān*) and the renewer of religion (*müceddid*). For further discussion of Mevlānā 'Īsā's work, see Cornell Fleischer, "The Lawgiver as Messiah: The Making of the Imperial Image in the Reign of Süleymân," in *Soliman le magnifique et son temps*, ed. Gilles Veinstein (Paris: Galeries Nationales du Grand Palais, 1992), 164–166.

53. It is true that Süleyman, like many other rulers of the Islamicate world at his time and before, ordinarily wore a turban and not a crown. Nevertheless, crowns continued to be recognized as symbols of temporal authority, as they were depicted time and again in images accompanying such classical texts as Firdawsī's *Shāhnāma*. Besides, the turban in essence is a translation of the crown. Like a crown, its form, material, and adornment communicated statements associated with ruling authority. For an inspiring account of the iconography of the turban, see Abolala Soudavar, *The Aura of Kings: Legitimacy and Divine Sanction in Iranian Kingship* (Costa Mesa: Mazda Publishers, 2003).

54. Soudavar mentions the Sasanian origins of the western European crown in his *The Aura of Kings*, in which he takes on an archeological study of the iconography of Divine Glory (*farr-izādī*). Soudavar, *The Aura of Kings*, 70.

55. For details, see Eryılmaz, "The Shehnamecis of Sultan Süleymān." For a study of the narration of Muṣṭafā's execution in Sulaymānnāma, see Fatma Sinem Eryılmaz, "Bir Trajedinin Kurgulanışı: 'Ārifī'nin Süleymānnāme'sinde (TSMK H. 1517) Şehzāde Muṣṭafā'nın Katlinin Ele Alınışı," in *Commemorative Gift to Filiz Çağman: Topkapı Palace Museum Communication Seminar on the Topkapı Palace and Ottoman Art* (forthcoming).

56. Emine Fetvacı, *Picturing History at the Ottoman Court* (Bloomington: Indiana University Press, 2013), especially chap. 1. In contrast to Fetvacı, who documents the wide circulation of books at the Ottoman court, Christine Woodhead considers the audience a small one. This difference seems partially due to a variance in reading similar data, or seeing the same glass as "half full or half empty." Woodhead also admits that "while there may have been little access to a finished *şehname*, its existence, magnificence and, perhaps, its message would have been no secret." Woodhead, "Reading Ottoman Şehnames," 67–80.

57. TPML, H. 1517, 6a.

58. TPML, H. 1517, 6a, esp. lines 5 and 6.

59. TPML, H. 1517, 6a, line 9.

7 The Challenge of Periodization

New Patterns in Nineteenth-Century Ottoman Historiography

Hakan T. Karateke

Ottoman historical consciousness and historiographical practices simultaneously underwent significant changes in the nineteenth century. This essay, conceived as the first in a series on new developments in Ottoman historiography during that century, concentrates on changes to Ottoman models of periodization for world history and aims to demonstrate that Ottoman historical consciousness entered a novel phase during the late nineteenth century. According to this new tripartite periodization model, world history was divided into "Ancient," "Medieval," and "New" periods, a departure from pre-nineteenth-century world histories, in which accounts of various dynasties had been given in roughly chronological fashion, with loose geographical groupings.

The choice of a new model for periodizing world history was a manifestation of a changing worldview, an indication of where the Ottomans located themselves in the emerging world civilization of the nineteenth century. Although that project was spearheaded by contemporary western European ideals, members of the Ottoman elite no doubt considered themselves a part of it. Moreover, the idea of a world civilization that was shared by, and common to, all leading nations of the world facilitated the appropriation of non-Ottoman models in many spheres, including historical periodization.

This essay investigates eight historians who published world histories or grappled with the topic of periodization in works written in the second half of the nineteenth century. Although their models seem largely similar, the small innovations introduced by each historian provide extraordinary insights into the nature of their concerns. Because the tripartite periodization model found resonance, was adopted with few alterations by later historians, and became the standard version taught in schools of the Turkish Republic, the variations that these historians proposed now seem all the more valuable historically. The model's later modifications, moreover, dominated and shaped Turkish historical consciousness in the twentieth century.

A number of reasons for such a development of a revised periodization model present themselves. One is the new source material that Ottoman historians began to appreciate and utilize in the nineteenth century. Sources doubtless have an effect on one's conception of historical periodization, but accepting a particular periodization of world history is a larger intellectual commitment than a mere replication of a European model. I consider the Ottomans' new periodization models to be a result of, and a vehicle for, a new notion of "universalism" in Ottoman historical consciousness. This new universalism was connected to the aforementioned idea of an emerging world civilization, and many Ottoman intellectuals regarded nineteenth-century modernization attempts as a step toward a common universal civilization project. The concept of westernization had not yet taken on negative connotations for non-Europeans, and hopes were high. Influenced by, and in negotiation with, the findings of the emerging professional discipline of history in Europe, the Ottomans felt the need for a "scientific" periodization that covered the entire known history of the world.[1]

Before the nineteenth century, Ottoman world histories had utilized a structure relating the rise and fall of individual dynasties in chronological order, with some geographical grouping. The loss of prestige of the monarchy as a form of government, and of individual dynasties as legitimate sovereigns, during the nineteenth century must have made the move away from historiographical practices closely associated with them natural and easy, rendering the models traditionally preferred in Ottoman court historiography obsolete. The Ottoman intellectual mind also gradually dispensed with its faith in the linearity and singularity of Ottoman history, and the centrality of Ottoman achievement to world history became an assumption fewer historians accepted as easily as their predecessors.

The tripartite division of world history and its later variations were adopted from European historiography. Several concepts of periodization based on Christian understandings of history and of the universe had been in use in Europe since the Middle Ages (e.g., the Four Kingdoms model or the Six Ages model). Christoph Cellarius's (d. 1707) tripartite model, dating from the late seventeenth century, is generally considered to be the first "secular" periodization of world history.[2] The Ottomans seem to have found it attractive only when it made its way into "scientific" nineteenth-century historiography. Oddly, the Ottoman mind had not been unfamiliar with tripartite taxonomies but classified many notions, including the histories of states, into three. Following the Ibn Khaldūnian scheme, for example, the historian Naʿīmā (d. 1716) viewed the rise, maturity, and decline of states as a reflection of the stages of a person's life.[3]

My goal is not to examine the validity or suitability of the tripartite periodization of world history, or to evaluate the dates and events taken as turning points in this division, but to consider the ways in which Ottoman historians and intellectuals presented and discussed this proposition. I would like to gauge, in light of these developments in history-writing in the Ottoman Empire, in which ways the Ottoman intellectual mind was ripe for, and receptive to, a new conceptualization of history.

Apart from Aḥmed Cevdet's (d. 1895) intelligent remarks quoted below, contemporary voices critical of the tripartite model are absent from this essay. This absence does not mean that resistance to the concept did not exist. The fact that I have not found any such criticism may be due to my inability to locate it, or to critics' reluctance to commit their opinions to paper. It is possible that there were intellectuals who found the new model unattractive, but there seems to have been no grave cultural conflict that would have caused its rejection. The view that many found the tripartite model practical is bolstered by the fact that most of the world histories composed during this time were for instructional purposes.

I will briefly discuss the structure and contents of a few pre-nineteenth-century universal histories as a point of departure for comparison with the new paradigms of the nineteenth century. The few histories cited here constitute a mere fraction of the total production of such works.[4] This discussion is not an extensive analysis of pre-nineteenth-century periodization models but an opportunity to establish that the later structures had indeed a novel character.

Periodization Models before the Nineteenth Century

Ottoman historiography traditionally considered itself and its major topic, the Ottoman dynasty, as a chapter of Islamic history. The narratives of pre-nineteenth-century universal histories began with the Creation, usually jumped to the rise of Islam, explored individual Islamic dynasties, and concluded with a considerably more detailed narration of the history of the Ottoman dynasty. Non-Islamic history generally featured only modestly in any Ottoman universal history, within particular contexts defined by time and space. Ottoman authors commonly consulted earlier sources—such as al-Ya'qūbī (d. after 905), al-Ṭabarī (d. 923), al-Mas'ūdī (d. 956), Ibn Athīr (d. 1233), and Rashīd al-Dīn (d. 1318)—for pre-Ottoman world history.[5] Their periodization scheme was thus based partially on the organizational schemes of these earlier models.

These prestigious pre-Ottoman world histories had some similarities in terms of their divisions of world history. However, based on whether the authors belonged to the Arabic or Persian cultural traditions, or simply as a result of their political orientations, they recounted recent and contemporary events in different ways. Rashīduddīn's *Jāmi' ul-Tawārīkh,* for instance, is a good example of an informative treatment of the Ilkhans by an insider who held administrative offices as high as grand vizier at the Ilkhanid court. Religious loyalties also made a difference when the author wrote in the Sunni or Shi'i tradition, evidenced, for example, by extra emphasis on the history of twelve imams by authors with Shi'i tendencies. These histories' cosmology derived from Islamic as well as biblical (or Islamicized biblical) traditions. The Old Testament was a common source for pre-Ottoman and Ottoman historians, and al-Ya'qūbī, for example, is known to have used apocryphal Psalms as well.[6]

A world history generally commenced with the creation of the light (*nūr*) of the Prophet Muhammad, angels, and souls, before continuing with the creation of the material world (although this arrangement differed slightly from work to work). Geographical data based on a few traditions (such as Ptolemaic or Iranian) was occasionally included in descriptions of the creation of the earth, the seas, the climes, and creatures. Tales of prophets would be told according to Islamic lore. A history of ancient nations was generally included in a section on the pre-Islamic era, incorporating basic information on the kings of ancient Mesopotamia, Persia, Israel, Greece, Rome, China, Byzantium, or Egypt.

Many of the prestigious histories written in Arabic or Persian were used extensively by Ottoman historians, especially by the more ambitious. Muṣṭafā ʿĀlī (d. 1600), for example, praises al-Ṭabari and Ibn Athīr, the latter for his extensive treatment of pre-Islamic and early Islamic history. He cites Ibn Athīr as a "historian without equal" (*müverriḫ-i bī-naẓīr*), praising the historian's detailed exposition of various peoples, events of ancient times, geographical knowledge, and "even" his case-by-case investigation of wonders and oddities.[7]

One implication of surveying world history before the rise of Islam in a cursory manner and exploring events thereafter in much more detail was that history could be presented as a divine plan. This approach originated in the medieval period but lived on in the Christian as well as the Islamic world into the early modern period. According to this view, it was mankind's task, and that of historians as their competent representatives, to try to discern God's plan for the universe and derive lessons from the past based on interpretation. This theme often surfaces in the introductory sections of Ottoman historical works, in which the author philosophizes about the uses and benefits of history. A related concept was the advance (although not necessarily "progress") of history toward its inevitable destination: the end of the world, or Judgment Day. The Eternal Ottoman State (*devlet-i ebed-müddet*) was implicitly considered the final phase of Islamic history.

A handful of histories penned from the fifteenth century on mark the emergence of Ottoman historiography. Şükrullāh (d. 1488), a member of the ulema class during Murad II's (r. 1421–1444 and 1446–1451) and Mehmed II's (r. 1444–1446 and 1451–1481) reigns, composed *Bahjat al-Tavārikh* (Splendor of Histories, ca. 1458) in Persian. *Bahjat,* a rather concise world history that was to become a prestigious source for later historians,[8] consisted of thirteen chapters and covered a period from the Creation to Mehmed II's enthronement in 1451. Şükrullāh claims in the introduction that his book would be a valuable source not only for history but for other sciences, such as astronomy, mathematics, or medicine, as well. The work begins with the creation of the universe, offers an Islamic cosmology, and explores the origins of some ancient peoples. After the second chapter, which depicts the history of the prophets according to Islamic lore, chapters 3 through 9 detail subjects in Islamic history centered around the Prophet, such as his genealogy, family, and companions. Chapters 8 and 9 also offer an excursus on the imams and notable sheikhs in Islamic history. An additional short chapter is on the "Most Significant Greek Philosophers," and chapter 11—"Kings of the Infidels and the Believers"—details the pre-Islamic Persian kings to the Sassanids. Şükrullāh again turns to Islamic history proper in chapter 12, which covers the

Umayyad, Abbasid, Fatimid, and Seljuk dynasties. Finally, the last chapter, which is also rather short, tells of the Ottomans up to the reign of Mehmed II.[9]

Although *Künhü'l-Aḫbār* (Essence of History), by Muṣṭafā ʿĀlī of Gallipoli (d. 1600), was published in five volumes in 1872, the author divided the book into four *rükns*, or pillars. ʿĀlī describes the first pillar as covering the period from the creation of the Light of Muhammad to the time of Adam. The section focuses on cosmology and the Creation; provides geographical information on the seas, islands, and climes; mentions some ancient nations; tells of the Flood; and records some tales of the prophets. The second pillar continues with stories of prophets and of Muhammad's life, gives an account of the rise of Islam and early Islamic history, and ends with a section about the Persian kings and Ptolemies. The third pillar is on Islamic dynasties that ruled in such locations as Egypt, Syria, and Anatolia. The Umayyads and Abbasids are treated in detail. After exploring certain smaller dynasties of the Islamic world and the characteristics of some European peoples, ʿĀlī ends this pillar with the Timurids and the Anatolian Seljuks, reserving the last and longest pillar for the history of the Ottoman dynasty.[10]

Ḳaraçelebizāde ʿAbdülʿazīz (d. 1658), born into a long-established ulema family, climbed the ladder of the ulema hierarchy, reaching the top and becoming *sheikhulislam* in 1651. His world history, *Ravżatü'l-Ebrār* (The Garden of the Pious), includes an informative and original section on recent Ottoman history and rather lengthy sections on the Mamluks and Safavids, which together compose more than half of the book. His treatment of pre-Ottoman times, however, is an uninspired and abridged replication of earlier world histories. The book is divided into four chapters (plus two appendices), the first of which covers the prophets mentioned in the Qur'an; the second, the life and achievements of the Prophet Muhammad; the third, pre-Ottoman Islamic dynasties; and the final and the longest chapter, the history of the Ottoman dynasty.[11]

Müneccimbaşı Aḥmed (d. 1702), a polymath of the late seventeenth century, was appointed chief astronomer in 1667 and held that office for twenty years. In addition to works in various other disciplines, he composed a massive world history in Arabic, entitled *Jāmiʿ al-Duwal* (A Compendium of States). Müneccimbaşı's history is divided into two main sections, the first of which concerns the Creation, the stories of prophets, and, in a much longer part, the vita of Prophet Muhammad. The second section is again divided into two parts: the first treats the dynasties and people that existed before Islam; the second, those that came after Islam. This section begins with a detailed account of the Umayyad and Abbasid dynasties. Müneccimbaşı then conducts something of a regional survey, within which he pursues a chronological treatment of the dynasties by centuries (*qarn*). As the title suggests, his exploration of individual dynasties is extensive: he not only includes numerous smaller Islamic dynasties but also incorporates the histories of European dynasties—Austrian, Spanish, English, Russian—up to his own time (despite the fact that he discusses them under the title "Dynasties before Islam"). Ancient dynasties and peoples, such as the Persians, Greeks, and Copts, had traditionally been mentioned in some detail in world histories since al-Ya'qūbī. Reporting on contemporary non-Islamic dynasties, particularly European examples, however, was a novelty. Müneccimbaşı was curious and studious enough to expand his list of dynasties and nations by consulting European sources and is known to have used a chronicle published in 1532 (in German) by Johannes Carion, who was an astronomer at the court of Brandenburg.[12] To recount the more recent history of certain European dynasties, however, Müneccimbaşı must have utilized other sources.[13]

The last example I would like to mention is *Gülşen-i Ma'ārif* (The Rose Garden of Knowledge) by Ferā'iżīzāde Meḥmed Sa'īd (d. 1835). Sa'īd was from Bursa and apparently lived there throughout his life, as the preacher at the Emir Sultan Mosque. He submitted his manuscript to Sultan Mahmud II (r. 1808–1839) and received encouragement and authorization to publish his work at the imperial press.[14] *Gülşen-i Ma'ārif* is rather less innovative as a world history than other contemporaneous examples. Quite religious in its tone, the two-volume work starts with sections on the qualities of God, the angels, and holy books, and then continues with biographies of the prophets. After recounting the prophets' lives through Muhammad and his age, Meḥmed Sa'īd turns back in time for a chronological digression about the ancient kings of Persia. The narrative then continues with the history of Islamic lands, by dynasty, and a detailed account of Ottoman history, which comprises three-fourths of the book. Although *Gülşen-i Ma'ārif* seems to be designed as a world history, the author's main objective was clearly arriving at Ottoman history as quickly as possible.[15]

Ottoman historians' concept of the periodization of world history was partially inherited from pre-Ottoman Muslim historians and partially shaped by what they regarded as decisive events of more recent history. The initial period began with the Creation and lasted until the next significant event in history: the Deluge. The prophets, for example, were usually classified as coming before or after the Deluge. Ancient nations of the antediluvian era also found some mention. 'Ālī, for one, surmises that before the Deluge people understood the descent of Adam to earth as the beginning of history. However, the historian reasons, because all of the documentation pertaining to the pre-Deluge era vanished in that catastrophe, the people living thereafter had to take the Deluge as the start of history.[16] Noah was occasionally mentioned by his epithet, the "second Adam" (*Ādem-i ṣānī*), which indicates the understanding that a completely new era had begun with him.[17]

The post-Deluge era stretched to the emergence of the Prophet Muhammad, or, more precisely, to his departure from Mecca to Medina (i.e., the Hegira). More pedantic historians broke down the period from Adam to Muhammad, which was believed to have lasted approximately six thousand years, into several eras: from Adam to the Deluge (2,256 years), from the Deluge to Abraham (1,079 years), from Abraham to Moses (565 years), from Moses to Suleiman (536 years), from Suleiman to Alexander the Great (770 years), from Alexander to Jesus (369 years), and from Jesus to Muhammad (550 years).[18]

While a proper chronology of events was considered one of the requirements of a good history, one did not need to seek hard evidence or documents to rectify the chronology of prehistoric events and people; this standard narrative relied heavily on Islamized biblical lore. Pre-Islamic Persian and Arabic history was also recounted, the degree of detail dependent on the historian's affiliation and prospects. The post-Hegira period was treated exclusively according to rulers or dynasties. A further topical classification might also be used to arrange the massive amount of material covered, such as "the dynasties of North Africa" or "the dynasties of India." When more recent events were recounted, some historians shifted to a detailed annalistic narrative. These latter annals were predominantly focused on wars, conquests, and political developments in the periods in question, again grouped by the reigns of individual sultans.

The post-Hegira period had one additional significant landmark for early Ottoman historians, whose first works date from the fifteenth century: the Mongol takeover of Baghdad and the fall of the Caliphate in 1258. The political and social transformations of the post-Mongol period must have given rise to an awareness of living in a different era than before.[19]

Muṣṭafā ʿĀlī's survey of historical events from different traditions, which he presents as epochal frontiers in history, gives us insight into his understanding of historical periodization. He mentions such events as the Pharaoh throwing Abraham into the fire, the Exodus, the first construction of the Kaʿaba, Alexander the Great's era (Romans and Greeks), the "Year of the Elephant" (ca. 570, Quraish tribe), and the reign of Kawadh I (d. 531), father of Anushirwan the Just (Persians). Finally, the Prophet Muhammad's departure from Mecca to Medina is mentioned as the first important political act of the budding Islamic state. This date was then taken as the "beginning of history," says ʿĀlī, and was used until his time.[20]

Only a few decades after the publication of *Gülşen-i Maʿārif* (1836), probably the last world history in the "old" tradition, a number of historians introduced an alternative periodization model for world history to the Ottoman intellectual public (initially through educational material): the tripartite division of world history. Although a dialogue continued for some time as to which events to accept as turning points in this tripartite division, the new model quickly found resonance.

New Periodization Models in the Later Nineteenth Century

Aḥmed Vefīḳ: Ḥikmet-i Tārīḫ *(The Philosophy of History), 1863*

One of the first to "officially" introduce a periodization model unfamiliar to the Ottoman tradition was the curiously erudite figure of Aḥmed Vefīḳ (d. 1891). Born to a family of interpreters for the imperial court, Vefīḳ was profoundly educated, especially in languages. In addition to perfecting his Arabic and Persian, he trained in Italian, Latin, and ancient Greek. Furthermore, he is said to have had substantial knowledge in Russian, German, Chagatai, and Hebrew. He was likely most skilled in French:

having attended high school for six years in Paris, he was apparently able to converse in French like a native.

Aḥmed Vefīḳ was appointed an official in the Department of Translation (*Tercüme Odası*) and served as a mediator in several foreign missions for the Ottoman state for more than three decades. He was one of the forty elected members of the Academy of Sciences (*Encümen-i Dāniş*), founded in 1851, the majority of whose activities concerned commissioning histories or translations from French, mostly on historical subjects.[21] For instance, Aḥmed Cevdet's twelve-volume Ottoman history, covering the years 1774–1826, was commissioned by the Academy of Sciences. Works on specialized topics in history, such as *Histoire naturelle* by Georges Louis Leclerc (Comte de Buffon, d. 1788), or on recent history (e.g., a book on the Napoleonic Wars) were among the books that the Academy supported. The Academy's activities over its short (about ten-year) life lead us to believe that "modern" historical approaches were strongly endorsed by the institution.

Aḥmed Vefīḳ did not become prolific until the 1860s. In 1863 he offered a series of lectures, entitled *Ḥikmet-i Tārīḫ* (The Philosophy of History), at the newly founded University (*Dārü'l-fünūn*). The lectures were one hour long, delivered twice a week, and continued only for a few weeks. Still, their introductory section, which was printed in the daily newspaper *Taṣvīr-i Efkār* the same month and appeared later as a separate booklet of forty-four pages,[22] has much to offer, particularly in terms of Vefīḳ's ideas about the periodization of world history. Lectures on such a subject were a novelty, as Ottoman education traditionally did not include any courses on the instruction of "history" per se.[23] The booklet gives one the impression that the lectures were designed as a class on "world civilization," rather than the philosophy of history, as scholars would characterize it today.

The sources and methodology of Ottoman historiography may well have been under discussion for some time. A reworking of periodization of world history, however, was apparently suggested only with *Ḥikmet-i Tārīḫ*. Vefīḳ not only proposes an adjusted periodization of the totality of world history but also discusses new types of sources and methodology for history-writing.[24]

Aḥmed Vefīḳ sees the arrival of the Prophet Muhammad as the most important landmark in the history of mankind. He justifies his choice of Prophet Muhammad's advent as a dividing line as follows: while the Arabs were a weak Bedouin tribe, prior to the Prophet's time, they managed to conquer the most fertile grounds of the world, and this conquest proved revolutionary for all nations. Except for China, he says, all parts of the world were affected by the coming of the Prophet Muhammad. Because all of the nations extant during Vefīḳ's time had come into existence after that momentous event, world history should be divided into two major parts. He classifies the fifty-six centuries from the Creation to the Hegira as the longer first period (*cüz-i ʿaẓīm*) and the thirteen centuries after the Prophet as the second. He labels the former the "Ancient Ages" (*ezmine-i muḳaddime*), and the latter the "Modern Ages" (*ezmine-i müteʾaḫḫire*).[25]

From time to time, Aḥmed Vefīḳ explains, the conditions of the world and of nations were transformed by "great events"; thus, it is necessary to subcategorize each of these two periods into four subsections, to which Vefīḳ attributes the following anthropomorphic designations:[26]

First era: The Period of Childhood (*faṣl-ı evvel-i şebābī*)
Second era: The Period of Growth (*faṣl-ı s̱ānī-i nemevī*)
Third era: The Period of Maturation (*faṣl-ı s̱ālis̱-i istivā*)
Fourth era: The Period of Descent (*faṣl-ı rābi'-i inḥiṭaṭī*)

However—and perhaps the note taker or editor is at fault—there seems to be a grave confusion in Aḥmed Vefīḳ's booklet. While at the outset he clearly discusses a division of world history into two periods, with the Hegira as the threshold, a few pages later his detailed list of events lays out a tripartite classification. Oddly, Vefīḳ does not address this discrepancy: he merely mentions that "some history books label this period the 'Middle Ages' and the subsequent one as 'Modern Ages'" and continues to list the events of these two periods.[27]

Aḥmed Vefīḳ does not claim that he is designing a new periodization model "from scratch." It is clear that he is quoting from "some histories" (*ba'żı tevārīḫ*) and relying on "scholars" (*erbāb-ı fenn*), whom he does not specify by title or name. He imports and domesticates models that were in circulation in nineteenth-century European historiography by inserting events pertinent to Islamic and Ottoman history in the Middle and Modern Ages sections. Vefīḳ seems to be adamant about the importance of the Prophet's advent for world history and the Hegira as the dividing line in his (earlier) bipartite periodization. (This insistence readily reminds one of the birth of Christ as the point of departure for Christian calendars. He integrates the Hegira into a "scientific" periodization of world history, although Christ's birth was not included in European historiography.)[28]

Aḥmed Ḥilmī (trans.): Tārīḫ-i 'Umūmī *(A World History), 1866–1878*

Although Aḥmed Vefīḳ's lectures and booklet may have had little effect, the following decade saw a lively discussion, as several additional translated works containing similar periodizations of world history were published. One of them was an adaptation of a "world history" by William Chambers (d. 1883)—a popular Scottish author and publisher of periodicals and encyclopedias—translated by Aḥmed Ḥilmī (d. 1878), an assistant clerk at the Translation Office. Apparently published with the encouragement of Minister of Education Kemal Efendi, between 1866 and 1878, this six-volume incomplete edition was the first translated universal history in Ottoman Turkish. While Aḥmed Ḥilmī mentions Chambers's name in the introduction, from which of his works Ḥilmī rendered the first two volumes of the book remains unclear.[29]

The first volume, which contains numerous illustrations of the remains of ancient cultures, begins with the ancient Egyptians and continues with the Phoenicians,

Assyrians, and Lydians. The second volume includes the ancient civilizations of the Iranians, Romans, Greeks, European and African nations, Scythians, Hindus, and Chinese. Ḥilmī concludes the second volume by reflecting that ancient history is largely based on tales and legendary accounts.[30] His tone makes clear that he views the "Ancient Ages" as times when common people suffered under absolute sovereigns, who ruled with injustice and coercion. Ḥilmī delivers the good news, though, that in the upcoming volumes the history of mankind will progress significantly. The sixth volume[31] recounts the Islamic history of the Middle Ages and ends with the fall of the Caliphate in Baghdad in 1258. The method of the book is noticeably different in this latter volume, which recounts the history of Islamic dynasties chronologically and with separate sections devoted to individual rulers. This volume does not seem to be a translation of Chambers's work but an adaptation from earlier chronicles available in the Ottoman realm. The translation project must have come to an end with Ḥilmī's death in 1878.

At the time, it was quite common for translators to intervene with, occasionally question, and even alter original works. Not surprisingly, then, Ḥilmī engages in a dialogue with Chambers's model of periodization: he employs Chambers's tripartite division without criticism, but considers the events Chambers chose to mark the beginnings and ends of those eras problematic. Ḥilmī mentions that one variant of periodization, conceivably the Ottoman example, divides history into the Ancient Ages (*ezmine-i müteḳaddime,* from the creation of Adam to the departure of the Prophet Muhammad from Mecca to Medina, i.e., the Hegira), the Middle Ages (*ezmine-i mütevassıṭa,* from the Hegira to the conquest of Constantinople), and the Modern Ages (*ezmine-i müte'aḫḫire,* from the conquest of Constantinople to the translator's time). However, as Ḥilmī mentions in passing, Chambers's original work suggests different events for these divisions: the "creation of Adam," the fall of the Roman Empire, and the discovery of the New World.[32]

Meḥmed ʿĀṭıf: Ḫulāṣatü't-Tevārīḫ *(A Summary of Histories), 1872–1873*

Another world history, penned by Meḥmed ʿĀṭıf of Candia (d. 1908 or 1909), appeared in 1872–1873. A civil servant by profession, the author apparently designed *Ḫulāṣatü't-Tevārīḫ* (A Summary of Histories) to comprise at least four volumes, only two of which appeared. ʿĀṭıf is not shy about invoking the ambition of his undertaking, namely his plans to write "a perfect universal history with no equal to date" (*misli nā-mevcūd bir tārīḫ-i mükemmel-i ʿumūmī*). ʿĀṭıf's confidence in his ability to produce a heretofore-unrivaled history is intriguing. His introduction suggests that what distinguishes his project might be the "new method" (*uṣūl-i cedīd*) in which he claims to be writing the book: ʿĀṭıf asserts that he compiled and translated his book from well-known Arabic, French, and Greek histories, due to a lack of histories written in the "new method" in Turkish. Unfortunately, he does not elaborate; however, it is conceivable that he is referring to the book's content: a new periodization model, the variety of civilizations covered, and presenting events' causal relationships.

Meḥmed 'Āṭıf also speculates about the model of tripartite periodization of world history used by European historians. The conventional division in Europe, he explains, offers the following historical eras, defined by specific events: Initial Ages (*ḳurūn-ı ūlā*), from the Creation to the fall of the Western Roman Empire; Middle Ages (*ḳurūn-ı vusṭā*), from the fall of the Western Roman Empire to the conquest of Constantinople by the Muslims; and Modern Ages (*ḳurūn-ı āḫire*), the period after the conquest of Constantinople. However, because "it would be more suitable for the glorious nation of Islam" (*millet-i celīle-i İslāmiyyece daha münāsib olduğundan*), he chose to replace the fall of the Western Roman Empire with the Hegira as the event marking the beginning of the Middle Ages.[33] 'Āṭıf does not otherwise alter the original periodization model; he also uses the Hegira calendar throughout the book. Hence, for example, the creation of Adam is dated 5,585 years before the Hegira.[34]

'Āṭıf also explores the subdivisions that European historians utilize, as well as shorter periods.[35] The book then continues with a long section on approximately twenty Greek, Roman, and Jewish historians, such as Herodotus, Thucydides, Plutarch, and Josephus (Yosef ben Matityahu), introducing each with a paragraph. Meḥmed 'Āṭıf's work resembles a somewhat detached compilation of sections from various sources. A chapter on "Tales of the Prophets" in the Islamic tradition is inserted into an otherwise largely Eurocentric narrative of pre-historic and ancient ages. Biblical stories on the Kingdom of Israel, Kingdom of Judah, and the destruction of the Temple of Jerusalem are followed by accounts of the Assyrians, Phoenicians, Lydians, Egyptians, and Sassanians. No further volumes to this world history appeared, and the work remains incomplete.

Süleymān Ḥüsnī: Tārīḫ-i 'Ālem, *1:* Ḳurūn-ı Ūlā *(A History of the World: The Initial Ages), 1876*

A few years after Meḥmed 'Āṭıf's universal history, Süleymān Ḥüsnī Pasha (d. 1892) published *Tārīḫ-i 'Ālem* (A History of the World), designed as a textbook for military high schools. The author, himself the director of the Military Academy (*mekātib-i 'askeriyye nāẓırı*), would also become an able commander during the Ottomans' war with Russia, which began a few months after the book's publication.[36] Ḥüsnī mentions that the textbook used in military schools (Ḥilmī's translation of Chambers) was a direct translation of European books, a fact that motivated him to compose *Tārīḫ-i 'Ālem*. The author leaves no doubt that he does not approve of the previous textbook's approach, which he describes as "contrary to Islamic principles and national values and the moral code."[37] He further notes that the textbook remained incomplete, in that only a few parts of the Ancient Ages section were translated. Süleymān Ḥüsnī used a number of recent universal histories in French in addition to Arabic and Ottoman sources, all of which he lists at the beginning of his volume. He then compiles information from a variety of primary and secondary sources and develops a narrative that he characterizes as compatible with Islamic and Ottoman values.

The beginning of the first volume lists the second volume, which would have been on the Middle Ages, as under preparation, but it seems to have never appeared. Ḥüsnī discusses the reasons he titled his work *Tārīḫ-i ʿĀlem* instead of *Tārīḫ-i ʿUmūmī* (General History): he viewed *Tārīḫ-i ʿĀlem, Tārīḫ-i ʿUmūmī,* and *Tārīḫ-i Ḫuṣūṣī* (Particular History) as subdivisions of political history (*Tārīḫ-i Siyāsī*). In explaining his choice of the title, Ḥüsnī provides a definition of the former two: *Tārīḫ-i ʿĀlem* narrates the events that happened from the time of the Creation, through the emergence of nations and states, to his own time. Although some historians would consider his account *Tārīḫ-i ʿUmūmī,* the latter would be, for Ḥüsnī, a full account of all of the events that took place during a specific period of time or in the course of a political rule.

Süleymān Ḥüsnī can be credited with some originality. In addition to his idiosyncratic definition of the generic term *Tārīḫ-i ʿUmūmī* as an account of world history, he lists somewhat unusual events as governing the tripartite division that he appropriates without comment. As far as I can detect, he is the only historian to take the rise of the Ottomans (ca. 1300) as the beginning of the Modern Age and the destruction of the Janissary corps as its end.[38]

Some topics, although identical in subject to the age-old tradition, were handled completely differently by Ḥüsnī. For example, although he begins his book with the Creation, nothing he tells in this section resembles traditional cosmologies of pre-nineteenth-century Ottoman historiography; instead, Ḥüsnī's Creation story builds on the latest scientific explanations in Europe. He describes a gas-liquid mass that cooled and turned into the earth over time and the elements that emerged. He covers the appearance of plants, mountain chains, animals, and, finally, humankind. Oddly, he also lists, clearly translating from European sources, the prehistoric period (Stone Age, Bronze Age) in a section just before his tripartite division of world history, the first part of which he wishes to call ancient history (*tārīḫ-i ḳadīm*). Biblical traditions predictably dominate the narrative's earlier portion; however, Ḥüsnī conspicuously cuts short the stories of the prophets. The book is further divided into thirteen chapters, each of which treats a separate people, starting with the ancient Egyptians and continuing to the Arabs of the pre-Islamic era.[39]

Rıfʿat Efendi: Naḳdü't-Tevārīḫ *(A Review of Histories), 1879*

In the 1870s, Aḥmed Rıfʿat (Yağlıkçızade, d. 1895), who served as a mid-level government official in Izmir, Crete, and Salonica, was working on his massive encyclopedic work, *Luġāt-i Tārīḫiyye ve Coğrāfiyye* (A Historical and Geographical Dictionary), which would appear a few years after *Naḳdü't-Tevārīḫ*. He informs the reader that the volume emerged as a byproduct of his studies on *Luġāt*.

Naḳdü't-Tevārīḫ is not a history per se but a chronological table of events from Adam to the year 1879. The work is interesting in that the blurb at the beginning of the book presents it as having been compiled in the "brand new style" (*ṭarz-ı nevīn*). While chronological tables are rare in Ottoman historiography, and none had been authored in the nineteenth century, the promotional language may be the publisher's commercial presentation, for the author himself does not discuss a "new method" and gives credit to another Ottoman historian, who, he says, inspired him to undertake this work.[40] The historian to whom he refers is Kātib Çelebi (d. 1657), whose chronology, *Taḳvīmü't-Tevārīḫ*, had found wide popularity due to its clear layout. Rıf'at's contribution, in his words, is that he tracked down many events that do not appear in Kātib Çelebi's work, notably some Islamic as well as non-Islamic (*ecnebī*, "foreign") historical events of the Ancient Ages.

Aḥmed Rıf'at elaborates on his dating system in the introduction to the book. He does not take the birth of Christ as the beginning of the calendar, as European (*ecnebī*) historians do, with the expressed intention of avoiding the trouble of reckoning forward and backward from that event.[41] Otherwise, he argues, it would have been suitable to take it as a turning point on the grounds that the events after Christ were recorded much more precisely than those before his birth. Therefore, although Rıf'at does not offer a separate periodization model in *Naḳdü't-Tevārīḫ*, he has a loose idea of the division of historical eras, based on the argument that historical accuracy is dependent on sources. A work such as *Naḳdü't-Tevārīḫ* further demonstrates that, in Rıf'at's mind, the focal point of world history was not an event in Islamic and Ottoman history. Rıf'at begins with the creation of Adam, marked as year zero; continues until the year 5595, at which point he begins providing the Christian calendar alongside it; then continues until the year 6215, when he switches to the Islamic and Gregorian calendars. The count from the Creation is not included thereafter.

Meḥmed Murād: Tārīḫ-i 'Umūmī *(A World History), 1880–1882*

Meḥmed Murād (d. 1917) taught courses in world history and geography at the School for Civil Servants (*Mekteb-i Mülkiyye*) from the time the school was restructured in 1877. Based on his lectures at the *Mekteb*, he composed a six-volume *Tārīḫ-i 'Umūmī* (A World History), the first edition of which was published between 1880 and 1882. The book enjoyed huge popularity and reached its third edition by 1910. It was also one of the rare world histories that was completed during the period under consideration. Murād planned to write an even longer, twelve-volume history of the Ottoman Empire, which remained unfinished but became quite popular nevertheless.[42]

Murād states that his world history project is an ambitious one. He mentions that his lectures had been approaching the matter in a completely new method, which no Ottoman historian had used before (*henüz lisānımızda yazılmamış bir ṭarzda*).[43] Despite his claims, the novelty of Murād's work, compared to the treatments of world history mentioned above, is not immediately apparent. According to Murād, there are two kinds of history: *Tārīḫ-i 'Umūmī* (A World History) is the general treatment of world history, whereas *Tārīḫ-i Ḫuṣūṣī* (Particular History) is a subdivision of the former, such as the history of a region or a country. He is to be credited for mentioning, possibly for the first time in Ottoman historiography, a variety of sources and auxiliary sciences that should be used in constructing a historical narrative, such as historical linguistics (*fenn-i elsine*), geology (*fenn-i ṭabaḳatu'l-'arż*), court records (*maḥkeme i'lāmatı*), and oral histories (*āṣār-ı menḳūle*).[44]

Murād begins his book with the narration of sacred history (*tārīḫ-i muḳaddes*), which he describes as events after the Creation for which no source exists other than sacred texts, especially the Old Testament.[45] Although he largely did not relate the stories of the prophets according to Islamic lore, Murād might have followed contemporaneous European historiography in creating a pre-history that heavily relied on biblical tradition. He also seems ambivalent about what to relate regarding the story of the Creation, as he briefly mentions that "according to the sacred texts" the universe was created in seven days but also mentions an account of earth's formation based on "the scientists' claims."[46]

As for his views on historical periodization, Murād does not differ much from the aforementioned history-writers. He chooses the Hegira as the beginning of the calendar, informing his readers of the traditions that take different important events to mark the start of their calendars. Among his examples are the Creation, the birth of the Christ, the founding of Rome, and the start of the ancient Olympic games.[47] By the time Murād wrote his book, the tripartite division of world history had already become a familiar model among Ottoman historians. So, he, too, uses it without further comment. The events he takes for his periodization are no different than those in one of the models circulating in Europe at the time: Ancient Ages (*ezmine-i müteḳaddime*), from Adam to the fall of the Western Roman Empire; Middle Ages (*ezmine-i mütevassıṭa*), from the fall of the Western Roman Empire to the conquest of Constantinople; and Modern Ages (*ḳurūn-ı cedīde* or *ezmine-i müte'aḫḫire*), from the conquest of Constantinople to modern times.[48]

Aḥmed Midḥat: Mufaṣṣal Tārīḫ-i Ḳurūn-ı Cedīde *(A Complete History of the Modern Ages), 1885–1888*

Aḥmed Midḥat (d. 1912) was a journalist who also published several popular history books, translated or adapted from French or composed by Midḥat himself. With his accessible, didactic style and wide readership, he is generally considered to have had substantial influence on the general reading public. He published a bulky *Mufaṣṣal Tārīḫ-i Ḳurūn-ı Cedīde* (A Complete History of the Modern Ages) first in his own newspaper, *Tercümān-ı Aḥvāl,* and later in book format. This unfinished three-volume work has an odd arrangement in that hundreds of long notes, which do not necessarily have direct relevance to the main text, run parallel to it and literally comprise one-half of the book. The main text recounts the rise of the Ottomans and the Byzantine Empire—from its break with the Roman Empire to the Latin invasion of Constantinople (395–1204)—and offers a survey of European nations and their state of affairs at the time of the conquest of Constantinople. Furthermore, Midḥat provides a history of

Istanbul as well as a narrative of the siege and the Byzantine intellectuals who fled to Europe after the fall of the city.[49]

Midḥat is critical of earlier Ottoman historians because of their failure to treat non-Islamic civilizations. He had also undertaken the initiative of printing—first in his newspaper and then in more than a dozen volumes—a series of histories titled *Kā'ināt* (The Universe) from 1871 to 1881. The first part (Europe) of that series includes histories of modern European nations published in several volumes; the second part (Asia) offers only one volume, devoted to the Ottoman Empire. Midḥat's volumes represented the rise of a new concept of universalism that did not see the history of the Ottoman Empire as a chapter within Islamic history.

Contributing to the manifestation of the idea of universalism was the periodization of world history, which Midḥat discusses in detail in his introduction to the first volume. "Is the division of history into periods arbitrary?" reads his title to the introduction. Midḥat is quite convinced that the tripartite division of world history is an absolute fact. According to him, "this division is not something subjective or an arbitrary choice of historians. All the historians (*cumhūr-i müverriḫīn*) agree on it."[50] Several mentions of "the historians" in his introduction, no doubt, refer to European historiographical production. Furthermore, "the unanimous agreement of the historians on the periodization of history," he declares, "grants almost a scientific nature (*fenniyyet*) to it. It is necessary to regard this structure as immutable (*lā-yataġayyer*)."[51]

However, Midḥat's presentation of the tripartite division as widely recognized among historians is only the first leg of his argument. He also considers this division natural. He argues that the earlier ages, for which there is little historical evidence, were the "obscure ages" (e.g., *ẓulmet-i mechūliyyet*), and that, accordingly, one should label the later periods, for which historical documentation does exist, as the "illuminated ages" (e.g., *ḳısm-ı münevver*). Because humankind did not leap from "Bedouinism" (a concept frequently used in opposition to "civilization" in the second half of the nineteenth century) to "civilization" at once, there should also be a period of transition. Therefore, according to Midḥat, a tripartite division can only be natural (*inḳısām-ı ṭabī'ī*). The fact that the three periods are not divided evenly in terms of their span also supports his argument. The events he takes for his tripartite periodization are no different than those in one of the contemporaneous European models: Ancient Ages (*ezmine-i müteḳaddime*), from Adam to the fall of the Western Roman Empire; Middle Ages (*ezmine-i mütevassıṭa*), from the fall of the Western Roman Empire to the conquest of Constantinople; and Modern Ages (*ezmine-i müte'aḫḫire*), from the conquest of Constantinople to modern times.[52]

Midḥat also offers his opinions as to which calendar to use for dating historical events. In a lengthy discussion, he objects to using the Hegira and the lunar calendar and defends the birth of Christ as the landmark for year zero in the solar calendar. This section must be a response to Meḥmed Murād's popular *Tārīḫ-i 'Umūmī*, which had appeared only a few years before and utilized the Islamic calendar for all of world history. Aḥmed Midḥat's justification seems to be based on practicality. Because of the ten days of difference between the two calendars, he argues, using the lunar calendar as opposed to the solar calendar is problematic.[53] If "we" accepted the birth of Christ as the start of the calendar, "we would neither be isolated from all the historians, nor would we have to alter the historical periodization which has been recognized by all."[54]

Aḥmed Cevdet: A Response to Aḥmed Midḥat, 1886

Aḥmed Midḥat sent a copy of the first few fascicles of his *Mufaṣṣal Tārīḫ-i Ḳurūn-ı Cedīde* (Complete History of the Modern Ages), along with a very humble letter, to Aḥmed Cevdet (d. 1895), the "grand historian" of the late nineteenth century. In the letter, Midḥat expresses great admiration for Cevdet's historianship, especially for rescuing "(Ottoman) historiography" (*fenn-i tārīḫ*) from mere tale-telling in favor of critical historianship through his opus magnum. The book to which he alludes is of course the *Tārīḫ-i Devlet-i ʿAliyye* (History of the Ottoman Empire), a twelve-volume work that covers the empire from 1774 to 1826. Cevdet may have been regarded as somewhat out of fashion by the new generation of history-writers in the 1880s, but apparently some still considered his blessings important and prestigious.

In his response, dated May 1886, Cevdet thanks Midḥat for his kind words and notes that he does not deem himself worthy of the exaggerated praises. He states that he read and studied Midḥat's book and offers some critical remarks on a few points, all of which pertain to the introductory section. As becomes clear from the tone of his polite, yet skeptical, response, Cevdet found the author's arguments naive, if not outright ignorant.

After a rather detailed and learned account of the emergence and use of the Julian and Gregorian calendars, Cevdet alludes to Midḥat's confusing the tripartite periodization with the Christian calendar, starting at Christ's birth. The latter was considered appropriate in Europe because of Christ's centrality to that culture. Accordingly, taking the Hegira for the start of the calendar would only be natural for Muslims. According to Cevdet, the difference between lunar and solar years is a non-issue. The period before the fifth century is also "quite obscure" in terms of historical knowledge; thus, Christ's birth was not considered the beginning of the Middle Ages.[55] He also does not consider the fall of the Western Roman Empire an event that had an important impact on world history: it may well have been a dramatic event for Europe but was not significant to world history in general (*ʿaleʾl-ʿumūm tārīḫ-i ʿālem için*).

Cevdet does not object to Midḥat's logical division of history into periods on the basis of the abundance of sound documentation. He has a modified model to offer, however: he divides history into two periods, Ancient and Modern, and proposes to regard the rise of Islam as the dividing line. He argues that the period from Adam to the rise of Islam is not sufficiently documented, and that the histories written before then were merely unreliable stories (*ḳuru ḥikāye*). According to Cevdet, it was only after the rise of Islam that historians examined the veracity of historical narration.

Before he finishes his letter—with the wise statement that all periodization is after all speculative (*bu mis̱illi taḳsīmler umūr-ı iʿtibāriyyedendir*), thus once again rejecting Midḥat's Eurocentric division of world history as an absolute truth—Cevdet makes one further, curious point. He proposes dividing the Modern Age into two sections, with the invention of the printing press as the dividing line. This logic is again in accordance with his division of world history into two periods, based on the availability of information about the period in question.[56]

Conclusion

Ottoman historiography traditionally took the Creation as the beginning of history and considered the lands and peoples that were under the influence of, or in direct contact with, Islamic states. The two historical turning points thereafter were the Flood and Prophet Muhammad's appearance. The first event was regarded as a logical second dawn of world history. As for the latter, it certainly was Islam centered, but because the message of the Prophet was regarded as universal, it was also seen as a landmark for world history. This model was gradually abandoned in the second half of the nineteenth century and a new scheme was adopted.

Another, albeit less common, scheme was to treat history after the rise of Islam by centuries. Müneccimbaşı, as we have seen above, chose to list the Islamic dynasties chronologically, grouped by centuries, after narrating the Umayyad and Abbasid dynasties in detail. Although dividing Islamic history into centuries was an approach that developed within the Islamic tradition, it became only somewhat popular. This division is usually understood to have risen from the concept that Islamic tradition expected a religious regeneration under the leadership of a spiritual (and/or political) ruler every hundred years after Hegira. Some nineteenth-century history-writers also experimented with this scheme with regards to Ottoman history. Aḥmed Vefīḳ, for example, grouped Ottoman sultans under centuries in his textbook *Feẕleke-i Tārīḫ-i ʿOs̱mānī* (A Résumé of Ottoman History, 1869). Aḥmed Cevdet, too, made use of the scheme in his *Tārīḫ*'s second edition (1884–1886).[57]

The shift from a long-established periodization scheme to a new model occurred as a result of several factors, among which new approaches to sources feature prominently. Changes in mentality and worldview do not occur over short periods of time, a statement especially valid for historical consciousness. In fact, emerging approaches to historical sources are evident before the period this essay focuses on, notably with Şānīzāde Meḥmed, a court annalist who composed his history in the early 1820s. Şānīzāde introduces and praises unusual sources for Ottoman historians as solid evidence that cannot be dismissed in historical writing: archeological finds (such as the Egyptian pyramids), statues, drawings, and inscriptions.[58]

By the last quarter of the nineteenth century, most Ottoman historians came to approach historical sources with a positivist perspective. A narrative of pre-historic times based on sacred texts gradually became impossible to substantiate. Consequently, the new qualification of sources led to a detachment of "sacred history" from the "history of civilizations," which would be the first step in completely removing such accounts as the stories of prophets from world histories,[59] as they came to be seen as stories without proper historical documentation.

A general disapproval of the traditional methodology of imperial annalists had already been on the rise in the 1840s. Although such criticism was not about periodization models per se, the general attitude can certainly be taken as evidence that the Ottoman intellectual mind was ripe for questioning long-established historical methods and patterns and apparently receptive to new ones. Criticism centered around the fact that the annalists recorded events in chronological order without seeking to elucidate any causal relationship between them, and that they were writing to justify the actions of powerful statesmen. Even an appointed imperial annalist, Recā'ī Meḥmed (d. 1874), found the tradition problematic by the late 1840s, as becomes clear from a petition he submitted to the grand vizier; he considered the unilateral nature of the sources to be the primary shortcoming of the annals written by his predecessors.[60]

Although Ottoman historians did not make use of the new types of sources directly, appreciation for them led to an admiration of historiography that utilized them extensively. Eventually, a periodization that partitioned all known history of the world in three main periods was adopted by Ottoman intellectuals who aspired to replicate a "scientific" historiography that became professionalized first in German academia and then in other places in Europe during the nineteenth century. The new historiography, an important component of which was the tripartite division, was accordingly labeled the "new method" (*uṣūl-i cedīd*) by several history-writers of the later nineteenth century.[61] It seems that the tripartite division as a format was imported rather mechanically and presented as absolute fact. No doubt it would have been impossible for Ottoman intellectuals to invent a much altered periodization scheme when European historiography made use of an overwhelming body of sources and auxiliary sciences. Ottoman scholarship had made no original contribution to non-Ottoman historiography by this time. Hence, major events that mark turning points in the European scheme were simply replaced with those from Islamic and Ottoman history. There seems to be a consensus that the scarcity or abundance of sources for each of these periods was the justification for the tripartite division.

Still, the ready acceptance of the tripartite division of history in the Ottoman intellectual milieu must be considered within the framework of Ottoman intellectual history and the emergence of a new notion of universalism. The new universalists did not consider Ottoman history the final phase of Islamic and world history, nor did they consider the world to be deteriorating toward its inevitable destruction, that is,

Judgment Day. The idea that by every lived day the world was approaching its cataclysmic end is deeply rooted in Christian and Islamic belief systems and can also be traced to Ancient Greek thought. History was now viewed as an optimistic story of progress—much in line with contemporary European views of history. Aḥmed Midḥat, for example, describes history as "the account of the progress of humankind and civilization." A progressive story of world history logically required a division that developed from old (ancient) to new (modern). The scheme that had partitioned Islamic history into centuries, as we have seen above, viewed Islamic history as a linear story, but not a progressive one.

There was also a political aspect to the idea of a progressive history. As mentioned, Aḥmed Ḥilmī explains at length—in an afterword to his discussion of the Ancient Ages—that the common people were oppressed and treated with injustice by absolute monarchs. Whatever the rulers proclaimed was taken as law, he laments. Ancient history can be characterized, in his words, by plundering, execution, injustice, and transgression—acts that conflicted with ideals such as "justice and humanity" (*ḥaḳḳaniyyet ve insāniyyet*).[62] Yet, the history of the Ancient Ages also proved that people in a state of savagery constantly strived to transform themselves into a state of civilization.[63] Surely, the monarchy's decline in popularity during the nineteenth century, and the growing admiration for popular participation in government, was the backdrop of such statements. History-writing was, as always, a medium that was used to reflect political views.

Another development that facilitated the rise of the "new method" in historiography was the democratization of historical writing in the Ottoman lands. Due to the educational policies of the nineteenth century and increasing printing opportunities, there was a rapid growth in the number of histories, the variety of subjects they covered, and the methodologies utilized. With new histories emerging in parallel, the city of Istanbul, the imperial court, and the central bureaucracy ceased to be the only centers of historical production. The professional background of history-writers changed, as well. In addition to historians from scribal careers, or those with close connections to the court, now freelance history-writers, modernizing military officers, and journalists (a new profession) composed or translated popular works or textbooks. The ulema, traditionally a prolific group in all kinds of writing activities, did not compose or translate any works in subjects under consideration here.

The tripartite division remained the only scheme used in modern Turkish historiography and had a great impact on Turkish historical consciousness throughout the twentieth century. Its adoption in the late nineteenth century was the result of an effort to integrate Ottoman-Turkish historiography with a tradition that claimed to have divided world history into periods "scientifically." Whether prompted by current historiographical outlooks on world history or by nationalistic incentives, many modern historians highlight the Eurocentric nature of the scheme and question the validity of such a model for world history.[64]

Appendix: Books Examined in This Essay

Historian	Work	Composed or Published	Period Covered
Şükrullāh (d. 1488)	*Bahjat al-Tawārikh*	late 1450s	from the Creation to the 1450s
Muṣṭafā ʿĀlī (d. 1600)	*Künhü'l-Aḫbār*	1590s	from the Creation to the late 1500s
Ḳaraçelebizāde ʿAbdülʿazīz (d. 1658)	*Ravżatü'l-Ebrār*	1648	from the Creation to 1646
Müneccimbaşı Aḥmed (d. 1702)	*Jāmiʿ al-Duwal*	1672	from the Creation to 1672
Ferā'iżīzāde Meḥmed Saʿīd (d. 1835)	*Gülşen-i Maʿārif*	completed 1834 published 1836	from Adam to 1774
Aḥmed Vefīḳ (d. 1891)	*Ḥikmet-i Tārīḫ*	lectures delivered at the University in March 1863	from the Creation to the Modern Ages
Aḥmed Ḥilmī (d. 1878)	*Tārīḫ-i ʿUmūmī*, 6 vols. (at least the first two volumes translated from William Chambers)	1866–1878	from the Ancient Ages to the Middle Ages (incomplete)
Meḥmed Āṭıf (d. 1908 or 1909)	*Ḫulāṣatü't-Tevārīḫ*	1872–1873	from the Creation to Ancient Greece (incomplete)
Süleymān Ḥüsnī (d. 1892)	*Tārīḫ-i ʿĀlem*, 1: *Ḳurūn-ı Ūlā*	1876	from the Creation to the Hegira (incomplete)
Rıfʿat Efendi (d. 1895)	*Naḳdü't-Tevārīḫ*	1879	from the Creation to 1879
Meḥmed Murād (d. 1917)	*Tārīḫ-i ʿUmūmī*	1880–1882	from the Creation to modern times
Aḥmed Midḥat (d. 1912)	*Mufaṣṣal Tārīḫ-i Ḳurūn-ı Cedīde*, 3 vols.	1885–1888	begins with the rise of the Ottomans
Aḥmed Cevdet (d. 1895)	Included in the *Teẕākir*	letter written in 1886	a critique of Aḥmed Midḥat's *Mufaṣṣal Ḳurūn-ı Cedīde Tārīḫi*

Notes

1. I have placed the adjective "scientific" in quotation marks because, while modern historians appreciate the limited validity (or invalidity) of all-encompassing historical models, the periodization scheme under consideration was accepted and promoted by members of the newly professional discipline of history in Europe, who conferred to it the illusion of scientific authority. A survey of developments in European historiography in the nineteenth and twentieth centuries can be found in

Georg Iggers, *Historiography in the Twentieth Century: From Scientific Objectivity to the Postmodern Challenge* (Hanover, N.H.: Wesleyan University Press, 1997).

2. For an overview of European periodizations of world history, see William A. Green, "Periodization in European and World History," *Journal of World History* 3, no. 1 (1992): 13–53, 16 ff.

3. *Na'īmā Tārīḫi* (Istanbul, 1281–1283/1864–1866), I, 26 f., quoted in Gottfried Hagen, "Afterword," in Robert Dankoff, *An Ottoman Mentality: The World of Evliya Çelebi* (Leiden: Brill, 2004), 242.

4. Franz Babinger, *Die Geschichtsschreiber der Osmanen und ihre Werke* (Leipzig: Otto Harrassowitz, 1927) lists at least a dozen universal histories alone for the sixteenth century.

5. An overview of various forms of early Islamic history-writing can be found in Franz Rosenthal, *A History of Muslim Historiography* (Leiden: Brill, 1968). Also see the individual articles for the abovementioned historians in the *Encyclopedia of Islam*, 2nd ed. For an evaluation and translation of chapters on non-Islamic history by these authors, see Karl Jahn, ed., *Die Frankengeschichte des Rašīd ad-dīn* (Vienna: Verlag der Österreichischen Akademie der Wissenschaften, 1977); Karl Jahn, ed., *Die Indiengeschichte des Rašid ad-Dīn: Einleitung, vollständige Übersetzung, Kommentar und 80 Texttafeln* (The Hague: Mouton, 1965); and other studies by Jahn. For al-Ya'qūbī, see Aḥmad ibn Abī Ya'qūb Ya'qūbī, *Ibn-Wādhih qui dicitur al-Ja'qubī historiae*, ed. M. Th. Houtsma (Leiden: Brill, 1883), part 1: Pre-Islamic History.

6. Camilla Adang, *Muslim Writers on Judaism and the Hebrew Bible, from Ibn Rabban to Ibn Hazm* (Leiden: Brill, 1996), 117–120.

7. Muṣṭafā 'Ālī, *Künhü'l-Aḫbār* (Istanbul: Taḳvīmḫāne-i Āmire, 1861), 1:262.

8. Cornell H. Fleischer, *Bureaucrat and Intellectual in the Ottoman Empire: The Historian Muṣṭafā 'Ālī (1541–1600)* (Princeton, N.J.: Princeton University Press, 1986), 240.

9. Şükrullāh, *Bahjat al-Tavārikh* (Splendor of Histories), composed ca. 1458. *Chapter 1 (bāb)*: Creation of the universe and creatures (in two versions), sky, stars, constellations, four elements, nature, people who live in the seven climes. Creation of the souls and bodies of humankind. Characteristics of humankind. Creation of the simple and complex limbs of humans. Earth. Seven seas. Seven climes. Inhabitants of the earth. China and Chinese people. The nine Turkish tribes. Greeks. Arabs. Hindus and Sinds. Abyssinians. Tekrur (Sudanese). People whose character does not conform to that of a human being. *Chapter 2:* History of the prophets mentioned in the Qur'an: Adam, Seth, Idris, Noah, Hud, Salih, Abraham, Ismail, Isaac, Joseph, Moses, Aaron, David, Suleiman, Jesus. *Chapter 3:* The genealogy of the Prophet Muhammad. Quraish Tribe. Sons of Hashim. *Chapter 4:* Birth of the Prophet Muhammad in seven subsections (*faṣl*). (1) Amina's pregnancy. (2) The miracles of the Prophet as recorded in the six reliable hadith collections. (3) The Prophet's battles. (4) His army. (5) His slaves. (6) His scribes and other servants. (7) His weapons. *Chapter 5:* (1) His wives. (2) His children. (3) His uncles and cousins. (4) His aunts. *Chapter 6:* The ten companions of the Prophet. Their genealogies, how long they lived. *Chapter 7:* (1) The rest of the companions of the Prophet. (2) The companions and the sequence of their death. (3) Those who memorized the Qur'an and those who were experts of law. (4) Those companions who transmitted sayings of the Prophet. *Chapter 8:* Imams: (1) Imams of the four schools of jurisprudence. (2) Six imams who compiled the sayings of the Prophet. (3) Eight imams whose fatwas are recognized. *Chapter 9:* Sheikhs. *Chapter 10:* Most significant philosophers of the Greeks and other people. *Chapter 11:* Kings of the infidels and the believers: (1) First dynasty of the Persian kings. (2) Kayanids. (3) Ashkanids (Parthia). (4) Sassanids. *Chapter 12:* Umayyads, Abbasids, Fatimids, Seljuks. *Chapter 13:* Ottomans until Sultan Mehmed II.

10. Muṣṭafā 'Ālī, *Künhü'l-Aḫbār* (Essence of Histories), composed 1590s. *Pillar 1:* The reason for composing the book. Layout of the book. General introduction. Benefits of historiography. The Creation: (several different traditions). The Prophet's light, this world and other world. The Throne. The *lawḥ*, that is, the tablet on which the predestination is inscribed, the throne of God. Skies and earth. Angels, jinns, Satan. Paradise and Hell. The Kaaba. The wonders of creation. Sun and moon,

rainbows, clouds, thunders, and so forth. Beasts. Sea creatures. Geography: the seas, islands, climes, countries. Ancient nations, their religion and customs. Syrians/Sabeans, Copts, Persians, Arabs, "Romans," Armenians, Russians, Khazars, Bulgars, Tatars, Circassians, Wallachians, Transylvanians, Moldavians, Jews, Greeks, Christians. Languages. Notes on historiography. Number of prophets. The descents of Gabriel. History of jinns and the Devil. The prophets before the Deluge: Adam, Seth, Idris, Noah. The Deluge. The sons of Noah (Sam, Japheth), and their descendants. The prophets after the Deluge: Hud, Salih, Alexander Dhulqarneyn, Abraham, Lot, Ismael, Isaac, Jacob, Joseph. Construction of Mecca. The non-Muslim postdiluvian kings: ancient Egypt, Coptic kings, Babylon. *Pillar 2:* The prophets (continued): Joseph, Job, Shuayb, Moses, Jonah, David, Suleiman, Zacharia, John, Jesus. Prophet Muhammad. His genealogy, miracles, night journey to the heavens, his slaves, and so forth. The four rightly guided Caliphs. The ten companions of the Prophet who were promised Paradise. Companions of the Prophet. The imams of the four schools of law. Experts of the Prophet's sayings. Those who memorized the Qur'an. Ḥasan and Ḥussain, the grandsons of the Prophet. The twelve imams. The Mahdi. The Persian kings and Ptolemies. The first dynasty, Kayanids, Ashkanids, Sassanids, Ptolemies. *Pillar 3:* The dynasties of North Africa, Egypt, and Syria: Tulunids, Ikhshidids, Fatimids, Ayyubids, Mamluks. The Circassian Mamluks. Caliphate until the fall of Baghdad: Umayyads, Abbasids. The dynasties of central and eastern Islamic world I: Timurids, Safavids, Shaybanids, Aqqoyunlu, Qaraqoyunlu, Dulkadrids, sultans of Hind, Gujarat, Jawnpur, Sind, Mazandaran, Turkomans, and so forth. The dynasties of central and eastern Islamic world II: Samanids, Danishmendids, Khwarazm Shahs, Ilkhanids, Mongols, Giray Khans, and so on. Two dynasties of the central and northwestern Islamic world: Timurids, Anatolian Seljuks. *Pillar 4:* Contemporary Islamic rulers and infidel rulers, indicating their relations with the Ottomans. The character of Albanians, Franks, Hungarians, Germans, and so forth, as state officials. Notes on physiognomy. The Ottomans: their genealogy, battles, important events, lists of scholars, and so on. A detailed account of Ottoman history until the 1590s classified according to the reigns of the sultans.

11. Ḳaraçelebizāde ʿAbdülʿazīz, *Ravżatü'l-Ebrār* (The Garden of the Pious), composed 1648. Chapters: the Prophets (Adam, Seth, Idris, Noah, etc.) (pp. 4–99); Prophet Muhammad, his family, wars, and so forth (pp. 99–126); the four rightly guided Caliphs (pp. 127–141); the rise and fall of the Islamic dynasties: Umayyads, Qarmatians, Ghaznavids, Buyids, Khwarezmian dynasty, Crusades, Ghurids, Abbasids, Seljuks, Karaman, Hulagu (pp. 141–275); the rise of the Ottomans (pp. 275–288); the fall of the Mamluks (pp. 288–319); Safavids (Ḳızılbaş) (pp. 319–338); a detailed account of Ottoman history (later sections recount contemporary history) (pp. 338–628).

12. Albert Dietrich, "A propos d'un précis d'histoire gréco-romaine dans la chronique universelle arabe de Müneccimbaşı," *V. Congrès international d'arabisants et d'islamisants: 31 août –septembre 1970, Bruxelles* (Bruxelles: Centre pour l'Étude des Problèmes du Monde Musulman Contemporain, 1971), 175–188.

13. For example, see the passage in which he narrates the Spanish kings until 1681, that is, the date that section was composed (mentioning the reigning Holy Roman Emperor Leopold I); cf. Müneccimbaşı Aḥmed, *Jamiʿ al-Duwal,* Süleymaniye Library, Istanbul. Esad Efendi 2101, fol. 136a. Partially condensed contents: sources, calendars. *Book 1. The Creation, Prophets:* The Creation. Prophet Adam and his descendants. Twenty-four other prophets. Prophets sent to the Israelites. Dynasties in the Arabian Peninsula before Islam. The origins of the tribe Quraish. History of Mecca. Birth of the Prophet Muhammad. His early childhood in Mecca. The four rightly guided Caliphs. *Book 2: 2a. Dynasties and Peoples before Islam:* The first dynasty (Pishdadiyan). Dynasties in ancient Syria. Ghassanids, Persians. Greeks, Amalekites, Copts. Hindus, Turks, Tatars, Turkoman tribes. Chinese, Bulgars, Russians, Georgians. Franks, English, Spaniards. History of the Black Sea, the Mediterranean, the Indian Ocean, and the Adriatic Sea. Sassanids. Ad, Tamud, and so forth. Ghassanids and ancient Arabian tribes. Byzantines. Austrians. Spaniards. Armenians. Egyptian history

before and after the Deluge. The tribes after the Deluge and the descendants of Israelites. Tribes in Mesopotamia. Rulers of India and China. *2b. Dynasties and Peoples after Islam:* Umayyads. Andalusian Umayyads. Abbasids. Aghlabids. Tahirids. Samanids. Rulers of Kirman. Gurgan, Kharezm, Simjurids, Ghaznawids. Tulunids. Hamdanids. Ihshidids. Basra, Wasit emirate. [*From here a division according to centuries commences:*] (Rulers in Gilan and Ruyan) Dabuyid dynasty, and so on. Rustamids. Idrisites. Daylamites, emirates in Sicily. North Africa. Ismailites. Buyids. Shaddadids. Seljuks. Danishmends. Emirs of Khuzistan, Khorasan. Kara Khitay. Almoravids, Almohads. Lurs, Kurds. Ghurids. Ayyubids. Circassians of Egypt. Sharifs of Makka and Madina. Principalities in the Persian Gulf. Mongols. Chagatais. Descendents of Genghis Khan. Chobanids, Ilkhanids, Jalayirids. Princes of Khorasan. Muzaffirids of Iran. Ahmarids of Andalusia. Marinids of North Africa. Zaydi sharifs of Yemen. Zaydi imams of Yemen. Rulers of the Island Hurmuz. Qaramanids. Principalities in Anatolia (Isfendiyar, Pervane, Aydın, Kermiyan, Menteşe, Hamid, Teke, Qarasi, Canik, Qadı Burhaneddin). Timurids. The emirates in India. Bahmanids. The emirates in Kashgar. Kashmir. Qaraqoyunlu. Aqqoyunlu. Dulqadrids. Banu Ramadan. Rulers of Shirvan. Safavids. Zaydis in Yemen. Sharifs of North Africa. [*Ottomans:*] Beginnings of the Ottomans: Ertugrul Gazi. Osman Gazi . . . a detailed history of individual sultans until the accession to the throne of Mehmed IV.

14. Abdülkadir Özcan, "Feraizizade Mehmed Said," *Türkiye Diyanet Vakfı İslam Ansiklopedisi,* 12 (1995), 366–67.

15. Ferā'iżīzāde Meḥmed Sa'īd, *Gülşen-i Ma'ārif* (The Rose Garden of Knowledge), published 1836. *Volume 1:* Articles of faith in Sunni Islam (p. 2); angels (pp. 4–6); holy books (pp. 6–7); the rest of the articles of faith (p. 8); prophets: Adam, Seth, Idris, Noah, Hud, Salih, Abraham, Ismail, Isaac, Jacob, Joseph, Moses, David, Suleiman, Jesus (pp. 9–63); life of the Prophet Muhammad (pp. 63–136); companions of the Prophet (pp. 136–175); the imams, sheikhs (pp. 176–223); Pihsdadiyan, Kayanids, Sassanids, Ashkanids, Umayyads, Abbasids, Samanids, Seljuks, rulers of Khwarezm, Khorasan, Kuhistan, and so forth. Turkish, Circassian, Genghisid, Timurid, Turkoman rulers (pp. 223–411); detailed account of Ottoman history (pp. 411–847). *Volume 2:* Detailed account of Ottoman history (pp. 850–1693).

16. Muṣṭafā 'Ālī, *Künhü'l-Aḫbār,* 1:260.

17. For example, Ḳaraçelebizāde 'Abdül'azīz, *Ravżatü'l-Ebrār* (Cairo: Maṭba'a-i Bulāḳ, 1832), 12; and Aḥmed Vefīḳ, *Ḥikmet-i Tārīḫ* (Istanbul, 1886), 29.

18. Muṣṭafā 'Ālī, *Künhü'l-Aḫbār,* 1:261.

19. Fleischer details the topic in his *Bureaucrat and Intellectual in the Ottoman Empire,* 273 ff. Adshead characterizes the Mongol conquests under Genghis Khan and his successors as a massive explosion that "started" history and affected even those parts of the world that were not physically penetrated by the Mongols. See Samuel Adrian M. Adshead, *Central Asia in World History* (New York: St. Martin's Press, 1993), 53.

20. Muṣṭafā 'Ālī, *Künhü'l-Aḫbār,* I, 260–261.

21. For some of the activities and publications of the Academy of Sciences, see Ahmet Karaçavuş, "Tanzimat Dönemi Osmanlı Bilim Cemiyetleri" (PhD diss., Ankara University, 2006), 112 ff., esp. 172 ff. Cf. Kenan Akyüz, *Encümen-i Dâniş* (Ankara: [Ankara Üniversitesi Eğitim Fakültesi Yayınları], 1975). See also Ahmet Hamdi Tanpınar, *XIX. Asır Türk Edebiyatı Tarihi,* ed. Abdullah Uçman (Istanbul: Yapı Kredi Yayınları, 2006), 139–141.

22. The booklet ends abruptly in the middle of a sentence, with a catchword for the next page, which might indicate that more was typeset but not printed. The reason why the booklet remained incomplete cannot be determined.

23. Somel disputes the assertion that history as a course was instructed as early as 1839 at schools, or even later during the 1850s. See Selçuk Akşin Somel, *The Modernization of Public Education in the Ottoman Empire, 1839–1908: Islamization, Autocracy, and Discipline* (Leiden: Brill, 2001), 194.

24. Oğuzhan Alpaslan, "A. Vefik Paşa ve Çağdaş Dönem ilk Osmanlı Tarih Metodolojisi Kitabı *Hikmet-i Tarih,*" *Muhafazakâr Düşünce* 2, no. 7 (2006): 197–218; cf. Tahir Nakıp, *Osmanlı Devletinde Geç Dönem Tarih-i Umumiler* (MA thesis, Marmara University, 2006), 26 ff.

25. Aḥmed Vefīḳ, *Ḥikmet-i Tārīḫ*, 7–8.

26. Ibid., 8.

27. Ibid., 13.

28. What follows is Aḥmed Vefīḳ's periodization of world history: *Ancient Ages* (*ezmine-i müteḳaddime*, or, alternatively, *ezmine-i ḳadīme*): First era (*faṣl*): 2550 years (Adam sent to earth; the Deluge; histories composed in Greece; end of the Assyrian Empire); Second era: 440 years (rise of the Achaemenid [Persian] Empire; Alexander halts the Persians); Third era: 300 years (founding of Rome; death of Alexander; birth of Christ); Fourth era: 622 years (fall of the Western Roman Empire; barbarian tribes invade Europe; Hegira). *Middle Ages* (*ezmine-i mütevassıṭa*): First era: two centuries (Islam spreads in Turkistan, Hindustan, and Europe; barbarian tribes in Europe); Second era: three centuries (the Caliphate splits in two; influence of the popes increases; rise of feudal lords); Third era: two centuries (Crusades; Genghis Khan; Holy Roman Empire); Fourth era: two centuries (Timur; advance of the Ottomans and Genoese; Renaissance and Reformation in Europe; invention of gunpowder and firearms). *Modern Ages* (*ezmine-i cedīde* or *mu'aḫḫara*): First era (conquest of Constantinople; discovery of the New World); Second era: 170 years (rise of Shi'ites in the East and Protestants in the West; rise of the Ottomans and Spain); Third era: 135 years (Mongol invasion of China; power of Hindustan, France, Netherlands, and Russia increases); Fourth era: 40 years (French Republic; Napoleonic Wars; founding of the United States; British naval power increases; the "Auspicious Event" [Abolition of the Janissary corps]).

29. Aḥmed Ḥilmī, *Tārīḫ-i 'Umūmī,* (Istanbul: Maṭba'a-i 'āmire, 1866–1878), 1:4.

30. Ibid., 2:334 ff.

31. I was not able to locate the third, fourth, and fifth volumes of this work.

32. William Chambers vs. Aḥmed Ḥilmī: Ancient Ages (from Adam to the fall of the Roman Empire) vs. *Ezmine-i müteḳaddime* (from Adam to the Hegira); Middle Ages (from the fall of the Roman Empire to the discovery of the New World) vs. *Ezmine-i mütevassıṭa* (from the Hegira to the conquest of Constantinople); Modern Ages (from the discovery of the New World to author's time) vs. *Ezmine-i müte'aḫḫire* (from the conquest of Constantinople to translator's time).

33. Meḥmed 'Āṭıf, *Ḫulāṣatü't-Tevārīḫ* (Istanbul: Muḥibb Maṭba'ası, 1872 or 1873), 3.

34. "European historians" vs. Meḥmed 'Āṭıf: Initial Ages (from the Creation to the fall of the Western Roman Empire) vs. *Ḳurūn-ı ūlā* (from the Creation to the Hegira); Middle Ages (from fall of the Western Roman Empire to the conquest of Constantinople) vs. *Ḳurūn-ı vusṭā* (from the Hegira to the conquest of Constantinople); Later Ages (from the conquest of Constantinople to author's time) vs. *Ḳurūn-ı āḫire* (from the conquest of Constantinople to the translator's time).

35. For example: Initial Ages (*ḳurūn-ı ūlā*): (1) Primary times (*ezmine-i evveliyye*): twenty-five centuries (events before the Deluge); (2) Mythical times (*ezmine-i esāṭiriyye*): seventeen centuries (from the establishment of historical states to the founding of Rome); (3) Historical times (*ezmine-i tārīḫiyye*): thirteen centuries (from the founding of Rome to the collapse of the Western Roman Empire).

36. The date 27 May 1876, which is recorded at the end of the book, must be the day on which the book went to press. However, the introduction includes a tribute to Murad V (p. 5), who would be enthroned on May 30 and rule as sultan until August 31, 1876. The introduction must have been adjusted after May 30.

37. Süleymān Ḥüsnī, *Tārīḫ-i 'Ālem,* 1: *Ḳurūn-ı Ūlā* (Istanbul: Mekteb-i Fünūn-ı Ḥarbiyye Maṭba'ası, 1876), 2.

38. Initial Ages (*ḳurūn-ı ūlā* or *tārīḫ-i ḳadīm*) (from Adam to the Hegira); Middle Ages (*ḳurūn-ı vusṭā*) (from the Hegira to the appearance of the Ottoman dynasty [ca. 1300]); Modern Ages (*ḳurūn-ı

aḫīre or *ḳurūn-ı cedīde*) (from the appearance of the Ottoman dynasty to the founding of the "Nizam-ı Cedid" and the destruction of the Janissary corps [1826]); Contemporary times (*tārīḫ-i ʿaṣr*) (from the destruction of the Janissary corps to the author's time).

39. Süleymān Ḥüsnī's division of pre-historic times, which differs somewhat from Meḥmed ʿĀṭıf's model, is as follows: Ancient History (*tārīḫ-i ḳadīm*): (1) Primary times (*ezmine-i evveliyye*): (a) the era of Adam (*ʿahd-i Ādem*) (events before the Flood), (b) the era of Noah (*ʿahd-i Nūḥ*) (until the establishment of the historical states); (2) Mythical times (*ezmine-i esāṭiriyye*) (from the establishment of historical states to the founding of Rome); (3) Historical times (*ezmine-i tārīḫiyye*) (from the founding of Rome to the Hegira).

40. Rıfʿat Efendi, *Naḳdüʾt-Tevārīḫ* (Istanbul: Yaḥyā Efendi Maṭbaʿası, 1879), 2.

41. Ibid., 3.

42. Christoph Herzog, *Geschichte und Ideologie: Meḥmed Murād und Celal Nuri über die historischen Ursachen des osmanischen Niedergangs* (Berlin: Klaus Schwarz, 1996).

43. Meḥmed Murād, *Tārīḫ-i ʿUmūmī* (Istanbul: Maḥmūd Bey Maṭbaʿası, 1880–1882), 1:2–3.

44. Ibid., 1:7.

45. Ibid., 1: 14.

46. Ibid., 1: 10–11.

47. Ibid., 1: 9.

48. Initial Ages (*ḳurūn-ı ūlā* or *ezmine-i müteḳaddime*) (from the Creation to the fall of the Western Roman Empire); Middle Ages (*ḳurūn-ı vusṭā* or *ezmine-i mütevassıṭa*) (from the fall of the Western Roman Empire to the conquest of Constantinople); Modern Ages (*ḳurūn-ı cedīde* or *ezmine-i müteʾaḫḫire*) (from the conquest of Constantinople to modern times).

49. On Aḥmed Midḥat's treatment of Byzantine history, see Michael Ursinus, "Byzantine History in Late Ottoman Turkish Historiography," *Byzantine and Modern Greek Studies* 10 (1986): 211–222.

50. Aḥmed Midḥat, *Mufaṣṣal Tārīḫ-i Ḳurūn-ı Cedīde* (Istanbul, 1885–1888), 1:7.

51. Ibid., 1: 9.

52. Ancient Ages (*ezmine-i müteḳaddime* or *ḳurūn-ı ḳadīme*) (from Adam to the fall of the Western Roman Empire); Middle Ages (*ezmine-i mütevassıṭa* or *ḳurūn-ı vusṭā*) (from the fall of the Western Roman Empire to the conquest of Constantinople); Modern Ages (*ezmine-i müteʾaḫḫire* or *ḳurūn-ı cedīde*) (from the conquest of Constantinople to modern times).

53. Midḥat cites a "witty" observation that the difference would create confusion in that both calendars would have the same date after centuries; Aḥmed Midḥat, *Mufaṣṣal Tārīḫ-i Ḳurūn-ı Cedīde* 1: 8. That would be the year 20,875 in the Gregorian calendar.

54. Aḥmed Midḥat, *Mufaṣṣal Tārīḫ-i Ḳurūn-ı Cedīde* 1:8–9: "*Cumhūr-ı müverriḫīnden ayrılmamış ve tārīḫiñ cümle nezdinde maḳbūl taḳsīmāt-ı esāsiyyesini . . .*"

55. Aḥmed Cevdet, *Tezākir 40-Tetimme*, ed. Cavid Baysun (Ankara: Türk Tarih Kurumu, 1991), 242.

56. Ancient Ages (*tārīḫ-i ʿatīḳ*) (from Adam to the rise of Islam); Modern Ages (*ʿaṣr-ı cedīd*) (from the rise of Islam to modern times, divided into two at the invention of the printing press).

57. Cf. Christoph Neumann, *Das indirekte Argument: ein Plädoyer für die* Tanẓīmāt *vermittels der Historie. Die geschichtliche Bedeutung von Aḥmed Cevdet Paşas* Taʾrīḫ (Münster: Lit, 1994), 105–106.

58. Şânîzâde Meḥmed Atâʾullah Efendi, *Şânîzâde Târîhî*, ed. Ziya Yılmazer (Istanbul: Çamlıca, 2008), 1:15 ff.

59. Several of the authors mentioned here discuss the separation of "sacred history" (*muḳaddes*) and "general history" (*ʿāmme*) (the latter also appearing as "history of civilization," *tārīḫ-i temeddün*); for example, cf. Aḥmed Ḥilmī, *Tārīḫ-i ʿUmūmī*, 2:334; Süleymān Ḥüsnī, *Tārīḫ-i ʿĀlem*, 1: *Ḳurūn-ı Ūlā*, 2, et. al.

60. Recorded in Meḥmed Cemāleddīn, *ʿOsmānlı Tārīḫ ve Müverriḫleri: Āyīne-i Ẓurefā* (Istanbul: İkdam, 1896–1897), 105–111. See Cemal Kafadar and Hakan Karateke, "Late Ottoman and Early

Republican Turkish Historiography," *The Oxford History of Historical Writing*, Volume 4: *1800–1945*, ed. Stuart Macintyre et. al. (New York: Oxford University Press, 2011), 559–577.

61. The term *uṣūl-i cedīd* was in circulation with respect to educational policies in the 1870s. The reflection in historiography can rightly be seen as a response to that policy. See Somel, *The Modernization of Public Education in the Ottoman Empire*, 169 ff.

62. Aḥmed Ḥilmī, *Tārīḫ-i 'Umūmī*, 2:339.

63. Aḥmed Ḥilmī, *Tārīḫ-i 'Umūmī*, 2:337: "*Tevārīḫ-i ḳadīme iṣbāt eder ki ḥāl-i vaḥşiyyetden çıḳan milletlerde müşāhede eyledigimiz teraḳḳī gibi milel-i ḳadīme daḫi vaḥşiyyet ḥālinde bulunduḳları zamānlarda medeniyyet-i ḥālete teraḳḳī eylemege sa'y ederler imiş*"; see also: Meḥmed Murād, *Tārīḫ-i 'Umūmī*, I, 4: "*Evlād-i beşeriñ ḥāl-i vaḥşet ve bedeviyyetden çıḳıp bugünkü 'umrān ve medeniyyet ḥāline gelinceye ḳadar teṣādüf eyledigi aḥvāl.*"

64. For a critical assessment of Eurocentric periodization of world history from an Islamic viewpoint, see Khalid Blankinship, "Islam and World History: Towards a New Periodization," *American Journal of Islamic Social Science* 8, no. 3 (1991), 423–439. For a rather blunt criticism of the Christian and Eurocentric nature of the tripartite periodization model, see Necmettin Alkan, "Tarihin Çağlara Ayrılmasında 'Üç'lü Sistem ve 'Avrupa Merkezci' Tarih Kurgusu," *Uluslararası Sosyal Araştırmalar Dergisi* 2, no. 9 (2009): 23–42.

Bibliography

Sources

ʿAbdüʾlvāsiʿ Çelebi. *Ḫalīlnāme*. Edited by Ayhan Güldaş. Ankara: T. C. Kültür Bakanlığı, 1996.

Aḥmed Cevdet. *Teẕākir*. Edited by Cavid Baysun. Ankara: Türk Tarih Kurumu, 1991.

Aḥmed Ḥilmī. *Tārīḫ-i ʿUmūmī*. 6 vols. Istanbul: Maṭbaʿa-i ʿāmire, 1866–1878.

Aḥmed Midḥat. *Mufaṣṣal Ḳurūn-ı Cedīde Tārīḫi*. 3 vols. Istanbul, 1885–1888.

Aḥmed Vefīḳ. *Ḥikmet-i Tārīḫ*. Istanbul, 1886.

Aḥmedī, Tāceʾd-Dīn İbrāhīm bin Ḫıżır. *İskender-nāme: İnceleme, Tıpkıbasım*. Edited by İsmail Ünver. Ankara: Türk Tarih Kurumu, 1983.

———. *Tevārīḫ-i Mülūk-i Āl-i ʿOs̱mān ve Ġazv-i İşān Bā-Küffār: Tāceʾd-Dīn İbrāhīm bin Ḫıżır Aḥmedī*. Critical edition by Kemal Silay. Cambridge, Mass.: Harvard University, Department of Near Eastern Languages and Civilizations, 2004.

Aḳsarāyī, Kerīmüddīn Maḥmūd. *Musāmarat al-akhbār*. In *Müsâmeret ül-ahbâr: Moğollar Zamanında Türkiye Selçukluları Tarihi*, edited by Osman Turan. Ankara: Türk Tarih Kurumu, 1944.

Al-Kisāʾī. *The Tales of the Prophets of al-Kisāʾī*. Translated by Wheeler M. Thackston, Jr. Boston: Twayne, 1978.

Al-Ṭabarī. *The History of al-Ṭabarī (Taʾrīkh al-rusul waʾl-mulūk)*. Translated by Franz Rosenthal. Vol. 1. Albany: State University of New York Press, 1989.

Anonymous. *Aḥvāl-i Sulṭān Meḥemmed bin Bāyezīd Ḫān*. Edited and translated by Dimitris Kastritsis as *The Tales of Sultan Meḥmed, Son of Bāyezīd Khan*. Cambridge, Mass.: Harvard University, Department of Near Eastern Languages and Civilizations, 2007.

———. *Baṭṭālnāme*. Edited and translated by Yorgos Dedes as *The Battalname, an Ottoman Turkish Frontier Epic Wondertale*. Part I. Cambridge, Mass.: Harvard University, Department of Near Eastern Languages and Civilizations, 1996.

———. *Cronaca dei Tocco di Cefalonia di anonimo*. Edited by Giuseppe Schirò. Rome: Accademia nazionale dei Lincei, 1975.

———. *Die altosmanischen anonymen Chroniken: Tevârîh-i Âl-i ʿOsmân*. Edited by Friedrich Giese. Breslau: self-published, 1922.

———. *Ġazavāt-ı Sulṭān Murād b. Meḥemmed Ḫān*. Edited by Halil İnalcık and Mevlud Oğuz. Ankara: Türk Tarih Kurumu, 1978.

———. *Ġurbetnāme-i Cem Sulṭān*. Edited by İsmail Hami Danişmend as "Gurbet-name-i Sultan Cem ibni Sultan Muhammed" in *Fatih ve İstanbul* 2, no. 12 (1954): 212–270.

———. *Mecmūʿa*. Oriental Institute in Sarajevo (Bosnian Manuscript Ingathering Project). MS 4811/II.

———. *Menāḳıb-ı Maḥmūd Paşa-yı Velī*. Istanbul, Süleymaniye Kütüphanesi, Ayasofya 1940/2, 68b–71a.

———. *Vilāyetnāme-i Demīr Baba*. In *Demir Baba Vilâyetnamesi*. Edited by Bedri Noyan. Istanbul: Can Yayınları, 1976.

[Oxford] Anonymous. Bodleian Library, Marsh 313. Published as *Rûhî Târîhi,* with facsimile and transcription, by Halil Erdoğan Cengiz and Yaşar Yücel in *Belgeler* 14/18 (1989–1992): 359–472.

[Oxford] Anonymous. Oxford University, Bodleian Library, Marsh 313. Published as *Rûhî Târîhi,* with transcription, by Halil Erdoğan Cengiz and Yaşar Yücel. Ankara: Türk Tarih Kurumu Basımevi, 1992.

ʿĀşıḳ Çelebi. *Meşāʿirü'ş-Şuʿarā.* Edited by G. M. Meredith-Owens. London: Luzac, 1971.

ʿĀşıḳpaşazāde [Dervīş Aḥmed]. *Die altosmanische Chronik des ʿĀşıḳpaşazāde.* Edited by Friedrich Giese. Leipzig: Harrassowitz, 1929.

———. *Tevārīḫ-i Āl-i ʿOsmān.* In *Osmanlı Tarihleri,* edited by N. Atsız. Istanbul: Türkiye Yayınevi, 1947.

———. *Tevārīḫ-i Āl-i ʿOsmān.* In *Osmanoğullari'nın Tarihi,* edited by K. Yavuz and M. A. Yekta Saraç. Istanbul: K Kitaplığı, 2003.

Celālzāde Muṣṭafā. *Cevāhirü'l-Aḫbār fī Ḫaṣā'ilü'l-Aḫyār.* Istanbul, Süleymaniye Library, Nuruosmaniye 2356.

———. *Geschichte Sultan Süleymān Ḳānūnīs von 1520 bis 1557, oder, Ṭabaḳāt ül-Memālik ve Derecāt ül-Mesālik / von Celālzāde Muṣṭafā genannt Ḳoca Nişāncı.* Edited by Petra Kappert. Wiesbaden: Steiner, 1981.

———. *Me'āṣir-i Selīm Ḫānī* (or *Selīmnāme*). London, British Museum Library, Add. 7848.

———. *Mevāhibü'l-Ḫallāḳ fī Merātibi'l-Aḫlāḳ.* Istanbul, Süleymaniye Library, Fatih 3521.

———. *Selīmnāme.* Edited by Ahmet Uğur and Mustafa Çuhadar. Istanbul: Milli Eğitim Bakanlığı, 1997.

Chalkokondyles, Laonikos. *Laonici Chalcocandylae historiarum demonstrationes,* Edited by Jeno Darkó. 2 vols. Budapest: Academia Litterarum Hungarica, 1922–1927.

Doukas. *Decline and Fall of Byzantium to the Ottoman Turks.* Translated by Harry J. Magoulias. Detroit: Wayne State University Press, 1975.

———. *Istoria Turco-Bizantină (1341–1462).* Edited by Vasile Grecu. Bucarest: Editura Academiei Republicii Populare Romîne, 1958.

Ebū'l-ḫayr-ı Rūmī. *Salṭuḳnāme.* Edited by A. H. Akalın. 3 vols. Ankara: Kültür ve Turizm Bakanlığı, 1987.

Elvān Çelebi. *Menāḳıbü'l-Ḳudsiyye fī Menāşıbü'l-Ünsiyye.* In *Menâkıbu'l-kudsiyye fî menâsıbi'l-ünsiyye: Baba İlyas-ı Horasânî ve Sülâlesinin Menkabevî Tarihi,* edited by İsmail Erünsal and Ahmet Yaşar Ocak. Istanbul: İstanbul Üniversitesi Edebiyat Fakültesi Yayınları, 1984.

Enverī. *Düstūrnāme.* In *Fatih Devri Kaynaklarından Düstûrnâme-i Enverî: Osmanlı Tarihi Kısmı (1299–1466),* edited by Necdet Öztürk. Istanbul: Kitabevi, 2003.

Ferā'iżīzāde Meḥmed Saʿīd. *Gülşen-i Maʿārif.* 2 vols. Istanbul: Maṭbaʿa-i ʿāmire, 1788.

Ferīdūn Aḥmed. *Münşe'ātü's-Selāṭīn. Mecmūʿa-i Münşe'āt-ı Ferīdūn Beg.* 2 vols. Istanbul: Dārü'ṭ-ṭıbāʿati'l-ʿāmire, 1264–1265 [1848–1849].

Georgius de Hungaria. *Tractatus de moribus, condictionibus et nequicia turcorum. Traktat über die Sitten, die Lebensverhältnisse und die Arglist der Türken.* Edited and translated by Reihhard Klockow. Wien: Böhlau, 1994.

Gerlach, Stefan. *Tagebuch der von zween Glorwüdrigsten Römischen Kaysern Maximiliano un Rudolpho . . . an die Ottomannische Pforte zu Constantinopel Abgefertigten.* Franckfurth am Mayn: Verlegung Johann David Zunners, 1674. Published as *Türkiye Günlüğü.* Edited by Kemal Beydilli. Translated by Türkis Noyan. 2 vols. Istanbul: Kitap Yayınevi, 2006.

Ḫalīl b. İsmāʿīl b. Şeyḫ Bedreddīn. *Menāḳıb-ı Şeyḫ Bedreddīn b. İsrāʾīl*. In *Simavna Kadısıoğlu Şeyh Bedreddin Manakıbı*. Edited by Abdülbaki Gölpınarlı and İsmet Sungurbey. Istanbul: Eti Yayınevi, 1967.

Ibn Khaldūn. *The Muqaddimah: An Introduction to History*. 2nd ed. Translated by Franz Rosenthal. Princeton, N.J.: Princeton University Press, 1967.

İbn-i Kemāl. *Tevārīḫ-i Āl-i ʿOs̱mān* (I. Defter). Edited by Şerafettin Turan. Ankara: Türk Tarih Kurumu, 1970.

Ḳaraçelebizāde ʿAbdüʾl-ʿazīz. *Ravżatüʾl-Ebrār*. Cairo: Maṭbaʿa-i Bulāḳ, 1832.

Laṭīfī. *Tez̠kiretüʾş-Şuʿarā*. Istanbul: İḳdām Maṭbaʿası, 1896–1897.

Manṣūrī, Baybars al-Dawādār. *Zubdat al-Fikrah fī Tārīkh al-Hijrah*. Berlin: Das arabische Buch, 1998.

Māzandarānī, ʿAbd Allāh ibn Muḥammad. *Die Resālä-ye Falakiyyä des ʿAbdollāh Ibn Mohammad Ibn Kiyā al-Māzandarānī: ein persischer Leitfaden des staatlichen Rechnungswesens (um 1363)*. Edited by Walther Hinz. Wiesbaden: Franz Steiner Verlag, 1952.

Meḥmed ʿĀṭıf. *Ḫülāṣatüʾt-Tevārīḫ*. Istanbul: Muḥibb Maṭbaʿası, 1872 or 1873.

Meḥmed Cemāleddīn. *ʿOs̱mānlı Tārīḫ ve Müverriḫleri: Āyine-i Zürefā*. Istanbul: İḳdām Maṭbaʿası, 1896–1897.

Meḥmed Murād. *Tārīḫ-i ʿUmūmī*. 6 vols. Istanbul: Maḥmūd Bey Maṭbaʿası, 1880–1882.

Müneccimbaşı. *Jāmiʿ al-Duwal*. Istanbul, Süleymaniye Library, Esad Efendi 2101–2103.

———. *Jāmiʿ al-Duwal*. In *Camiüʾd-düvel: Osmanlı Tarihi, 1299–1481*, edited and translated by Ahmet Ağırakça. Istanbul: İnsan Yayınları, 1995.

———. *Jāmiʿ al-Duwal*. In *Müneccimbaşı als Historiker: Arabische Historiographie bei einem osmanischen Universalgelehrten des 17. Jahrhunderts: Ǧāmiʿ ad-duwal (Teiledition 982/1574–1082/1672)*, edited by Hatice Arslan-Sözüdoğru. Berlin: Klaus Schwarz Verlag, 2009.

———. *Ṣaḥāʾif ül-Aḫbār* [Ottoman Turkish translation of *Jāmiʿ al-duwal*]. Translated by Nedīm. 3 vols. Istanbul: Maṭbaʿa-i ʿāmire, 1285/1868.

Murād b. ʿAbdullāh. *Kitāb Tesviyetüʾt-Teveccüh Ilāʾl-Ḥaḳḳ*. London, British Library, Add. 19894.

Muṣṭafā ʿĀlī. *Künhüʾl-Aḫbār*. 5 vols. Istanbul: Taḳvīmḫāne-i Āmire, 1861.

———. *Naṣīḥatüʾl-Selāṭīn*. In *Muṣṭafā ʿĀlī's Counsel for Sultans of 1581*, edited and translated by Andreas Tietze. 2 vols. Vienna: Verlag der Österreichischen Akademie der Wissenschaften, 1978, 1982.

Neşrī [Mevlānā Meḥemmed]. *Ǧihânnümâ: Die altosmanische Chronik des Mevlânâ Meḥemmed Neschrî*. Edited by Franz Taeschner. 2 vols. Leipzig: Harrassowitz, 1951–1959.

———. *Kitâb-ı Cihan-nümâ. Neşrî Tarihi*. Edited by Faik Reşit Unat and Mehmed A. Köymen. 2 vols. Ankara: Türk Tarih Kurumu, 1949–1957.

Nicolay, Nicolas de. *The Nauigations into Turkie*. London: 1585. New ed. Amsterdam: Da Capo Press, 1968.

Oruç bin ʿĀdil. *Die frühosmanischen Jahrbücher des Urudsch nach den Handschriften zu Oxford und Cambridge erstmals herausgegeben und eingeleitet*. Edited by Franz Babinger. Hannover: H. Lafaire, 1925.

———. *Oruç Beğ Tarihi*. Edited by Nihal Atsız. Istanbul: Tercüman, 1972.

———. *Oruç Beğ Tarihi*. Edited by Necdet Öztürk. Istanbul: Çamlıca, 2007.

Qazwīnī. *The Geographical Part of the Nuzhat-al-qulūb composed by Ḥamd-Allah Mustawfī of Qazwīn in 740 (1340)*. Edited and translated by Guy Le Strange. 2 vols. Leiden and London: Brill and Luzac & Co., 1915–1919.

Rashīd al-Dīn, Fadlallāh. *Geschichte Ġāzān-Ḫān's aus dem Ta'rih-i-Mubārak-i-Ġāzānī.* Edited by Karl Jahn. London: E. J. W. Gibb Memorial, 1940.

Rıf'at Efendi. *Naḳdü't-Tevārīḫ.* Istanbul: Yaḥyā Efendi Maṭba'ası, 1879.

Şānīzāde Meḥmed 'Aṭā'ullāh Efendi. *Şānīzāde Tārīḫi.* Edited by Ziya Yılmazer. Istanbul: Çamlıca, 2008.

Sehī. *Tezkire-i Sehī.* Istanbul: Maṭba'a-i Āmidī, 1907.

Serrāc b. 'Abdullāh. *Mecmū'atü'l-Leṭā'if.* Sofia, SS Cyril and Methodius National Library, Oriental Collection, Or. 2461.

Seydī 'Alī Re'īs. *Mir'ātü'l-Memālik.* In *Mir'âtü'l-Memâlik: İnceleme, Metin, İndeks,* edited by Mehmet Kiremit. Ankara: Atatürk Kültür Dil ve Tarih Yüksek Kurumu, 1999.

Seyyid Mūrādī. *Ġazavāt-ı Ḫayreddīn Paşa.* In *Barbaros Hayreddin Paşa'nın Hatıraları,* edited by M. Ertuğrul Düzdağ. Vol. 1. Istanbul: Tercüman, n.d.

Şükrullāh. *Bahjat al-Tawārīkh.* Excerpt edited and translated by Theodor Seif. In "Der Abschnitt über die Osmanen in Šükrüllāh's persischer Universalgeschichte." *Mitteilungen zur osmanischen Geschichte* 2 (1923–1926): 63–128.

———. *Bahjat al-Tawārīkh.* Vienna, Österreischiche Nationalbibliothek, MS. No. H.O.1.

Süleymān I [Ottoman ruler]. *Dîvân-ı Muhibbî (Kanunî Sultan Süleyman'ın Şiirleri).* Edited by Vahit Çabuk. 3 vols. Istanbul: Tercüman, 1980.

Süleymān Ḥüsnī. *Tārīḫ-i 'Ālem,* 1: *Ḳurūn-ı Ūlā.* Istanbul: Mekteb-i Fünūn-ı Ḥarbiyye Maṭba'ası, 1876.

Sūzī Çelebi. *Ġazavātnāme-i Miḫāloğlu 'Alī Beg.* In *Ġazavāt-nāmeler ve Mihaloğlu Ali Bey'in Ġazavāt-nāmesi,* 2nd ed., edited by Agah Sırrı Levend. Ankara: Türk Tarih Kurumu, 2000.

'Umarī. *Masālik al-Abṣār fī Mamālik al-Amṣar.* Excerpt edited by Franz Taeschner. In *Al-'Umarī's Bericht über Anatolien in seinem Werke Masālik al-abṣār fī mamālik al-amṣār.* Leipzig: Otto Harrassowitz, 1929.

———. "Notice de l'ouvrage qui a pour titre Masalek alabsar fi memalek alamsar, Voyages des yeux dans les royaumes des différentes contrées (ms. Arabe 583)." Translated by E. Quatremère. *Notices et Extraits des manuscrits de la Bibliothèque du Roi* 13 (1838): 151–384.

Ya'qūbī, Aḥmad ibn Abī Ya'qūb. *Ibn-Wādhih qui dicitur al-Ja'qubī historiae.* Edited by M. Th. Houtsma. Leiden: Brill, 1883.

Studies

Abel, A. "Un Ḥadīṯ sur la Prise de Rome dans la Tradition Eschatologique de l'Islam." *Arabica* 5, no. 1 (1958): 1–14.

Ács, Pál. "Tarjumans Mahmud and Murad: Austrian and Hungarian Renegades as Sultan's Interpreters." In *Europe und die Türken in der Renaissance,* edited by B. Guthmüller and W. Kühlmann, 307–316. Tübingen: Max Niemeyer Verlag, 2000.

Adang, Camilla. *Muslim Writers on Judaism and the Hebrew Bible: From Ibn Rabban to Ibn Hazm.* Leiden: Brill, 1996.

Adshead, Samuel Adrian M. *Central Asia in World History.* New York: St. Martin's Press, 1993.

Ágoston, Gábor. "Information, Ideology, and the Limits of Imperial Policy: Ottoman Grand Strategy in the Context of Ottoman-Habsburg Rivalry." In *The Early Modern Ottomans: Remapping the Empire,* edited by Virginia Aksan and Daniel Goffman, 75–102. Cambridge: Cambridge University Press, 2007.

Akman, Mehmet. *Osmanlı Devletinde Kardeş Katli.* Istanbul: Eren, 1997.
Aksan, Virginia, and Daniel Goffman, eds. *The Early Modern Ottomans: Remapping the Empire.* Cambridge: Cambridge University Press, 2007.
Akyüz, Kenan. *Encümen-i Dâniş.* Ankara: Ankara Üniversitesi Eğitim Fakültesi Yayınları, 1975.
Alexandrescu-Dersca Bulgaru, Marie Mathilde. *La campagne de Timur en Anatolie (1402).* Bucharest: Monitorul Oficial si Imprimeriile Statului, 1942.
Alkan, Necmettin. "Tarihin Çağlara Ayrılmasında 'Üç'lü Sistem ve 'Avrupa Merkezci' Tarih Kurgusu." *Uluslararası Sosyal Araştırmalar Dergisi* 2, no. 9 (2009): 23–42.
Alpaslan, Oğuzhan. "A. Vefik Paşa ve Çağdaş Dönem ilk Osmanlı Tarih Metodolojisi Kitabı *Hikmet-i Tarih.*" *Muhafazakâr Düşünce* 2, no. 7 (2006): 197–218.
Alpay, Günay. "Abdülvâsi Çelebi'nin Eseri ve Nüshaları." *Türk Dili Araştırmaları Yıllığı: Belleten* 33 (1969): 201–226.
Andrews, Walter G. "Literary Art of the Golden Age: The Age of Süleymân." In *Süleymân the Second and His Time,* edited by Halil İnalcık and Cemal Kafadar, 353–368. Istanbul: Isis Press, 1993.
———. *Poetry's Voice, Society's Song: Ottoman Lyric Poetry.* Seattle: University of Washington Press, 1985.
Ankersmit, Frank N. *Historical Representation.* La Jolla: Stanford University Press, 2001.
Arbel, Benjamin. "Maps of the World for Ottoman Princes? Further Evidence and Questions Concerning 'The Mappamondo' of Hajji Ahmed." *Imago Mundi* 54 (2002): 19–29.
Artuk, İbrahim, and Cevriye Artuk. *İstanbul Arkeoloji Müzeleri: Teşhirdeki İslami Sikkeler Kataloğu.* Istanbul: T.C. Millî Eğitim Bakanlığı, Eski Eserler ve Müzeler Genel Müdürlüğü, 1970–1973.
Atıl, Esin. *Süleymanname: The Illustrated History of Süleyman the Magnificent.* New York: Harry N. Abrams, Inc., 1986.
Ayhan, Aydın, and Tuncer Şengün. "Anadolu Beyliklerinin ve Osmanlı Beyliği'nin İlhanlılar Adına Kestirdiği Sikkeler." In *XIII. Türk Tarih Kongresi (Ankara: 4–8 Ekim 1999)—Kongreye Sunulan Bildiriler.* Vol. 3, Part 2, 1161–1171. Ankara: Türk Tarih Kurumu, 2002.
Babinger, Franz, ed. *Die Frühosmanischen Jahrbücher des Urudsch nach den Handschriften zu Oxford und Cambridge erstmals herausgegeben und eingeleitet.* Hannover: H. Lafaire, 1925.
———.*Die Geschichtsschreiber der Osmanen und ihre Werke.* Leipzig: Otto Harrassowitz, 1927.
Bağcı, Serpil. "Visualizing Power: Portrayals of the Sultans in Illustrated Histories of the Ottoman Dynasty." *Islamic Art* 6 (2009): 113–127.
Bağcı, Serpil, Filiz Çağman, Günsel Renda, and Zeren Tanındı. *Osmanlı Resim Sanatı.* Istanbul: T.C. Kültür ve Turizm Bakanlığı Yayınları, 2006.
Barthe, Pascale. "An Uncommon Map for a Common World: Hajji Ahmed's Cordiform Map of 1559." *L'Esprit Créateur* 48, no. 1 (2008): 32–44.
Beldiceanu-Steinherr, Irène. *Recherches sur les actes des règnes des sultans Osman, Orkhan et Murad I.* Munich: Societatea Academică Română, 1967.
Bellingeri, Giampiero. "Fascie 'altaiche' del mappamondo turco-veneziano." In Giampiero Bellingeri, *Turco-Veneta,* 61–81. Istanbul: Isis Press, 2003.
Blankinship, Khalid. "Islam and World History: Towards a New Periodization." *The American Journal of Islamic Social Science* 8, no. 3 (1991): 423–439.
Borzsák, István. "A 'Hungarian History' through Turkish Eyes and the Alexander the Great Tradition." In *Occident and Orient: A Tribute to the Memory of Alexander Scheiber,* edited by R. Dán, 31–38. Budapest: Akadémiai Kiadá, 1998.

Bosworth, Clifford Edmund. *The New Islamic Dynasties: A Chronological and Genealogical Manual.* New York: Columbia University Press, 1996.
Brubaker, Rogers, and Frederick Cooper. "Beyond 'Identity.'" *Theory and Society* 29, no. 1 (2000): 1–47.
Buzov, Snježana. "The Lawgiver and His Lawmakers: The Role of Legal Discourse in the Change of Ottoman Imperial Culture." PhD diss., University of Chicago, 2005.
Cahen, Claude. *The Formation of Turkey: The Seljukid Sultanate of Rūm: Eleventh to Fourteenth Century.* Translated and edited by P. M. Holt. Harlow: Longman, 2001.
Carboni, Stefano, ed. *Venice and the Islamic World, 828–1797.* New Haven, Conn.: Yale University Press, 2007.
Casale, Giancarlo. "The Ethnic Composition of Ottoman Ship Crews and the 'Rumi' Challenge to Portuguese Identity." *Medieval Encounters* 13 (2007): 122–144.
———. *The Ottoman Age of Exploration.* Oxford: Oxford University Press, 2010.
———. "16. Yüzyıla Ait Türkçe Dünya Haritasında Avrupa Düşüncesi." In *Harp ve Sulh: Avrupa ve Osmanlılar,* edited by Dejanirah Couto, translated by Şirin Tekeli, 56–81. Istanbul: Kitap Yayınevi, 2010.
Clark, Elizabeth A. *History, Theory, Text: Historians and the Linguistic Turn.* Cambridge, Mass.: Harvard University Press, 2004.
Çıpa, H. Erdem. "The Centrality of the Periphery: The Rise to Power of Selīm I, 1481–1512." PhD diss., Harvard University, 2007.
———. "Contextualizing Şeyẖ Bedreddīn: Notes on Ḫalīl b. İsmāʿīl's Menāḳıb-ı Şeyẖ Bedreddīn b. İsrāʾīl." In *Şinasi Tekin'in Anısına: Uygurlardan Osmanlıya,* 285–295. Istanbul: Simurg, 2005.
Danişmend, İsmail Hami. *İzahlı Osmanlı Tarihi Kronolojisi.* Vol. 2. Istanbul: Türkiye Basımevi, 1948.
Darling, Linda. "Contested Territory: Ottoman Holy War in Comparative Context." *Studia Islamica* 91 (2000): 133–163.
Darwin, John. *After Tamerlane: The Global History of Empire since 1405.* London: Allen Lane, 2007.
Davis, James C. *Pursuit of Power: Venetian Ambassadors' Reports on Turkey, France, and Spain in the Age of Philip II, 1560–1600.* New York: Harper Torchbooks, 1970.
Delilbaşı, Melek. "Christian *Sipahis* in the Tırhala Taxation Registers (15th and 16th Centuries)." In *Provincial Elites in the Ottoman Empire,* edited by A. Anastasopoulos, 87–114. Herakleion: Crete University Press, 2005.
DeWeese, Devin. *Islamization and Native Religion in the Golden Horde.* University Park: Pennsylvania State University Press, 1994.
Dietrich, Albert. "A propos d'un précis d'histoire gréco-romaine dans la chronique universelle arabe de Müneccimbaşı." In *V. Congrès international d'arabisants et d'islamisants: 31 août–septembre 1970, Bruxelles,* 175–188. Bruxelles: Centre pour l'Étude des Problèmes du Monde Musulman Contemporain, 1971.
Dobrovits, Mihály. "The Turco-Mongolian Tradition of Common Origin and the Historiography in Fifteenth Century Central Asia." *Acta Orientalia Academiae Scientiarum Hungaricae* 48 (1994): 269–277.
Dressler, Markus. "Inventing Orthodoxy: Competing Claims for Authority and Legitimacy in the Ottoman Safavid Conflict." In *Legitimizing the Order: The Ottoman Rhetoric of State Power,* edited by H. Karateke and M. Reinkowski, 151–176. Leiden: Brill, 2005.

Emecen, Feridun M. *Zamanın İskenderi, Şarkın Fatihi: Yavuz Sultan Selim.* Istanbul: Yitik Hazine Yayınları, 2010.

Emiralioğlu, Pınar. "Cognizance of the Ottoman World: Visual and Textual Representations in the Sixteenth-Century Ottoman Empire, 1514–1596." PhD diss., University of Chicago, 2005.

Eryılmaz, Fatma Sinem. "Bir Trajedinin Kurgulanışı: 'Ārifī'nin Süleymānnāme'sinde (TSMK H. 1517) Şehzāde Muṣṭafā'nın Katlinin Ele Alınışı." In *Commemorative Gift to Filiz Çağman: Topkapı Palace Museum Communication Seminar on the Topkapı Palace and Ottoman Art.* Forthcoming.

———. "The Shehnamecis of Sultan Süleymān: 'Ārif and Eflatun and Their Dynastic Project." PhD diss., University of Chicago, 2010.

Fabris, Antonio. "The Ottoman Mappa Mundi of Hajji Ahmed of Tunis." *Arab Historical Review for Ottoman Studies* 7–8 (1993): 31–37.

Fasolt, Constantin. *The Limits of History.* Chicago: University of Chicago Press, 2004.

Fetvacı, Emine. "The Office of the Ottoman Court Historian." In *Studies on Istanbul and Beyond. The Freely Papers,* edited by Robert G. Ousterhout. Vol. 1, 6–21. Philadelphia: University of Pennsylvania Museum of Archaeology and Anthropology, 2007.

———. *Picturing History at the Ottoman Court.* Bloomington: Indiana University Press, 2013.

———. "Viziers to Eunuchs: Transitions in Ottoman Manuscript Patronage, 1566–1617." PhD diss., Harvard University, 2005.

Finkel, Caroline. *Osman's Dream.* New York: Basic Books, 2006.

Fleischer, Cornell. *Bureaucrat and Intellectual in the Ottoman Empire: The Historian Mustafa Âli (1541–1600).* Princeton, N.J.: Princeton University Press, 1986.

———. "The Lawgiver as Messiah: The Making of the Imperial Image in the Reign of Süleyman." In *Soliman le magnifique et son temps,* edited by Gilles Veinstein, 159–177. Paris: Galeries Nationales du Grand Palais, 1992.

———. "Mahdi and Millenium: Messianic Dimensions in the Development of Ottoman Imperial Ideology." In *The Great Ottoman-Turkish Civilization,* edited by Kemal Çiçek. Vol. 3, 42–54. Ankara: Yeni Türkiye, 2000.

———. "Preliminaries to the Study of Ottoman Bureaucracy." *Journal of Turkish Studies* 10 (1986): 135–141.

———. "Seer to the Sultan: Haydar-i Remmal and Sultan Süleyman." In *Cultural Horizons: Festschrift in Honor of Talat S. Halman,* edited by Jayne S. Warner. Vol. 1, 290–299. Syracuse, N.Y.: Syracuse University Press, 2001.

———. "Shadows of Shadows: Prophecy and Politics in 1530s Istanbul." *International Journal of Turkish Studies* 13, no. 1–2 (2007): 52–57.

Fleischer, Cornell, and Kaya Şahin. "Süleyman the Magnificent." In *The Princeton Encyclopedia of Islamic Political Thought,* edited by Gerhard Bowering et al. Princeton, N.J.: Princeton University Press, 2012.

Flemming, Barbara. "Public Opinion under Sultan Süleymân." In *Süleymân the Second and His Time,* edited by Halil İnalcık and Cemal Kafadar, 59–67. Istanbul: Isis Press, 1993.

———. "Ṣāḥib-ḳırān und Mahdī: Türkische Endzeiterwartungen im ersten Jahrzehnt der Regierung Süleymāns." In *Between the Danube and the Caucasus,* edited by György Kara, 43–62. Budapest: Akadémiai Kiadá, 1987.

Geary, Patrick J. *Phantoms of Remembrance: Memory and Oblivion at the End of the First Millennium.* Princeton, N.J.: Princeton University Press, 1994.

Goffman, Daniel. *The Ottoman Empire and Early Modern Europe.* Cambridge: Cambridge University Press, 2002.
Gökbilgin, T. M. "Rüstem Paşa ve Hakkındaki İthamlar." *Tarih Dergisi* 8 (1955): 11–50.
Green, William A. "Periodization in European and World History." *Journal of World History* 3, no. 1 (1992): 13–53.
Grube, Ernst J. *Islamic Paintings from the Eleventh to the Eighteenth Century in the Collection of Hans P. Kraus.* NewYork: H. P. Kraus, 1972.
Hagen, Gottfried. "Afterword." In Robert Dankoff, *An Ottoman Mentality: The World of Evliya Çelebi.* Leiden: Brill, 2004.
Halasi-Kun, Tibor. "Gennadios' Turkish Confession of Faith." *Archivum Ottomanicum* 12 (1987–1992): 5–7.
Hammer-Purgstall, Joseph von. *Geschichte des Osmanischen Reiches.* 10 vols. Pest: C. A. Hartleben, 1827–1835.
Hanna, Nelly. *In Praise of Books: A Cultural History of Cairo's Middle Class, Sixteenth to the Eighteenth Century.* Syracuse, N.Y.: Syracuse University Press, 2003.
Hathaway, Jane. "The *Evlâd-i 'Arab* ('Sons of the Arabs') in Ottoman Egypt: A Rereading." In *Frontiers of Ottoman Studies,* edited by Colin Imber and Keiko Kiyotaki. Vol. 1, 203–216. London: I. B. Tauris, 2005.
Hattox, Ralph. *Coffee and Coffeehouses: The Origins of a Social Beverage in the Medieval Near East.* Seattle: University of Washington Press, 1985.
Hay, Denys. *Europe: The Emergence of an Idea.* Edinburgh: Edinburgh University Press, 1968.
Helmy, N. Mahmoud. "Membré, Michele." In *Dizionario Biografico degli Italiani,* http://www.treccani.it/enciclopedia/michele-membre_(Dizionario-Biografico)/
Herbert, John, ed. *Christie's Review of the Season 1977.* London: Studio Vista, 1977.
Herzog, Christoph. *Geschichte und Ideologie: Mehmed Murad und Celal Nuri über die historischen Ursachen des osmanischen Niedergangs.* Berlin: K. Schwarz, 1996.
Iggers, Georg. *Historiography in the Twentieth Century: From Scientific Objectivity to the Postmodern Challenge.* Hanover, N.H.: Wesleyan University Press, 1997.
Imber, Colin. "Ideals and Legitimation in Early Ottoman History." In *Süleyman the Magnificent and His Age: The Ottoman Empire in the Early Modern World,* edited by Metin Kunt and Christine Woodhead, 138–153. London: Longman, 1995.
———. "The Legend of Osman Gazi." In *Studies in Ottoman History and Law,* 323–331. Istanbul: Isis Press, 1996.
———. *The Ottoman Empire 1300–1481.* Istanbul: Isis Press, 1990.
———. "What Does *ghazi* Actually Mean?" In *The Balance of Truth: Essays in Honour of Professor Geoffrey Lewis,* edited by Ç. Balım-Harding and Colin Imber, 165–178. Istanbul: Isis Press, 2000.
İnalcık, Halil. "How to Read 'Āşık Paşa-zāde's History." In *Studies in Ottoman History in Honour of Professor V. L. Ménage,* edited by Colin Heywood and Colin Imber, 139–156. Istanbul: Isis Press, 1994.
———. "Osmān Ghāzī's Siege of Nicaea and the Battle of Bapheus." In *The Ottoman Emirate (1300–1389),* edited by Elizabeth Zachariadou, 77–99. Rethymnon: Crete University Press, 1993.
———. *The Ottoman Empire: The Classical Age.* New York: Praeger, 1973.
———. "The Policy of Mehmed II toward the Greek Population of Istanbul and the Byzantine Buildings of the City." *Dumbarton Oaks Papers* 23 (1969–1970): 229–249.

———. "The Rise of Ottoman Historiography." In *Historians of the Middle East,* edited by Bernard Lewis and Peter M. Holt, 152–167. London: Oxford University Press, 1962.
———. "Stefan Duşan'dan Osmanlı İmparatorluğuna: XV. Asırda Rumeli'de Hıristiyan Sipâhiler ve Menşeleri." In *Fatih Devri Üzerinde Tetkikler ve Vesikalar,* 137–184. Ankara: Türk Tarih Kurumu, 1954.
Jahn, Karl, ed. *Die Frankengeschichte des Rašīd ad-dīn.* Vienna: Verlag der Österreichischen Akademie der Wissenschaften, 1977.
———, ed. *Die Indiengeschichte des Rašid ad-Dīn: Einleitung, vollständige Übersetzung, Kommentar und 80 Texttafeln.* The Hague: Mouton, 1965.
Kafadar, Cemal. *Between Two Worlds: The Construction of the Ottoman State.* Berkeley: University of California Press, 1995.
———. "Osman Beg and His Uncle: Murder in the Family?" In *Studies in Ottoman History in Honour of Professor V. L. Ménage,* edited by Colin Heywood and Colin Imber, 157–163. Istanbul: Isis Press, 1994.
———. "A Rome of One's Own: Reflections on Cultural Geography and Identity in the Lands of Rum." *Muqarnas* 24 (2007): 7–25.
———. "Self and Others: The Diary of a Dervish in Seventeenth Century Istanbul and First-Person Narratives in Ottoman Literature." *Studia Islamica* 69 (1989): 121–150.
Kafadar, Cemal, and Hakan Karateke. "Late Ottoman and Early Republican Turkish Historiography." In *The Oxford History of Historical Writing,* edited by Stuart Macintyre et al. Vol. 4, *1800–1945,* 559–577. New York: Oxford University Press, 2011.
Kafescioğlu, Çiğdem. *Constantinopolis/Istanbul—Cultural Encounters, Imperial Vision, and the Construction of the Imperial Capital.* University Park: Pennsylvania State University Press, 2009.
Kagan, Richard L. *Clio and the Crown: The Politics of History in Medieval and Early Modern Spain.* Baltimore: Johns Hopkins University Press, 2009.
Karaçavuş, Ahmet. "*Tanzimat Dönemi Osmanlı Bilim Cemiyetleri.*" PhD diss., Ankara University, 2006.
Karatay, Fehmi Edhem. *Topkapı Sarayı Müzesi Kütüphanesi Arapça Yazmalar Kataloğu.* Istanbul: Topkapı Sarayı Müzesi, 1966.
———. *Topkapı Sarayı Müzesi Kütüphanesi Farsça Yazmalar Kataloğu.* Istanbul: Topkapı Sarayı Müzesi, 1961.
Kastritsis, Dimitris. "Çelebi Meḥemmed's Letter of Oath (*Sevgendnāme*) to Ya'ḳūb II of Germiyan: Notes and a Translation Based on Şinasi Tekin's Edition." In *Şinasi Tekin'in Anısına: Uygurlardan Osmanlıya,* 442–444. Istanbul: Simurg, 2005.
———. "The Revolt of Şeyh Bedreddin in the Context of the Ottoman Civil War of 1402–13." In *Halcyon Days in Crete 7: Political Initiatives "From the Bottom Up" in the Ottoman Empire,* 233–250. Rethymno: University of Crete Press, 2012.
———. *The Sons of Bayezid: Empire Building and Representation in the Ottoman Civil War of 1402–1413.* Leiden: Brill, 2007.
Khoury, Dina Rizk. "Who Is a True Muslim? Exclusion and Inclusion among Polemicists of Reform in Nineteenth-Century Baghdad." In *Early Modern Ottomans,* edited by Virginia Aksan and Daniel Goffman, 256–274. Cambridge: Cambridge University Press, 2007.
Kim, Sooyong. "Minding the Shop: Zati and the Making of Ottoman Poetry in the First Half of the Sixteenth Century." PhD diss., University of Chicago, 2005.

Kiprovska, Mariya. "The Mihaloğlu Family: Gazi Warriors and Patrons of Dervish Hospices." *Osmanlı Araştırmaları* 32 (2008): 193–222.

Kırzıoğlu, Fahrettin. *Osmanlı'nın Kafkas-Elleri'ni Fethi (1451–1590).* Ankara: Sevinç Matbaası, 1976.

Kish, George. "The Cosmographic Heart: Cordiform Maps of the 16th Century." *Imago Mundi* 19 (1965): 13–21.

———. *The Suppressed Turkish Map of 1560.* Ann Arbor: William Clements Library, 1957.

Köprülü, Mehmet Fuat. *Osmanlı Devleti'nin Kuruluşu.* Ankara: Türk Tarih Kurumu, 1959.

———. "Osmanlı İmparatorluğu'nun Etnik Menşei Meseleleri." *Belleten* 7 (1943): 219–303.

Krstić, Tijana. *Contested Conversions to Islam: Narratives of Religious Change and Communal Politics in the Early Modern Ottoman Empire.* Palo Alto, Calif.: Stanford University Press, 2011.

———. "Illuminated by the Light of Islam and the Glory of the Ottoman Sultanate: Self-Narratives of Conversion to Islam in the Age of Confessionalization." *Comparative Studies in Society and History* 51, no. 1 (2009): 35–63.

——— "Narrating Conversions to Islam: The Dialogue of Texts and Practices in the Early Modern Ottoman Balkans." PhD diss., University of Michigan, 2004.

———. "Of Translation and Empire: Sixteenth-Century Ottoman Imperial Interpreters as Renaissance Go-Betweens." In *The Ottoman World,* edited by Christine Woodhead, 130–142. Abingdon: Routledge, 2011.

Kunt, Metin. "Ethnic-Regional (Cins) Solidarity in the Seventeenth-Century Ottoman Establishment." *International Journal of Middle East Studies* 5 (1974): 233–239.

Leaman, Oliver. *A Brief Introduction to Islamic Philosophy.* Malden, Mass.: Blackwell, 1999.

Levenson, Jay A., ed. *Encompassing the Globe: Portugal and the World in the 16th and 17th Centuries.* Washington, D.C.: Smithsonian, 2007.

Lewis, Bernard. *Islam from the Prophet Muhammad to the Capture of Constantinople.* Vol. 1. New York: Harper and Row, 1974.

Lindner, Rudi Paul. "Between Seljuks, Mongols and Ottomans." In *The Great Ottoman-Turkish Civilization,* edited by Kemal Çiçek. Vol. 1, 116–122. Ankara: Yeni Türkiye, 2000.

———. *Explorations in Ottoman Prehistory.* Ann Arbor: University of Michigan Press, 2007.

———. "How Mongol were the Early Ottomans?" In *The Mongol Empire and Its Legacy,* edited by Reuven Amitai-Preiss and David O. Morgan, 282–289. Leiden: Brill, 1999.

Lowry, Heath W. *The Nature of the Early Ottoman State.* New York: State University of New York Press, 2003.

Lynch, John, ed. *Monarquía e Imperio: El Reinado de Carlos V.* Madrid: El Pais, 2007.

———. *Spain 1516–1598: From Nation to World Empire.* Oxford: Blackwell, 1994.

Manners, Ian, ed. *European Cartographers and the Ottoman World, 1500–1750: Maps from the Collection of O. J. Sopranos.* Chicago: Oriental Institute, 2007.

Mantran, Robert. "L'historiographie ottomane à l'époque de Soliman le Magnifique." In *Soliman le Magnifique et son temps,* edited by Gilles Veinstein, 25–32. Paris: La Documentation Française, 1992.

Matschke, Klaus-Peter. *Die Schlacht bei Ankara und das Schicksal von Byzanz: Studien zur spätbyzantinischen Geschichte zwischen 1402 und 1422.* Weimar: Bohlau, 1981.

Matuz, Josef. *Das Kanzleiwesen Sultan Süleymans des Prächtigen.* Wiesbaden: F. Steiner, 1974.

Ménage, V. L. "The Beginnings of Ottoman Historiography." In *Historians of the Middle East,* edited by Bernard Lewis and Peter M. Holt, 168–179. London: Oxford University Press, 1962.

———. "The Map of Hajji Ahmed and Its Makers." *Bulletin of the School of Oriental and African Studies* 21 (1958): 291–314.

———. "The Menākib of Yakhshi Faqīh." *Bulletin of the School of Oriental and African Studies* 26 (1963): 50–54.

———. *Neshrī's History of the Ottomans: The Sources and Development of the Text.* London: Oxford University Press, 1964.

———. "Review." *Bulletin of the School of Oriental and African Studies* 47, no. 1 (1984): 154–157.

Milstein, Rachel, Karin Rührdanz, and Barbara Schmitz. *Stories of the Prophets: Illustrated Manuscripts of the Qiṣaṣ al-Anbiyā'.* Costa Mesa: Mazda Publishers, 1999.

Minkov, Anton. *Conversion to Islam in the Balkans:* Kisve Bahası *Petitions and Ottoman Social Life, 1670–1730.* Brill: Leiden, 2004.

Moačanin, Nenad. "Mass Islamization of the Peasants in Bosnia: Demystifications." In *Melanges Professor Machiel Kiel,* 353–358. Zaghouan: Fondation Temimi, 1999.

Nakıp, Tahir. *"Osmanlı Devletinde Geç Dönem Tarih-i Umumiler."* MA thesis, Marmara University, 2006.

Necipoğlu, Gülru. *The Age of Sinan.* Princeton, N.J.: Princeton University Press, 2005.

———. "A Kânûn for the State, a Canon for the Arts: Conceptualizing the Classical Synthesis of Ottoman Arts and Architecture." In *Soliman le Magnifique et son temps,* edited by Gilles Veinstein, 195–216. Paris: La Documentation Française, 1992.

———. "Süleyman the Magnificent and the Representation of Power in the Context of Ottoman-Hapsburg-Papal Rivalry." *Art Bulletin* 71, no. 3 (1989): 401–427.

Neumann, Christoph. *Das indirekte Argument: ein Plädoyer für die Tanẓīmāt vermittels der Historie. Die geschichtliche Bedeutung von Aḥmed Cevdet Paşas Ta'rīḫ.* Münster: Lit, 1994.

Newman, Andrew J. *Safavid Iran: Rebirth of a Persian Empire.* London: I. B. Tauris, 2006.

Ng, Su Fang. "Alexander the Great and Early Modern Classicism from the British Isles to the Malay Archipelago." *Comparative Literature* 58, no. 4 (2006): 293–312.

Niewöhner-Eberhard, Elke. *Osmanische Polemik gegen die Safawiden im 16. Jahrhundert nach arabischen Handschriften.* Freiburg: Schwarz, 1970.

Noever, Peter, ed. *Global Lab: Art as a Message, Asia and Europe 1500–1700.* Wien: MAK/Hatje Cantz, 2009.

Ocak, Ahmet Y. *Osmanlı Toplumunda Zındıklar ve Mülhidler (15.–17. Yüzyıllar).* Istanbul: Tarih Vakfı Yurt Yayınları, 1998.

Ölçer, Cüneyt. *Yıldırım Bayezid'in Oğullarına Ait Akçe ve Mangırlar.* Istanbul: Yenilik Basımevi, 1968.

Osterhout, Robert. "The East, the West and the Appropriation of the Past in Early Ottoman Architecture." *Gesta* 43, no. 2 (2004): 165–176.

Özbaran, Salih. *Bir Osmanlı Kimliği: 14.–17. Yüzyıllarda Rûm/Rûmi Aidiyet ve İmgeleri.* Istanbul: Kitap Yayınevi, 2004.

Özcan, Abdülkadir. "Feraizizade Mehmed Said." *Türkiye Diyanet Vakfı İslam Ansiklopedisi* 12 (1995): 366–367.

———. "Historiography in the Reign of Süleyman the Magnificent." In *The Ottoman Empire in the Reign of Süleyman the Magnificent,* edited by Tülay Duran, 165–222. Istanbul: Historical Research Foundation, Istanbul Research Center, 1988.

Pagden, Anthony, ed. *The Idea of Europe: From Antiquity to the European Union.* Cambridge: Cambridge University Press, 2002.

Piterberg, Gabriel. *An Ottoman Tragedy: History and Historiography at Play.* Berkeley: University of California Press, 2003.

Posch, Walter. "Der Fall Alkâs Mîrzâ und der Persienfeldzug von 1548–1549: ein gescheitertes osmanisches Projekt zur Niederwerfung des safavidischen Persiens." PhD diss., University of Bamberg, 1999.

Raby, Julian. "El Gran Turco, Mehmet the Conqueror as a Patron of the Arts of Christendom." PhD diss., Oxford University, 1980.

———. "Mehmed the Conqueror's Greek Scriptorium." *Dumbarton Oaks* 37 (1983): 15–34.

Rambo, Lewis R., and Charles E. Farhadian. "Converting: Stages of Religious Change." In *Religious Conversion, Contemporary Practices and Controversies*, edited by Christopher Lamb and M. Darrol Bryant, 23–34. New York: Cassell, 1999.

Remler, Philip. "New Light on Economic History from Ilkhanid Accounting Manuals." *Studia Iranica* 14, no. 2 (1985): 157–177.

Rosenthal, Franz. *A History of Muslim Historiography*. Leiden: Brill, 1968.

Sabev, Orlin. "The Legend of Köse Mihal: Additional Notes." *Turcica* 34 (2002): 241–252.

Salzmann, Ariel. *Tocqueville in the Ottoman Empire: Rival Paths to the Modern State*. Leiden: Brill, 2004.

Schlegell, Barbara Rosenow von. "Sufism in the Ottoman Arab World: Shaykh ʿAbd al-Ganī al-Nābulsī (d. 1143/1731)." PhD diss., University of California, Berkeley, 1997.

Schmidt, Jan. *Mustafa Âli's Künhül-Ahbar and Its Preface According to the Leiden Manuscript*. Leiden: Nederlands Instituut voor het Nabije Oosten, 1987.

———. *Pure Water for Thirsty Muslims: Muṣṭafā ʿĀlī of Gallipoli's Künhü'l-Aḫbār*. Leiden, Het Oosters Instituut, 1991.

Smith, John Masson, Jr. "Mongol Nomadism and Middle Eastern Geography: qīshlāqs and tümens." In *The Mongol Empire and Its Legacy*, edited by Reuven Amitai-Preiss and David O. Morgan, 39–56. Leiden: Brill, 1999.

Somel, Selçuk Akşin. *The Modernization of Public Education in the Ottoman Empire, 1839–1908: Islamization, Autocracy, and Discipline*. Leiden: Brill, 2001.

Soudavar, Abolala. *The Aura of Kings: Legitimacy and Divine Sanction in Iranian Kingship*. Costa Mesa: Mazda Publishers, 2003.

Spiegel, Gabrielle M. *The Past as Text: The Theory and Practice of Medieval Historiography*. Baltimore: Johns Hopkins University Press, 1997.

———, ed. *Practicing History: New Directions in Historical Writing after the Linguistic Turn*. New York and London: Routledge, 2005.

Stavrides, Theoharis. *The Sultan of Vezirs: The Life and Times of the Ottoman Grand Vezir Mahmud Pasha Angelović (1453–1474)*. Leiden: Brill, 2001.

Stone, Michael E., and Theodore A. Bergen. *Biblical Figures Outside of the Bible*. Harrisburg: Trinity Press International, 1998.

Subrahmanyam, Sanjay. "Connected Histories: Notes towards a Reconfiguration of Early Modern Eurasia." *Modern Asian Studies* 31, no. 3 (July 1997): 735–762.

———. "Cránica and Tārīkh in the Sixteenth-Century Indian Ocean World." *History and Theory* 49 (2010): 118–145.

———. "Sixteenth Century Millenarianism from the Tagus to the Ganges." In *Explorations in Connected History*. Vol. 2, *From the Tagus to the Ganges*, 102–137. New Delhi: Oxford University Press, 2007.

Sümer, Faruk. "Anadolu'da Moğollar." *Selçuklu Araştırmaları Dergisi* 1 (1969): 1–147.

———. *Safevi Devletinin Kuruluşu ve Gelişmesinde Anadolu Türklerinin Rolü*. Ankara: Güven Matbaası, 1976.

Şahin, Kaya. "Âşıkpaşa-zâde as Historian: An Analysis of the Tevârih-i Âl-i Osman [The History of the Ottoman House] of Âşıkpaşa-zâde." MA thesis, Sabancı University, 2000.
———. "Constantinople and the End Time: The Ottoman Conquest as a Portent of the Last Hour." *Journal of Early Modern History* 14, no. 4 (2010): 317–354.
———. "In the Service of the Ottoman Empire: Celālzāde Muṣṭafā, Bureaucrat and Historian." PhD diss., University of Chicago, 2007.
Şehsuvaroğlu, Bedi. "Kanuni Devrinde Yazılmış ve Şimdiye Kadar Bilinmeyen bir Coğrafya Kitabı." In *Kanuni Armağanı*, 207–225. Ankara: Türk Tarih Kurumu, 1970.
Taeschner, Franz, and Paul Wittek. "Die Vezirfamilie der Ğandarlyzāde (14./15. Jhdt.) und ihre Denkmäler." *Der Islam* 18 (1929): 60–115.
Tanındı, Zeren. *Siyer-i Nebī.* Istanbul: Hürriyet Vakfı Yayınları, 1984.
Tanpınar, Ahmet Hamdi. *XIX. Asır Türk Edebiyatı Tarihi.* Edited by Abdullah Uçman. Istanbul: Yapı Kredi Yayınları, 2006.
Tekin, Şinasi. "Fatih Sultan Mehmed Devrine Âit bir İnşâ Mecmuası." *Journal of Turkish Studies* 20 (1996): 267–311.
Terzioğlu, Derin. "Man in the Image of God in the Image of the Times: Sufi Self-Narratives and the Diary of Niyāzī Mişrī (1618–94)." *Studia Islamica* 94 (2002): 139–165.
———. "Sufis in the Age of State Building and Confessionalization." In *The Ottoman World*, edited by Christine Woodhead. Abingdon: Routledge, 2011.
Tezcan, Baki. "The Politics of Early Modern Ottoman Historiography." In *The Early Modern Ottomans*, edited by Virginia Aksan and Daniel Goffman, 167–198. Cambridge: Cambridge University Press, 2007.
———. *The Second Ottoman Empire: Political and Social Transformation in the Early Modern World.* New York: Cambridge University Press, 2010.
———. "Some Thoughts on the Politicization of Early Modern Science." *Journal of Ottoman Studies* 36 (2010): 135–156.
Thomas, Lewis V. *A Study of Naima.* New York: New York University Press, 1972.
Tietze, Andreas. *Mustafa 'Ālī's Description of Cairo of 1599: Text, Translation, Notes.* Wien: Verlag der Österreichischen Akademie der Wissenschaften, 1975.
Togan, Ahmet-Zeki Velidî. "Die Vorfahren der Osmanen in Mittelasien." *Zeitschrift der deutschen morgenländischen Gesellschaft* 95 (1941): 367–373.
———. "Mogollar Devrinde Anadolu'nun İktisadî Vaziyeti." *Türk Hukuk ve İktisat Tarihi Mecmuası* 1 (1931): 1–42 [translated by Gary Leiser as "Economic Conditions in Anatolia in the Mongol Period" in *Annales Islamologiques* 25 (1991): 203–240].
———. *Umumî Türk Tarihine Giriş.* Vol. 1, *En Eski Devirlerden 16. Asra Kadar.* Istanbul: Hak Kitabevi, 1946.
Tulum, Mertol. "Elvan Çelebi'nin Menâkıbu'l-kudsiyye Adlı Eserinin İkinci Baskısı Münasebetiyle—III." *Türk Dünyası Araştırmaları* 106 (1997): 53–104.
Turan, Ebru. "The Marriage of Ibrahim Pasha (ca. 1495–1536): The Rise of Sultan Süleyman's Favorite, Ibrahim Pasha, to the Grand Vizirate and the Politics of Elites in the Early Sixteenth-Century Ottoman Empire." *Turcica* 41 (2009): 3–36.
———. "The Sultan's Favorite: İbrahim Pasha and the Making of Ottoman Universal Sovereignty in the Reign of Sultan Süleyman (1516–1526)." PhD diss., University of Chicago, 2007.
———. "Voices of Opposition in the Reign of Sultan Süleyman. The Case of İbrahim Pasha (1523–36)." In *Studies on Istanbul and Beyond: The Freely Papers*, edited by Robert G.

Ousterhout. Vol. 1, 23–35. Philadelphia: University of Pennsylvania Museum of Archaeology and Anthropology, 2007.

Turan, Osman. *Selçuklular Zamanında Türkiye: Siyasî Tarih, Alp Arslan'dan Osman Gazi'ye (1071–1318).* Istanbul: Turan Neşriyat Yurdu, 1971.

Ursinus, Michael. "Byzantine History in Late Ottoman Turkish Historiography." *Byzantine and Modern Greek Studies* 10 (1986): 211–222.

———. "From Süleyman Pasha to Mehmet Fuat Köprülü: Roman and Byzantine History in Late Ottoman Historiography." *Byzantine and Modern Greek Studies* 12 (1988): 305–314.

Uzunçarşılı, İsmail Hakkı. *Çandarlı Vezir Ailesi.* Ankara: Türk Tarih Kurumu, 1974.

———. "Onaltıncı Asır Ortalarında Yaşamış Olan İki Büyük Şahsiyet: Tosyalı Celâl zâde Mustafa ve Salih Çelebiler." *Belleten* 22, no. 87 (1958): 391–441.

———. *Osmanlı Devletinin Merkez ve Bahriye Teşkilatı.* Ankara: Türk Tarih Kurumu, 1989.

———. *Osmanlı Tarihi.* Vol. 1. Ankara: Türk Tarih Kurumu, 1947.

———. *Osmanlı Tarihi.* Vol. 2. Ankara: Türk Tarih Kurumu, 1943.

Walsh, John R. "The Historiography of Ottoman-Safavid Relations in the Sixteenth and Seventeenth Centuries." In *Historians of the Middle East,* edited by Bernard Lewis and Peter M. Holt, 197–211. London: Oxford University Press, 1962.

White, Hayden V. *The Content of the Form: Narrative Discourse and Historical Representation.* Baltimore: Johns Hopkins University Press, 1987.

Wittek, Paul. *The Rise of the Ottoman Empire.* London: Royal Asiatic Society, 1938.

Woodhead, Christine. "After Celalzade: The Ottoman *Nişancı* c. 1560–1700." *Journal of Semitic Studies,* Supplement 23 (2007): 295–311.

———. "An Experiment in Official Historiography: The Post of Şehnameci in the Ottoman Empire, c. 1555–1605." *Wiener Zeitschrift für die Kunde des Morgenlandes* 75 (1983): 157–182.

———. "From Scribe to Litterateur: The Career of a Sixteenth Century Ottoman *Kātib.*" *Bulletin of the British Society for Middle Eastern Studies* 9, no. 1 (1982): 55–74.

———. "Perspectives on Süleyman." In *Süleyman the Magnificent and His Age,* edited by Metin Kunt and Christine Woodhead, 164–190. London: Longman, 1995.

———. "Reading Ottoman Şehnames: Official Historiography in the Late Sixteenth Century." *Studia Islamica* 104/105 (2007): 67–80.

Woods, John E. *The Aqquyunlu: Clan, Confederation, Empire.* Salt Lake City: University of Utah Press, 1999.

Yerasimos, Stephane. *La fondation de Constantinople et de Sainte-Sophie.* Paris: Institute Français d'etudes anatoliennes d'Istanbul, 1990.

Yılmaz, Hüseyin. "The Sultan and the Sultanate: Envisioning Rulership in the Age of Süleyman the Lawgiver (1520–1566)." PhD diss., Harvard University, 2004.

Yılmaz, Mehmet Şakir. "'Koca Nişancı' of Kanuni: Celalzade Mustafa Çelebi, Bureaucracy and 'Kanun' in the Reign of Süleyman the Magnificent (1520–1566)." PhD diss., Bilkent University, 2006.

Yücel, Yaşar. *Kadı Burhaneddin Ahmed ve Devleti (1344–1398).* Ankara: Ankara Üniversitesi Basımevi, 1970.

Yürekli, Zeynep. "Legend and Architecture in the Ottoman Empire: The Shrine of Seyyid Gazi and Hacı Bektaş." PhD diss., Harvard University, 2005.

Zachariadou, Elizabeth. "Manuel II Palaeologos on the Strife between Bayezid and Kadi Burhan al-Din Ahmad." *Bulletin of the School of Oriental and African Studies* 18 (1980): 471–481.

———. "Süleyman Çelebi in Rumili and the Ottoman Chronicles." *Der Islam* 60, no. 2 (1983): 268–290.

Zhelyazkova, Antonina. "Islamization in the Balkans as a Historiographical Problem: The Southeast-European Perspective." In *The Ottomans and the Balkans,* edited by Suraiya Faroqhi and Fikret Adanır, 223–266. Leiden: Brill, 2002.

Contributors

H. Erdem Çıpa is Assistant Professor of Ottoman History in the Departments of History and Near Eastern Studies, University of Michigan, Ann Arbor. He is currently working on a book project entitled "The Making of Selim 'the Grim': The History and Historiography of a Succession Struggle."

Emine Fetvacı is Assistant Professor of Islamic Art at Boston University and author of *Picturing History at the Ottoman Court* (Indiana University Press, 2013).

Giancarlo Casale is Associate Professor of the History of the Islamic World at the University of Minnesota, where he has taught since 2005. He is the author of *The Ottoman Age of Exploration* and executive editor of the *Journal of Early Modern History.*

Fatma Sinem Eryılmaz is a postdoctoral fellow at the Scuola Normale Superiore, Pisa. Currently she is working on a monograph on ʿĀrif's *Anbiyanama.*

Hakan T. Karateke is Associate Professor of Ottoman and Turkish Culture, Language and Literature, Department of Near Eastern Languages and Civilizations, University of Chicago. He recently published an annotated edition of *An Ottoman Protocol Register* from the Ottoman State Archives.

Dimitris Kastritsis is Lecturer in Ottoman and Middle Eastern History at the University of St. Andrews, Scotland. His publications include *The Sons of Bayezid: Empire Building and Representation in the Ottoman Civil War of 1402–1413* and *The Tales of Sultan Mehmed, Son of Bayezid Khan: Annotated English Translation, Turkish Edition, and Facsimiles.*

Tijana Krstić is Associate Professor of Ottoman History at Central European University in Budapest and author of *Contested Conversions to Islam: Narratives of Religious Change and Communal Politics in the Early Modern Ottoman Empire.*

Kaya Şahin is Assistant Professor of History at Indiana University, Bloomington, and author of *Empire and Power in the Reign of Süleyman: Narrating the Sixteenth-Century Ottoman World.*

Baki Tezcan is Associate Professor of History and of Religious Studies at the University of California, Davis, and author of *The Second Ottoman Empire: Political and Social Transformation in the Early Modern World.*

Index

Page numbers in *italics* indicate illustrations.

Printed and bound by CPI Group (UK) Ltd, Croydon, CR0 4YY

13/04/2025

14656534-0001